Debugging ASP.NET

Contents At a Glance

Part I   ASP Debugging Basics

1   Conceptual Framework   3

2   Traditional Approaches to Debugging in ASP   9

3   Debugging Strategies   23

4   Code Structure that Eases Debugging   39

Part II   ASP.NET Debugging Tools

5   Conditional Compiling   69

6   Tracing   79

7   Visual Studio .NET   97 Debugging Environment

8   Leveraging the Windows 2000 Event Log   119

Part III   Debugging the New ASP.NET Features

9   Debugging Server-Side Controls   141

10   Debugging Data-Bound Controls   157

11   Debugging User Controls   173

12   Caching Issues and Debugging   189

Part IV   Debugging Related Technologies

13   Debugging Web Services   203

14   Debugging .NET Components and HttpHandlers   231

15   COM+ Issues   253

16   Debugging ADO.NET   273

Part V   Appendix

A   Issues that Arise When Migrating from ASP to ASP.NET   305

Index   325

Debugging
ASP.NET

Jonathan Goodyear
Brian Peek
Brad Fox

New Riders
www.newriders.com
201 West 103rd Street, Indianapolis, Indiana 46290
An Imprint of Pearson Education
Boston • Indianapolis • London • Munich • New York • San Francisco

Debugging ASP.NET

International Standard Book Number: 0-7357-1141-0

Library of Congress Catalog Card Number: 00-110030

06 05 04 03 02   7 6 5 4 3 2 1

Interpretation of the printing code: The rightmost double-digit number is the year of the book's printing; the right-most single-digit number is the number of the book's printing. For example, the printing code 02-1 shows that the first printing of the book occurred in 2002.

Printed in the United States of America

Trademarks

Warning and Disclaimer

Publisher
David Dwyer

Associate Publisher
Stephanie Wall

Managing Editor
Kristy Knoop

Acquisitions Editor
Deborah Hittel-Shoaf

Development Editor
Chris Zahn

Product Marketing Manager
Stephanie Layton

Publicity Manager
Susan Nixon

Copy Editor
Krista Hansing

Indexer
Chris Morris

Manufacturing Coordinator
Jim Conway

Book Designer
Louisa Klucznik

Cover Designer
Brainstorm Design, Inc.

Composition
Jeff Bredensteiner

❖

To my beautiful, dedicated, and supportive wife, Joy. The only person who has ever left me speechless.
Jonathan Goodyear

To Bunk, my dog—keep fighting.
Brian Peek

To my Wonderful, Supportive and Beautiful wife Wendy, who has helped me become the man I am today and helped me achieve my goals in life. Thank you so much for being there for me, I know it was a difficult journey and you stood by me every step of the way. Thank you!

To my sons, Brandon and Travis, I love you guys very much!

And Finally, thank you Mom and Dad for your support and inspiration.
Brad Fox

❖

TABLE OF CONTENTS

I ASP Debugging Basics   1

1 Conceptual Framework   3
Understanding Server-Side Events   3
New Language Options   7
Summary   8

2 Traditional Approaches to Debugging in ASP   9
Structure of Pre–ASP.NET Pages   9
Problems and Shortcomings   13
Old Strategies That Still Do the Job Well   14
An ASP Debug Object   16
Summary   22

3 Debugging Strategies   23
Tier Sandboxes   24
Divide and Conquer   29
Simple Before Complex   32
Turtle Makes the Wiser   36
Summary   37

4 Code Structure That Eases Debugging   39
Code Partitioning   39
Control-of-Flow Guidelines   53
Structured Exception Handling   58
Global Exception Handling   59
Summary   64

II ASP.NET Debugging Tools 67

5 Conditional Compiling 69

What Is Conditional Compiling? 69

Other Preprocessor Directives 76

Summary 78

6 Tracing 79

Configuration 80

Trace Output 81

Setting Trace Messages 85

Trace Viewer 91

Tracing via Components 93

Tips for Using Trace Information 95

Summary 96

7 Visual Studio .NET Debugging Environment 97

Introduction to Features 97

Attaching to Processes 101

Setting It All Up 103

Inline Debugging of ASP.NET Pages 103

Inline Debugging of Components 111

Remote Debugging 116

Summary 117

8 Leveraging the Windows 2000 Event Log 119

The Windows 2000 Event Log Defined 119

Web Applications Can Use the Event Log 120

The System.Diagnostics Event Log Interface 120

Custom Event Logs 121

Handling Different Types Of Events 124

Access Event Log Data via the Web 129

Summary 136

III Debugging the New ASP.NET Features 139

9 Debugging Server-Side Controls 141
Creating the Project 142
Debugging the Control 151
Summary 155

10 Debugging Data-Bound Controls 157
Data-Bound Controls 157
Debugging Templates 162
Namespace Issues 164
XML Binding 168
Summary 172

11 Debugging User Controls 173
User Control Basics 174
Adding Properties and Methods 175
Dynamic User Controls 184
Summary 187

12 Caching Issues and Debugging 189
Output Caching 190
The Caching API 196
Summary 200

IV Debugging Related Technologies 201

13 Debugging Web Services 203
Web Services Stumbling Blocks 203
Error Messages 205
Problems Working with XMLSerializer 214
Working with Errors in SOAP 215
Error Returning Certain Types of Data 219
Working with Streams 220
Tools 225
Basic Web Services Debugging 226
Problems Deploying Your Web Service? 230
Summary 230

14 Debugging .NET Components and HttpHandlers 231

The Component   231

Interfaces   242

HttpHandlers   243

State-Management Issues   246

.NET Components Versus Registered COM Components   249

Summary   252

15 COM+ Issues   253

Role-Based Security   253

Transaction Issues   264

Summary   272

16 Debugging ADO.NET   273

Understanding the System.Data Namespace   275

Catching SQL Errors   275

New Connection Components   280

Issues with the DataReader Class   281

Working with Transactions   281

Error Codes and How to Debug Them   284

Common Pitfalls   295

SQL ADO.NET Objects Versus OleDb ADO.NET Objects   300

Summary   301

V Appendix   303

A Issues That Arise When Migrating from ASP to ASP.NET   305

Moving from ASP to ASP.NET   305

Moving from VBScript to Visual Basic   311

Opting for C#   318

Summary   323

Index   325

About the Authors

Jonathan Goodyear began his career as a software developer at Arthur Andersen after receiving a degree in accounting and information technology from Stetson University. He has also worked as a consultant for PricewaterhouseCoopers and as the Internet architect for the Home Shopping Network's e-commerce presence (http://www.hsn.com). Presently, he works as an independent consultant through his consulting practice, ASPSoft, focusing on developing web applications with ASP.NET.

Jonathan is a contributing editor for *Visual Studio Magazine* (http://www.vbpj.com) and is a charter member of the Visual Studio 6 MCSD certification. He is also the founder and editor of *angryCoder* (http://www.angrycoder.com), the first eZine written completely in ASP.NET.

When not hunched over a keyboard, Jonathan likes to spend time going to theme parks with his family near his home in Orlando, Florida.

Brian Peek is a senior software developer with Rapid Application Developers, Inc. (http://www.rapiddevelopers.com/) located in Troy, New York. He specializes in developing *n*-tiered applications, web-based applications, wireless applications, and any other projects that happen to come along. Additionally, he is the owner and lead programmer of Ganksoft Entertainment (http://www.ganksoft.com/), a small video game–development company dedicated to producing high-quality games for video game consoles using only freely available tools and documentation. He holds a bachelor's degree in computer science from Union College in Schenectady, New York, his hometown. When not coding for work or coding games that he wishes would be published commercially, he can often be found practicing magic, learning to play piano, or playing his latest favorite video game. He can be reached at brian@ganksoft.com or brian@rapiddevelopers.com.

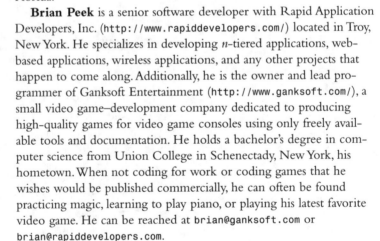

Brad Fox started programming in BASIC at the age of 12. Since then, computers and technology have played an integral part in his life. Brad joined the Army right out of high school and served in the 82nd Airborne Division. Since then he has gone on to become a Microsoft Certified Solution Developer. Currently, Brad is CEO of Digital Intelligence, Inc., where he spends most of his time developing cutting-edge technology for the financial industry.

About the Technical Reviewers

These reviewers contributed their considerable hands-on expertise to the entire development process for *Debugging ASP.NET*. As the book was being written, these dedicated professionals reviewed all the material for technical content, organization, and flow. Their feedback was critical to ensuring that *Debugging ASP.NET* fits our reader's need for the highest-quality technical information.

Diane Stottlemyer is presently an online teacher for Learning Tree, Capella University, Connected University, Franklin University, CalCampus, and ElementK. She enjoys teaching online and feels that her diverse background enables her to teach many different courses and add variety to them.

Diane fees that her biggest strength as an online teacher is her ability to present the student materials with life skills and to help her students understand the material so that they can process it and use it. Diane is also an adjunct professor for Mary Baldwin College, Piedmont Valley Community College, and James Sprunt Community College. She teaches several course on testing, management, programming, and advanced computer skills. She is an avid reader and keeps up on new technology, new software, and new hardware.

Diane is a professor of computer science and a Certified Software Test Engineer; she just completed her doctorate in computer science. She received her undergraduate degree from Indiana University and received masters and Ph.D. degrees in computer science from Lacrosse University. She believes that education is the door to future opportunities and that you are never too young or old to learn.

Diane's first book, entitled *Automated Web Testing Toolkit: Expert Methods for Testing and Managing Web Applications*, will be released this month. She is excited about the book and feels that it will be a great addition to anyone's library. She also just signed a contract for her second book on testing .NET applications.

Steve Platt has been around computers for the last 17 years; he got in through the back door after studying chemistry and chemical engineering with Pilkington Brothers, a well-known glass manufacturer. While writing some of their financial systems in CICS/COBOL and other obscure languages, such as Gener/OL and FOCUS, he rose from junior programmer to Senior Analyst/Programmer. Deciding that contracting was the way to go, he started a career that brought him into contact with quite a number of blue-chip companies: Shell Chemicals, American Express, Shell Oils, and Lloyds Bank. All these companies were mainframe users, but the projects were varied, including a huge data transfer from legacy systems to DB2, production support firefighting, and some data warehousing using Prism. Steve has spent the last few years in the Internet arena, working with Victoria Real (who created the UK's BigBrother site), on Iceland online shopping and the shopping portal Ready2Shop using UNIX, Perl, Oracle 8i, and JavaScript. More recently, he joined RDF Consulting, a Brighton-based organization and Microsoft solution provider that specializes in the e-commerce needs of financial organizations such as Legal & General and Northern Rock. There, Steve uses his skills as a configuration/build manager and Oracle DBA.

Steve has a wife and daughter, and he is interested in fitness and the martial arts. He is passionate about motorcycling and new technology, and he can be found on many an evening coding into the early hours. He would dearly love to emigrate to Australia.

Acknowledgments

We would all like to thank the following people at New Riders Publishing for their tireless work towards making this book a reality.

- Acquisitions Editor: Karen Wachs
- Acquisitions Editor: Deborah Hittel-Shoaf
- Development Editor: Chris Zahn
- Managing Editor: Kristy Knoop
- Copy Editor: Krista Hansing
- Indexer: Chris Morris
- Compositor: Jeff Bredensteiner
- Technical Reviewers: Diane Stottlemeyer, Steve Platt

Jonathan Goodyear

Many people have helped lift me to where I am today. I would like to thank Darren Jensen, Paula Stana, and John Wagner at Arthur Andersen for patiently mentoring me while I was a development rookie. Without your help, I would have become an employment casualty early in my career.

I would like to thank Robert Teixeira for filling in the gaps in my knowledge while I was at PricewaterhouseCoopers. You have an amazing gift for distilling complex concepts into understandable information.

From The Home Shopping Network, I would like to thank Nick Ruotolo for taking a chance on a young, but ambitious, kid. I would also like to thank Ken McNamee for lending me the server that I used to test this book's code.

At *Visual Studio Magazine* (formerly *Visual Basic Programmer's Journal*), I would like to thank Susannah Pfalzer. With your help, my writing has improved tenfold. It has been a pleasure to work with you and the rest of the VSM staff (particularly Patrick Meader and Elden Nelson) over the past couple of years.

My co-authors, Brian Peek and Brad Fox, deserve a special thank-you for their help in bringing my book idea to life. You guys stepped in and did a fantastic job.

On a personal level, I would like to thank some of my lifelong friends for everything that they have done for me throughout the years. They are Stephen Ferrando, Patrick Tehan, Jamie Smith, James Rowbottom, and Damian Jee. You guys are the best!

To my wife, Joy, thank you for your endless patience while I pursue my career dreams. Without you, none of this would have been possible. I would like to thank my 1-year-old son, CJ, for opening my eyes to the wonders of fatherhood. Lastly, I would like to thank my sister-in-law, Cherie. Your relentless pursuit of your Olympic dreams in gymnastics has been an inspiration to me.

Brian Peek

This book, and life in general, would not be possible without the help and support of quite a few people. At the very top of that list would be Jonathan for giving me the opportunity to co-author this book with him.

Thanks to my parents for providing me with daily encouragement while writing. A thank you to Jennifer Trotts not only for coming back, but for making me cookies. I missed you. Thank you to Mark Zaugg, a great friend who has guided me through some tough times and who continues to be highly mellifluous (and Canadian). I would like to thank Stacy Tamburrino for teaching me a great deal about myself, and for many wonderful times and memories that I will always treasure. Thank you to Matthew Kennedy for being a great friend and sharing my cynicism toward the planet. I thank Arden Rauch for giving me confidence in my abilities at an early age. Thanks to Bob Thayer for putting up with my anal retentiveness on graphic layouts.

A big thank-you to my grandparents for putting me through college.

And finally, a short hello and thank you to my friends that have supported me in my endeavors: Adina Konheim, Jason Sawyer, Danette Slevinski, David Wallimann, Robert Sharlet, Michael Kilcullen, Girish Bhatia, Chuck Snead, Justin Whiting, Clare Mertz-Lee, Ed O'Brien, Jon Rodat, Dionne Ehrgood, Patricia Hoffman, Andy Lippitt, and the rest of the RAD staff.

Brad Fox

Every time you read these things, they seem so cliché, but what can you do? I will try to make mine interesting. First of all, I have to thank Jonathan Goodyear—yes, the author of this book, for giving me the opportunity to co-author with him. This has been a dream of mine for half my life, and he has helped me to accomplish it. Thank you, Jonathan. J

Next, I would like to thank David Waddleton for helping me with Chapter 13, "Debugging Web Services."

I would also like to thank Shannon McCoy for his support and the knowledge that I was able suck from his brain. Not to mention, he's the best friend anyone could have. I love ya, buddy.

A few individuals at Microsoft that were instrumental in making this book a success. These include Scott Guthrie, Rob Howard, Susan Warren, Shaykat Chaudhuri, and Dmitry Robsman. Thanks to all of you for your help on this book.

Tell Us What You Think

As the reader of this book, you are the most important critic and commentator. We value your opinion and want to know what we're doing right, what we could do better, what areas you'd like to see us publish in, and any other words of wisdom you're willing to pass our way.

As the Associate Publisher for New Riders Publishing, I welcome your comments. You can fax, email, or write me directly to let me know what you did or didn't like about this book—as well as what we can do to make our books stronger.

Please note that I cannot help you with technical problems related to the topic of this book, and that due to the high volume of mail I receive, I might not be able to reply to every message.

When you write, please be sure to include this book's title and author as well as your name and phone or fax number. I will carefully review your comments and share them with the author and editors who worked on the book.

Fax: 317-581-4663
Email: stephanie.wall@newriders.com
Mail: Stephanie Wall
            Associate Publisher
            New Riders Publishing
            201 West 103rd Street
            Indianapolis, IN 46290 USA

Introduction

Over the last year or so, an incredible amount of industry attention has been paid to Microsoft's new .NET Framework. It is the platform that will drive Microsoft's technology direction for at least the next five years. With so much at stake, developers have been clamoring to get their hands on anything and everything .NET.

The web portion of the multidimensional .NET Framework is ASP.NET. ASP.NET is the next generation of the Active Server Pages web-development platform, and it represents a quantum leap forward with respect to its feature set and scalability. With its newfound power, however, comes increased complexity.

This book is designed to address many of the problems and issues that developers will most assuredly face as they begin developing web applications using ASP.NET. Specifically, it introduces tried-and-true web-development strategies that reduce the risk of bugs and also enable bugs to be tracked down more easily when they do occur. This book also introduces the myriad new debugging tools that are available in ASP.NET and demonstrates how to use them effectively. Finally, this book tackles the issues and problems associated with each aspect of ASP.NET, showing potential error messages and explaining how to fix their causes.

By no means is this book a troubleshooting compendium. There is simply no way to account for all possible errors and bugs that can be encountered in an ASP.NET web application. Instead, this book gives solid advice on how to build bug-free web applications, gives you a firm understanding of the debugging tools that are at your disposal, and explains how to handle some of the more common errors and bugs that occur. When you finish this book, you should be confident enough to find and eliminate any bug that you encounter in your ASP.NET web application.

Who Will Benefit from This Book?

The intended audience for this book is intermediate to experienced developers and project managers. The persons responsible for establishing project coding standards, mentoring junior-level developers, and debugging web applications will get the most benefit from this book. The reader should be familiar with developing ASP.NET web applications with either Visual Basic .NET or C# (all code examples are provided in both languages). Some of the key skills that the reader will learn from this book are listed here:

- How to write code that reduces the chance of bugs
- Solid strategies for debugging large web applications
- How to leverage the many debugging tools available in ASP.NET, such as tracing, event logging, and conditional compiling

- How to track down bugs associated with specific parts of ASP.NET, such as User Controls, caching, ADO.NET, and web services
- Some of the caveats and issues common to migrating traditional ASP web applications to ASP.NET

Who Is This Book Not For?

This book is not for junior-level developers or for developers who are not relatively comfortable developing web applications with ASP.NET. It is not an ASP.NET tutorial; many other books on the market accomplish this task very well. Likewise, this book assumes that the reader is familiar with either Visual Basic .NET, C#, or both. The reader will not be able to understand and use the code examples without this knowledge.

Organization of This Book

The book parts and chapters are outlined in the next several sections.

Part I: ASP Debugging Basics

Chapter 1, "Conceptual Framework," explains some of the new concepts introduced with ASP.NET, such as server-side events, the ASP.NET page life cycle, and the new language options available.

Chapter 2, "Traditional Approaches to Debugging in ASP," covers some of the approaches used to debug traditional ASP web applications. It highlights several of the problems and shortcomings with the limited tools that were available.

Chapter 3, "Debugging Strategies," outlines several plans of attack for debugging ASP.NET web applications. This includes debugging application tiers individually and distilling complex code into smaller, more manageable pieces.

Chapter 4, "Code Structure That Eases Debugging," gives advice on how to build code that is both less likely to contain bugs and easier to debug when bugs creep in. Topics include code partitioning, control-of-flow guidelines, structured exception handling, and global exception handling.

Part II: ASP.NET Debugging Tools

Chapter 5, "Conditional Compiling," covers how to take advantage of function attributes and preprocessor directives to dynamically add debugging code to your web applications.

Chapter 6, "Tracing," shows you how to use the new `TraceContext` object available in ASP.NET and interpret its results. Trace configuration at both the page and the application levels is covered, as is using the Trace Viewer utility.

Chapter 7, "Visual Studio .NET Debugging Environment," introduces all the powerful debugging features packed into the Visual Studio .NET IDE. Some of the topics covered include how to set breakpoints, the call stack, the watch window, inline ASP.NET page debugging, and how to attach to processes.

Chapter 8, "Leveraging the Windows 2000 Event Log," explains how to write data to the Windows 2000 Event Log. Some of the things you will learn in this chapter include how to create custom event logs, how to handle both expected and unexpected events, and how to access the contents of the Windows 2000 Event Log via the web.

Part III: Debugging the New ASP.NET Features

Chapter 9, "Debugging Server-Side Controls," takes you through the process of creating a custom server control, outlining many of the issues that you might encounter. Practical advice and solutions for these issues are provided.

Chapter 10, "Debugging Data-Bound Controls," takes a close look at some of the common mistakes that can be made while using data-bound server controls. DataGrid, DataList, and the XML data binding are a few of the topics covered.

Chapter 11, "Debugging User Controls," covers many of the issues that you might encounter while building user controls. The basics are covered, as are properties, methods, and dynamic user control issues.

Chapter 12, "Caching Issues and Debugging," delves into the types of issues that crop up when leveraging caching in ASP.NET web applications. Highlights of this chapter include cache dependencies, output caching, the caching API, expiration callbacks, and declarative attributes.

Part IV: Debugging Related Technologies

Chapter 13, "Debugging Web Services," uncovers and offers solutions for many of the problems that you might encounter while building and implementing web services. Several different error messages are discussed. Some of the other topics covered are the XMLSerializer, SOAP, and UDDI.

Chapter 14, "Debugging .NET Components and HttpHandlers," explains how to use the `StackTrace` and `TextWriterTraceLister` objects to track down bugs in .NET components and `HttpHandlers`. The chapter also discusses issues with interfaces and state management.

Chapter 15, "COM+ Issues," covers the problems and issues that can occur when setting up components to leverage COM+. It also covers some of the runtime anomalies that might occur in the context of COM+.

Chapter 16, "Debugging ADO.NET," helps you interpret ADO.NET error messages, as well as track down bugs associated with each of the new ADO.NET objects. Database permissions issues are also briefly discussed.

Appendix

Appendix A, "Issues That Arise When Migrating from ASP to ASP.NET", is a collection of issues that you are likely to run into while porting your traditional ASP web applications to ASP.NET. The new declaration syntax for script blocks is discussed along with many other useful topics, such as page declaratives, events, and cookies.

Source Code and Errata

All the source code provided in this book can be downloaded from `www.debuggingasp.net`. Also available at the site are any corrections and updates to the text. The errata will be updated as issues are discovered and corrected.

Conventions

This book follows these typographical conventions:

- Listings, functions, variables, and other "computer language" are set in a fixed-pitch font—for example, "you should note the addition of the `RUNAT="server"` parameter added to each control."

- Code Continuation characthers ➥ are inserted into code when a line is too wide to fit into margins.

I

ASP Debugging Basics

1 Conceptual Framework

2 Traditional Approaches to Debugging in ASP

3 Debugging Strategies

4 Code Structure that Eases Debugging

1

Conceptual Framework

ASP.NET IS THE NEXT STAGE IN THE Active Server Page evolutionary process. It extends the existing ASP framework into a whole new realm of power. Now you can use ASP in a true three-tier architecture. With ASP.NET, you will be able to harness the power of a true programming language, such as Visual Basic .NET or C#, instead of VBScript. Is ASP.NET easy to use? Yes. Is it the same as ASP? Not even close. But do not fret. In this chapter, we discuss some of the new features of the ASP.NET framework and show how it differs from the ASP framework that you currently know and love—or at least know and use. First we focus on server-side events, and then we discuss new language options for use with the .NET version of ASP.

Understanding Server-Side Events

Server-side events are one of the fundamental changes in the ASP.NET architecture, compared to older versions of ASP. These server-side events provide for a programming model that is very similar to that of a traditional event-model Visual Basic application. The code for these events is generally stored in a separate file called a code-behind file. This allows for separation between your client and server code, making things much more organized and structured. The code-behind file simply contains everything that used to be contained within the <%%> files in your old ASP pages; however, it is strictly code without any HTML.

Now let's see what events are available to you on the server and how you can exploit them to your advantage.

Differences from Client-Side Events

The major difference between client-side events and server-side events, obviously, is that server-side events are handled on the server. This adds a great degree of flexibility and power to the existing ASP framework. It also provides for far more structured code.

Client-side events are part of the DHTML standard. They can be scripted in either JavaScript or VBScript, and they are embedded directly in the HTML of your page. These events allow you to trap button clicks, tab out of text boxes, detect the presence of the mouse cursor over certain controls, and handle other events that involve a user changing something on the client-side interface.

Server-side events enable you to respond to similar events, such as changing a text box or clicking a button, but, obviously, these are handled on the server instead of the client. Because a trip to the server is required to activate these events, only a small subset of events is available. These are generally limited to "click-type" events rather than "mouse-over" events. Imagine having to make a trip to the server every time your mouse moved 1 pixel!

Types of Server-Side Events

The types of events available on the server are very basic. For example, you will be able to respond to button clicks, text box changes, and drop-down box changes.

Take a look here at what one of these events looks like on the server. Listing 1.1 shows a very simple ASP page that contains a form with a text box and a Submit button.

Listing 1.1   **Simple ASP Page with a Form**

```
<HTML>
<BODY>
    <FORM ACTION="form.aspx" METHOD="POST" RUNAT="server">
        <INPUT TYPE="text" ID="txtText" RUNAT="server">
        <INPUT TYPE="submit" ID="btnSubmit" RUNAT="server">
    </FORM>
</BODY>
</HTML>
```

You will notice that this looks like some plain old HTML. However, you should note the addition of the RUNAT="server" parameter added to each control. This enables you to trap the events on the server and respond to them appropriately.

Now take a look at a server-side event associated with both the text box and the Submit button. Listing 1.2 shows this in C#.

Listing 1.2   **Server-Side Events in C#**

```
public void btnSubmit_ServerClick(sender As Object, e as EventArgs)
{
    txtText.Value = "You clicked the Submit button!";
}


protected void txtText_TextChanged(object sender, EventArgs e)
{
    Response.Write("TextChanged: " + txtText.Value);
}
```

Listing 1.3 shows the same event examples in Visual Basic.

Listing 1.3   **Server-Side Events in Visual Basic .NET**

```
Private Sub btnSubmit_ServerClick (sender As Object, e as EventArgs)
    txtText.Value = "You clicked the Submit button!"
End Sub

Sub txtText_TextChanged(sender Object, e As EventArgs)
    Response.Write("TextChanged: " & txtText.Value)
End Sub
```

In each of these examples, two separate events are being handled on the server: a Submit button being clicked and the value of a text box being changed. Each event that is handled on the server takes the `Object` and `EventArgs` arguments. The object is simply the object that sent you the event (for example, the button, the text box, and so on). The `EventArgs` argument contains any event- or object-specific arguments that are relevant to the object being acted upon.

ASP.NET Page Life Cycle

The life cycle of an ASP.NET page is similar to that of an ASP page. However, you can hook into a few new events as well. Table 1.1 runs down the events of an ASP.NET page.

Table 1.1   **Events in the Life Cycle of an ASP.NET Page**

Event	Description
Page_Init	This is the first event to be called in the process. Here you should provide any initialization code required for instantiation of the page.
Page_Load	At this point, control view state is restored. You can now read and update control properties.
Page_PreRender	This event is raised before any page content is sent to the browser.
Page_Unload	This is the very last event to be raised. At this point, you should clean up everything you have used, including closing connections and dereferencing objects.

In terms of the life cycle of your ASP.NET application, quite a few new events can be used inside the global.asax file. The events that can be hooked into in global.asax are described in Table 1.2.

Table 1.2   **Events That Can Be Used Inside global.asax**

Event	Description
Application_Start	Raised only once, when the application starts for the first time. Initialize application-wide things here.
Session_Start	Raised when a new user's session begins.
Application_End	Raised when your application shuts down or is reset. Clean up here.
Session_End	Raised when a user's session times out or is reset.
Application_Error	Raised when an unhandled exception is raised (those not caught in a try/catch block). You could call a logging routine here.
Application_BeginRequest	Raised every time a new request is received at the server.
Application_Authenticate	Raised when the request is to be authenticated. You can provide custom authentication code here.
Application_AuthorizeRequest	Raised when the request is to be authorized. Again, you can provide custom authorization code.

`Application_ResolveRequestCache`	Raised to enable you to stop the processing of requests that are cached.
`Application_AcquireRequestState`	Raised to enable you to maintain state in your application (session/user state).
`Application_PreRequestHandlerExecute`	The last event to be raised before the request is processed by the ASP.NET page or a web service.
`Application_PostRequestHandlerExecute`	Raised after the handler has finished processing the request.
`Application_ReleaseRequestState`	Raised to enable you to store the state of your application.
`Application_UpdateRequestCache`	Raised when processing is complete and the page is going into the ASP.NET cache.
`Application_EndRequest`	Raised at the very end of your request.
`Application_PreRequestHeadersSent`	Raised before HTTP headers are sent to the client. Here you can add custom headers to the list.

Now you can't say that you don't have enough control of what happens when and where in your ASP.NET application. These events also provide excellent places to hook into the ASP.NET processing chain for debugging, as you will see in some later chapters.

New Language Options

ASP.NET gives you unprecedented flexibility in that it enables you to use any .NET-enabled language as your server-side code. Out of the box, you'll be able to use Visual Basic, C#, JScript, and C++ with managed extensions as your server-side language. Note that we said *Visual Basic,* not *VBScript.* ASP.NET finally enables you to use a real programming language, not a scripted language. This offers a huge benefit in a couple areas.

First, you gain the speed of a compiled language versus an interpreted language. Because no time is wasted in parsing the scripted code, and because your code is compiled down into native machine code, you get a very significant speed increase.

Another benefit to using a real programming language is that you have real data types. If you're familiar with ASP, you will remember that every variable is of type Variant. ASP.NET enables you to use typed languages to your advantage. Now you will never need to question whether your variable is really a String or an Integer internally because you will be able to specify its type before it is assigned.

Summary

This chapter discussed server-side events and showed how they change the way an ASP.NET page is processed versus a traditional ASP page. It also discussed the advantages of using a real programming language to write your server code. The next chapter takes a look at some existing ways to debug ASP code that can be easily used in the ASP.NET environment. Later chapters discuss debugging techniques that are new and specific to ASP.NET only.

2

Traditional Approaches to Debugging in ASP

IF YOU HAVE EVER USED A PREVIOUS version of ASP, you are already aware of the nightmare that debugging a traditional ASP application can become. This chapter explains some of the shortcomings of the original ASP technology, the potential problems and pitfalls involved in debugging a typical ASP application, and a few ways to overcome these obstacles. At the end of the chapter, you'll find a debugging object that can be used in tandem with a traditional ASP page to display a great deal of useful information for tracking down those pesky errors in your ASP code.

Structure of Pre–ASP.NET Pages

As you will soon see, the structure of a page in previous versions of ASP is quite different from that of an ASP.NET page. Pre–ASP.NET pages are severely lacking in the structure department. Although there are a few ways to make your ASP code slightly structured, several lines become blurred. This section talks about a few of the common problems that developers run into when developing with previous versions of ASP.

The Great Monolith

So how do you currently write ASP pages? Well, if you're anything like us—and let's hope that you're not, in some respects—your ASP pages have the structure of a 50-story skyscraper made out of Popsicle sticks. Now, don't get us wrong: A certain degree of structure can be attained with standard ASP programming, but it is not the type of structure and organization that is obtained with a real programming language. The fact is, there just isn't any great way to write extremely structured code in ASP like there is in Visual Basic or C#.

For example, if you have a series of "global" functions that are used throughout your application, you probably shove them into an .asp file and use the `#include file` directive to bring them into the rest of your .asp pages to avoid code repetition. Although this might get the job done, you might not realize what is happening behind the scenes with the script parser.

By including pages in this manner, they simply get tacked on at the point where you include them. This means that the entire included page is parsed and processed even if only a single constant declaration, for example, is used out of it. Luckily, because ASP.NET uses true, compiled languages, it gets you out of this bind.

Pasta Nightmare

You probably have heard the expression "spaghetti code," which is code that lacks structure and clear separation among the main elements. Traditional ASP code is the epitome of spaghetti code. Code does not get much more tangled up in any language quite like it does in ASP. The main reason for this is the lack of a distinct separation between client-side presentation code and server-side business/logic code.

In the traditional ASP environment, you generally wind up mixing your HTML presentation layer with your VBScript server code, as shown in Listing 2.1.

Listing 2.1   **A Typical ASP Page**

```
<HTML>
<BODY>
<%
    Dim pvNameArray
    pvNameArray = Array("Jonathan Goodyear", "Brian Peek", "Brad Fox")
    Response.Write "<select name='Author'>"
    For i = 0 to 2
        Response.Write "<option value='" & i & "'>" & pvNameArray(i) &
        ➥"</option>"
    Next
%>
</BODY>
</HTML>
```

As you can see, instead of a very clear distinction between the HTML that creates the drop-down box and the code that fills it, the two are very much intertwined. This type of coding conflicts with the basic principles of "three-tier" programming. The theory of three-tier programming is that there is a distinct separation among the client presentation layer, the server business logic layer, and the database layer. In ASP, the lines between these layers can very easily become blurred. In the previous example, you are doing work that could and should be performed at the business logic layer instead of at the client layer.

The Inclusion Conclusion

Code reuse is a very important part of writing any type of application. No one wants to rewrite the same code to perform the same function time and time again. Most programming languages provide a way for developers to include libraries of functions in their applications, saving them from having to reinvent the wheel every time they need to do something simple. ASP allows for something similar, but it has one very major flaw.

For example, imagine that you are writing a screen for an application that needs to pull several ADO recordsets from a database and display them to the user in a table. The code to grab the recordset from the database might look similar to Listing 2.2.

Listing 2.2   **Code to Retrieve an ADO Recordset**

```
<%
Const adLockReadOnly = 1
Const adLockPessimistic = 2
Const adLockOptimistic = 3
Const adLockBatchOptimistic = 4

Const adOpenForwardOnly = 0
Const adOpenKeyset = 1
Const adOpenDynamic = 2
Const adOpenStatic = 3

Const adCmdText = 1
Const adCmdTable = 2
Const adCmdStoredProc = 4
Const adCmdUnknown = 8
%>
<HTML>
<BODY>
<%
    Set poCon = Server.CreateObject("ADODB.Connection")
    poCon.Open "Driver=
    ➥{SQL Server};Server=(local);Database=Pubs;UID=sa;PWD="
```

continues

```
Set poRS = Server.CreateObject("ADODB.Recordset")
poRS.Open "SELECT * FROM authors ORDER BY au_lname", poCon,
➥adOpenKeyset, adLockReadOnly, adCmdText
Do While Not poRS.EOF
        Response.Write poRS.Fields("au_fname").Value & " " &
        poRS.Fields("au_lname").Value & "<br>"
        poRS.MoveNext
    Loop
%>
</BODY>
</HTML>
```

Every time you need to retrieve an ADO recordset, you must rewrite the code that creates the connection object, opens the connection, creates the recordset object, and opens the recordset. So how do you solve this in traditional ASP? Well, you can write some generic routines that open connections or open recordsets and put them in a separate file. Then you can use the #include file="<filename>" directive to pull this file into the page that is about to be displayed to the user. However, this scenario contains one major downfall: Every page that is included in this fashion is parsed in its entirety. So, if you created an ASP page that included all your database routines for your entire application, and you then included it on a page on which only one of the functions is used, the ASP processor still would parse the entire page and work its way through all the unused code before giving you what you need. Without a doubt, this is terribly inefficient. So how do you combat that in ASP?

The way to currently work around this problem in ASP is to move your business logic code into components. From ASP, you can create an instance of your component and call methods on it just as you would from Visual Basic. With this approach, you gain the benefit of a compiled language—that is, increased speed and decreased memory usage. However, this approach suffers from a number of downfalls. First, you will be forced to compile your code every time you want to make a change instead of just editing a text file. This can become quite cumbersome if your site undergoes many changes before becoming stable.

Second, when the object is instantiated in your ASP page, you get only a generic object that pretends to be the real object. Because of this, every time you call a method on that object, the GetIDsOfNames API call is fired to locate the position of the method in the object's vtable. This is a definite performance hit.

Finally, deploying components can be a difficult process. Access to the server is required to register the resulting DLLs. This runs contrary to the simple process of copying assemblies to the server in the case of a ASP.NET application, which can even be done through a simple shared drive or folder.

Problems and Shortcomings

Although ASP is a very powerful technology, it suffers from a number of problems and shortcomings. It lacks separation of client- and server-side code, it does not allow for structured programming, and it does not follow an event-style programming model, among other issues. Luckily, ASP.NET addresses many of these problems and turns ASP into an even more powerful and easy-to-use technology for today's high-powered web-based applications.

No Events

If you're a Visual Basic programmer, you are quite familiar with event-based programming. For example, if you drop a button on a form in Visual Basic, then when a user clicks it, it generates a `Click` event that you can respond to and act on appropriately. In ASP, this type of programming model is nonexistent, even though the same types of events are taking place in your web page–based application. That is, buttons are being clicked, users are entering and leaving fields, and so on. Why shouldn't you have the capability to answer these events in a similar manner? This is one area in which ASP.NET really shines.

Includes Eat Up Memory

As discussed in the previous section, "includes" are a horribly inefficient way to do something that is inherently very simple. As an ASP programmer, you should be able to link a library of functions into the main application without a detrimental performance hit. Most programming languages allow for dynamically or statically linked libraries that contain commonly called functions directly to the application only once, in the case of static linking, or that allow them to be called from an external binary file in the scenario of dynamic linking.

An excellent example of a bloated include file is the ADOVBS.INC file provided by Microsoft, which defines an ASP interface for ADO. This file is huge, and most people will use only a few items out of the myriad of things it declares. Even though you might use only those very few items, however, the entire page is parsed every single time it is referenced.

In a real programming language, such as Visual Basic or C, you would compile against a library containing pointers for the real versions of the functions in precompiled DLLs. In this way, you are never wasting time accessing any portion of the ADO library that you don't explicitly request.

Scripted Language Versus Compiled Language

One of the major problems with ASP is that it is a scripted language rather than a compiled language. This involves an enormous and severe performance hit, for a number of reasons.

First, the script parser needs to parse the entire page top to bottom before any of the code can be executed. Second, when the code is parsed, it is not generated into a native machine code that can be executed directly every time thereafter. This process must be repeated every single time that the page is rendered, which is obviously incredibly inefficient.

Old Strategies That Still Do the Job Well

Although a variety of new debugging features in the Visual Studio .NET IDE can be used in debugging your ASP.NET applications, some old methods and tricks from the days of ASP are still worthwhile.

Using the *Response* Object

Previous versions of ASP are built on the foundation of five objects: Response, Request, Server, Application, and Session. The Response object is used to send information from the server down to the client's browser. The Write method of the Response object can be used to dynamically write content to the client's browser. This is one of the easiest ways to debug standard ASP pages and is still applicable in the new architecture.

The problem with this approach is that it isn't very pretty. At the end of debugging a long logic process, you will wind up with a pile of if/then statements and Response.Write() calls littered throughout your .asp pages. This output can get lost inside the HTML if it's not placed properly. A better approach is to create a specific debugging object that outputs important and pertinent information but handles it in a much nicer and cleaner fashion. You will write an object like this later in the chapter so that you can use it very easily in your ASP debugging procedures.

Using the *Server* Object

Internet Information Server (IIS) 5.0 included a new method on the Server object, called GetLastError. This method returns an ASPError object that contains almost everything you need to know about the error except how to correct it. Table 2.1 shows what properties are available on the ASPError object.

Table 2.1   **Properties of the *ASPError* Object**

ASP Code	Error Code from IIS
Number	COM error code
Source	Source of line that caused error
Category	Type of error (ASP, script, object)
File	ASP file where error occurred
Line	Line number where error occurred

Column	Column where error occurred
Description	A text description of the error
ASPDescription	Detailed description if error was ASP-related

You will notice that the information returned in the object is the same information that is presented to you in a standard ASP error page. However, with this information at your disposal, you can create a custom error page that is displayed instead of the standard ASP error page. You can set the error to your own custom page by using the IIS Admin tool. If a custom page is selected, then when the server encounters an error, it will perform a `Server.Transfer` to the error page, maintaining all state information to the new page. This enables you to get an instance of the `ASPError` object and pull out the pertinent information for display as a debugging guide. Listing 2.3 shows such a page.

Listing 2.3   **Sample ASP Error Page Using the *ASPError* Object**

```
<%
    Dim Err
    Set Err = Server.GetLastError()
%>
<HTML>
<HEAD>
<TITLE>Error</TITLE>
</HEAD>
<BODY>
    An error has occurred!
    <p>
    <table border>
        <tr>
            <td>Description</td>
            <td><%=Err.Description%></td>
        </tr>
        <tr>
            <td>Number</td>
            <td><%=Err.Number%></td>
        </tr>
        <tr>
            <td>Category</td>
            <td><%=Err.Category%></td>
        </tr>
        <tr>
```

continues

Listing 2.3 **Continued**

```
            <td>File</td>
            <td><%=Err.File%></td>
        </tr>
        <tr>
            <td>Line</td>
            <td><%=Err.Line%></td>
        </tr>
        <tr>
            <td>Column</td>
            <td><%=Err.Column%></td>
        </tr>
            <td>Source</td>
            <td><%=Err.Source%></td>
        </tr>
        <tr>
            <td>ASP Description</td>
            <td><%=Err.ASPDescription%></td>
        </tr>
    </table>
</BODY>
</HTML>
<%  Set Err = Nothing%>
```

An ASP Debug Object

In preparation for the debugging and tracing tools available to you in ASP.NET, you'll now create a debug object that works in previous versions of ASP. For this example, you will need to have VBScript 5.0 or higher running on your server. VBScript 5.0 introduced classes into the scripting language, and you will be taking advantage of that here.

First, take a look at the code of your object, shown in Listing 2.4.

Listing 2.4 *clsDebug* **Source Code (***clsDebug.asp***)**

```
<style type="text/css">
        span.trace__ { background-color:white; color:black;font: 10pt
    ➥ verdana, arial; }
        span.trace__ table { font: 10pt verdana, arial; cellspacing:0;
    ➥ cellpadding:0; margin-bottom:25;}
        span.trace__ tr.subhead { background-color:cccccc;}
        span.trace__ th { padding:0,3,0,3 }
```

```
      span.trace__  th.alt { background-color:black; color:white;
      ➥padding:3,3,2,3; }
      span.trace__  td { padding:0,3,0,3 }
      span.trace__  tr.alt { background-color:eeeeee }
      span.trace__  h1 { font: 24pt verdana, arial; margin:0,0,0,0}
      span.trace__  h2 { font: 18pt verdana, arial; margin:0,0,0,0}
      span.trace__  h3 { font: 12pt verdana, arial; margin:0,0,0,0}
      span.trace__  th a { color:darkblue; font: 8pt verdana, arial; }
      span.trace__  a { color:darkblue;text-decoration:none }
      span.trace__  a:hover { color:darkblue;text-decoration:underline; }
      span.trace__  div.outer { width:90%; margin:15,15,15,15}
      span.trace__  table.viewmenu td { background-color:006699; color:white;
      ➥padding:0,5,0,5; }
      span.trace__  table.viewmenu td.end { padding:0,0,0,0; }
      span.trace__  table.viewmenu a {color:white; font: 8pt verdana,arial; }
      span.trace__  table.viewmenu a:hover {color:white; font: 8pt verdana,
      ➥arial; }
      span.trace__  a.tinylink {color:darkblue; font: 8pt verdana, arial;
      ➥text-decoration:underline;}
      span.trace__  a.link {color:darkblue; text-decoration:underline;}
      span.trace__  div.buffer {padding-top:7; padding-bottom:17;}
      span.trace__  .small { font: 8pt verdana, arial }
      span.trace__  table td { padding-right:20 }
      span.trace__  table td.nopad { padding-right:5 }
</style>
<%

      Class clsDebug
              Dim mb_Enabled
              Dim md_RequestTime
              Dim md_FinishTime
              Dim mo_Storage

              Public Default Property Get Enabled()
                      Enabled = mb_Enabled
              End Property

              Public Property Let Enabled(bNewValue)
                      mb_Enabled = bNewValue
              End Property
```

continues

Listing 2.3 **Continued**

```
                    Private Sub Class_Initialize()
                        md_RequestTime = Now()
                        Set mo_Storage =
                        ➥Server.CreateObject("Scripting.Dictionary")
                    End Sub


        Public Sub Print(label, output)
            If Enabled Then
                Call mo_Storage.Add(label, output)
            End If
    End Sub


        Public Sub [End]()
            md_FinishTime = Now()
        If Enabled Then
            Response.Write "<p><span class='trace__'>" & vbCrLf
            Call PrintSummaryInfo()
            Call PrintCollection("VARIABLE STORAGE", mo_Storage)
            Call PrintCollection("QUERYSTRING COLLECTION",
            ➥Request.QueryString())
            Call PrintCollection("FORM COLLECTION", Request.Form())
            Call PrintCollection("COOKIES COLLECTION", Request.Cookies())
            Call PrintCollection("SERVER VARIABLES COLLECTION",
            Request.ServerVariables())
             Response.Write "</span>"
        End If
    End Sub


    Private Sub PrintSummaryInfo()
        Dim i


        PrintTableHeader("SUMMARY INFO")

Response.Write("<tr><td>Start Time of Request</td><td>" & md_RequestTime
➥ & "</td></tr>" & vbCrLf)
Response.Write("<tr class='alt'><td>Finish Time of Request</td><td>" &
➥ md_FinishTime & "</td></tr>" & vbCrLf)
Response.Write("<tr><td>Elapsed Time</td><td>" & DateDiff("s",
➥ md_RequestTime, md_FinishTime) & "</td></tr>" & vbCrLf)
Response.Write("<tr class='alt'><td>Request Type</td><td>" &
➥ Request.ServerVariables("REQUEST_METHOD") & "</td></tr>" & vbCrLf)
Response.Write("<tr><td>Status Code</td><td>" & Response.Status &
➥ "</td></tr>" & vbCrLf)
```

```
            Response.Write "</tr></table>"
    End Sub

    Private Sub PrintCollection(Byval Name, ByVal Collection)
        Dim vItem
        Dim i

        PrintTableHeader(Name)

        For Each vItem In Collection
            If i mod 2 = 0 Then
                Response.Write("<tr>")
            else
                Response.Write("<tr class='alt'>")
            end if
            Response.Write("<td>" & vItem & "</td><td>" & Collection(vItem)
            ➥ & "</td></tr>" & vbCrLf)
            i = i + 1
        Next

        Response.Write "</tr></table>"
    End Sub

    Private Sub Class_Terminate()
        Set mo_Storage = Nothing
    End Sub

    Private Sub PrintTableHeader(ByVal Name)
Response.Write "<table cellpadding='0' width='100%' cellspacing='0'>" &
➥ vbCrLf
Response.Write "<tr><th class='alt' colspan='10' align='left'><h3><b>" &
➥ Name & "</b></h3></th></tr>" & vbCrLf
Response.Write "<tr class='subhead' align='left'><th
➥ width='10%'>Name</th><th width='10%'>Value</th></tr>" & vbcrlf
    End Sub
End Class
%>
```

Using this object for debugging and tracing is extremely simple. All you need to do is include the page at the top of the ASP page that you want to track, instantiate an instance of the object in your ASP page, enable it, and then call the Print method to output your own debugging information. When you're finished, call the End method to display the collection information. Finally, set it equal to Nothing to destroy it. Another nice feature of this object is that it can be enabled and disabled at will. If you tossed in a few Debug.Print calls for testing and did not want them output for a demo, for example, you could simply disable the debug object on that page to stop the output from appearing instead of manually removing all the lines that reference it.

As an additional guide, take a look at Listing 2.5, which shows an example ASP page where the debug object that you just built is being used.

Listing 2.5   **Sample ASP Page Using clsDebug (*DebugTest.asp*)**

```
<%@ Language=VBScript %>
<%Option Explicit%>
<!—#include file="clsDebug.asp"—>

<%
    Dim Debug
    Dim x

    Set Debug = New clsDebug    ' Instantiate it
    Debug.Enabled = True        ' Enable it

    ' Set a test cookie
    Response.Cookies("TestCookie") = "This is a test cookie!"
%>
<HTML>
<HEAD>
<TITLE>Test Page</TITLE>
</HEAD>
<BODY>
<%
    x = 10

    ' Output a debug string
    Debug.Print "x before form", x
%>
    <form method="POST" action="DebugTest.asp" name="frmForm1"
➥ id="frmForm1">
        <input type="text" name="txtText1" id="txtText1">
        <input type="submit" name="btnSubmit1" id="btnSubmit1">
    </form>

    <form method="GET" action="DebugTest.asp" name="frmForm2"
➥ id="frmForm2">
```

```
            <input type="text" name="txtText2" id="txtText2">
            input type="submit" name="btnSubmit2" id="btnSubmit2">
      </form>
<%

    x = 20

    Debug.Print "x after form", x

    ' Close it all up
    Debug.End
    Set Debug = Nothing
%>
</BODY>
</HTML>
```

After calling the End method, all information regarding form submissions, the query string, cookies, server variables, and your own variable-tracking statements is displayed. The output is almost identical to the trace output that is included as part of the ASP.NET functionality that you will be looking at in Chapter 6, "Tracing." The output of this object can be seen in Figure 2.1.

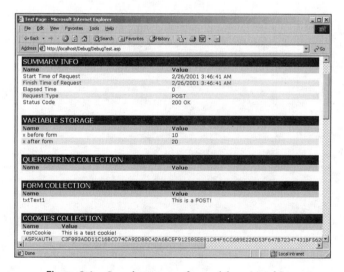

Figure 2.1   Sample output of your debugging object.

Summary

This chapter looked at problems and shortcomings of previous ASP versions, issues with debugging it, and several solutions to these problems, including a tool that you can use to help find problems in your own ASP code. You also learned about the problems inherent in "including" files, the shortcomings of a scripting language versus a compiled language, and the lack of an event programming model in the existing ASP framework.

The next chapter discusses some general strategies for debugging applications. With this information in mind, you will be ready to tackle the brave new world of ASP.NET debugging.

3

Debugging Strategies

DEBUGGING WEB APPLICATIONS IS AN ART very much like warfare. Before entering into a battle, you create a plan of attack and then execute it to defeat your enemy. Few would consider such an engagement without a plan—thoughts of doing so conjure up images of soldiers blindly running at the enemy and throwing themselves into the path of gunfire. Yet, many developers attempt to engage in a debugging battle without any such plan or method.

Debugging under these circumstances might consist of randomly attempting different things, in vain hope that one of them (or a random combination of them) will solve the problem. Although sometimes this works (hey, somebody wins the lottery), it all too often leads to long, frustrating hours yielding little, if any, meaningful progress. Even a slightly more intuitive approach, such as basing your debugging efforts on past experiences, falls short of the ideal. This is because working with newer technologies reduces the effectiveness of the experience factor. We need more than a collection of memorized "fixes" to problems. We need a complete process to track down and eliminate bugs in code.

In this chapter, we introduce some tried-and-true methods for debugging web applications. These methods link together to form a complete approach to narrowing and eliminating those hard-to-find problems. They all aim to reduce the amount of time required to find bugs in code. The chapter is oriented more toward overall methodology than technical implementation, so we will keep the examples simple.

We will demonstrate more complex examples of each of these methods, as well as the overall approach, throughout the book as we go into more detail on debugging specific parts of ASP.NET. We will be sure to mention which method or methods we are using so that you can keep track of them. Note also that the following methods are designed mostly to track down semantic errors. These are runtime or logic errors. Syntax or compile-time errors will be discussed in the context of each technology covered in the following chapters.

Tier Sandboxes

The first question that must be answered to fix a bug is, "Where is it?" Most ASP.NET web applications have three (or more) tiers to them, so finding a bug (particularly a subtle one) in such a large system can at first appear to be a daunting task. The first thing that you can do to get a better handle on the situation is break the system into parts. Because web applications are typically broken into logical tiers already, it only makes sense to use this as the first level of debugging segmentation. For the purposes of this book, we assume a system containing three tiers: a data tier, a business object tier, and a user interface (for example, web page) tier. You can then test each tier and eliminate the ones that are not contributing to the problem. This will leave the tier(s) that you need to concentrate more debugging effort on.

Data Tier

In the context of an ASP.NET web application, the data tier is usually represented by a relational database, but it could also be represented by another data source, such as an Exchange server or Directory Services. Regardless of the data source, to eliminate the data tier from the list of suspects, you must determine three things. The first is whether the data is set up properly in the data source. We can't tell you how many times we have been frustrated to the point at which we are contemplating tossing the monitor out the window, only to discover that the data was not set up properly or had been changed or removed by one of the other developers on the team. The moral of the story is to establish one or more known test scenarios and verify the data setup for each of the scenarios each time before you run it.

The second thing that you must determine to verify that the data tier is not the source of your problem is to make sure that you can connect to the data source. How you do this is largely determined by the nature of your data source. As an example, if you are connecting to an OLEDB data source, it helps to verify that your connection string is properly formatted and that it contains valid server information and security credentials. A good way to do this is to create what is known as a data link file. To do this, right-click the desktop, select New, and then select Text Document. Rename the new text file that is created to test.udl. During this process, the warning prompt (shown in Figure 3.1) will be displayed.

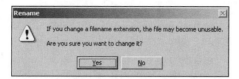

Figure 3.1   Warning prompt displayed when changing filenames.

Click Yes, or just press the Enter key. If you double-click the test.udl file that you just created, the Data Link Properties dialog box is displayed. Select an appropriate data source from the Provider tab, and fill in the connection information on the Connection tab. The Connection tab for a SQL Server connection would look like the one shown in Figure 3.2.

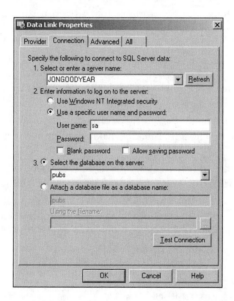

Figure 3.2   Dialog box used to set the properties of the data link file.

After you finish this, you can test whether a connection to the data source can be achieved by clicking the Test Connection button. A failure at this level indicates that you are unable to even talk to your data source, let alone exchange information with it.

A Convenient Data Link File Feature

A nice feature about data link files is that after you create a connection string that works, you can open the file in Notepad and extract a perfectly formatted connection string to use in your ASP.NET code. If you are going to do this, however, be sure to check the Allow Saving Password check box on the Connection tab so that your password information is stored in the data link file.

If a connection to the data source can be successfully achieved, then you can run some tests on your data conversations to make sure that they are working properly. As an example, you could execute a SQL Server 2000 stored procedure directly in Query Analyzer with hard-coded parameters to determine whether the results returned are what you expected. Be sure not to test your data conversations through any data component layers such as ADO, ADO.NET, or custom data extraction components because this adds an additional level of ambiguity to your test. Right now, you just want to determine whether the data tier is doing its job. After you have checked the data tier, the business object tier is next.

Business Object Tier

The business object tier is the glue that holds the entire web application together. Because of this, you must determine not only whether there are bugs internal to the tier, but also whether there are bugs in the communication layers between it and the other tiers in the web application. Luckily, making this multifaceted determination is relatively straightforward.

The most common object used as a communication layer between the business object tier and the data tier is ADO. Microsoft's new .NET architecture comes with a new version of this popular library, ADO.NET. We'll go into more detail about ADO.NET in later chapters in the book, and we'll focus on debugging issues with it in Chapter 16, "Debugging ADO.NET." For now, you can use a simple test to see whether ADO.NET is capable of connecting to your data source properly, as shown in Listings 3.1 and 3.2.

Listing 3.1   **A Simple Test to See Whether ADO.NET Connects to the Data Source Properly (C#)**

```
<%@ Page Language="C#" ClientTarget="DownLevel" %>
<%@ Import Namespace="System.Data" %>
<%@ Import Namespace="System.Data.OleDb" %>

<%
string conString = "Provider=SQLOLEDB.1;" +
     "Persist Security Info=True;" +
     "User ID=sa;" +
     "Password=;" +
```

```
        "Initial Catalog=pubs;" +
        "Data Source=localhost";


OleDbConnection cn = new OleDbConnection(conString);
cn.Open();


if(cn.State==ConnectionState.Open)
{
        Response.Write("Success!");
}


cn.Close();
%>
```

Listing 3.2   **A Simple Test to See Whether ADO.NET Connects to the Data Source Properly (Visual Basic .NET)**

```
<%@ Page Language="VB" ClientTarget="DownLevel" %>
<%@ Import Namespace="System.Data" %>
<%@ Import Namespace="System.Data.OleDb" %>


<%
Dim conString As String = "Provider=SQLOLEDB.1;" & _
        "Persist Security Info=True;" & _
        "User ID=sa;" & _
        "Password=;" & _
        "Initial Catalog=pubs;" & _
        "Data Source=localhost"


Dim cn As OleDbConnection = New OleDbConnection(conString)
cn.Open()


If cn.State = ConnectionState.Open Then
        Response.Write("Success!")
End If


cn.Close()
%>
```

If "Success!" gets rendered to the browser, then you know that ADO.NET (your communication layer between the business object tier and the data tier) is working properly. We'll go into reasons why it might not be working properly when we discuss ADO.NET debugging more thoroughly in Chapter 16.

The meat of the business object tier is comprised of two major parts. First, there is the intrinsic ASP.NET functionality, such as server controls, user controls, and data binding. Second, there are custom components. The bulk of the rest of this book (Parts III, "Debugging the New ASP.NET Features," and IV, "Debugging Related Technologies," in particular) is dedicated to dissecting each of these topics one at a time, covering how to find bugs in each and how to solve them. For now, suffice it to say that if you have established that your data tier and communication layers are working properly and you are still seeing peculiar or incorrect behavior in your web application, then the business object tier is most likely the source.

Communication with the user interface tier is usually handled through the intrinsic ASP.NET `Response` object, so this layer is usually working just fine. A simple call to `Response.Write()` can confirm this. Most of the problems with communicating with the bottom tier of your web application occur for one of two reasons. First, you might not be conveying the proper information. As an example, one gotcha that will plague you in your development efforts (although it is easy to solve) occurs when you forget to add the `runat=server` attribute to your ASP.NET server controls. This causes server event handlers to fail, and the page cannot maintain state.

The second reason why you might have trouble communicating with the bottom tier of your web application arises in the case of nonuser interface communication such as web services. We will discuss the nuances of debugging web services in Chapter 13, "Debugging Web Services."

User Interface Tier

Although this book focuses on server-side ASP.NET debugging, it is helpful to know when you are dealing with a bug on the client side (user interface tier). As a general rule, if you are prompted with an error dialog box similar to the one shown in Figure 3.3, then you have a problem with your client-side script.

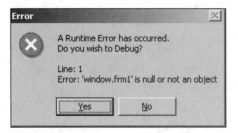

Figure 3.3   An example of a client-side runtime error dialog box.

Unfortunately, not all client-side bugs will generate error dialog boxes. The user interface tier is subject to many of the same subtle logic and functionality bugs that can occur on the data tier and the business object tier. The concepts introduced in this chapter are generic enough to be applied to all tiers in a web application, although a good book on VBScript or JavaScript will provide a better reference on the nuances of client-side programming and its object model.

Divide and Conquer

Now that you a have a list of tiers that might be causing problems, the next step is to trace the path of execution that the "buggy" functionality is following. When you have a list of objects, functions, stored procedures, and so on that are being used, you can divide them and attack them individually. The advantage to taking this encapsulated debugging approach is that you can effectively granulize the problem into tiny chunks of code that either work or don't work. The most effective place to start (where else?) is at the beginning. Regardless of the code encountered, the same strategies can be applied.

Logic Test

Before rushing in and making changes to a section of code, take a step back and look at the big picture. What are you trying to accomplish with the code? A good way to clarify this is to create a "mission statement" for the code segment. It sounds cheesy, but it actually works well. Before you begin debugging, add this mission statement as a comment at the top of the code segment. It makes you think about what the code needs to get done, and it provides you with a reference to look back on if the toils of developing and debugging give you a temporary case of vertigo. Take care to state not only all the tasks that the code should accomplish, but also in what order they are to be done.

Plan for Debugging from the Start
Ideally, you should create code mission statements at the initial development time as well so that you don't forget what the code's original purpose was when you return to debug it later.

Now compare the mission statement that you just created with what the code is actually doing. Sometimes this is easier said than done. It sometimes helps to traverse the code, line by line, adding comments about what the code is doing. When you get done, you can compare the sum total of the line-level comments to the mission statement at the top of the code. Not surprisingly, many problems can be diagnosed right off the bat because a piece of logic was either omitted or included in the wrong order. If your logic stands up to the test, though, don't despair. You have only just begun to fight.

Inputs and Outputs

Perfect logic doesn't mean a hill of beans if you are working with incorrect data. The old adage "Garbage in, garbage out" definitely applies here. You need to verify that the data that is going into your code is correct, or else you cannot expect the results to be what you want. A good place to start testing inputs is right in the beginning of the code block that you are testing. Take a look at how the code in Listings 3.3 and 3.4 accomplishes this.

Listing 3.3   **Validating the Input of a Method (C#)**

```
<script language="C#" runat="server">
class foo
{
       public int CalcThis(int a, int b)
       {
              if(a < 7) throw new Exception("a=" + a.ToString() +
                 " is too small");
              if(b > 2) throw new Exception("b=" + b.ToString() +
                 " is too big");

              return(a + b);
       }
}
</script>
```

Listing 3.4   **Validating the Input of a Method (Visual Basic .NET)**

```
<script language="VB" runat="server">
Class foo
       Public Function CalcThis(a as Integer, b as Integer) _
              as Integer

              If a < 7 Then Throw New Exception("a=" & CStr(a) & _
                    " is too small")
              If b > 2 Then Throw New Exception("b=" & CStr(b) & _
                    " is too big")

              CalcThis = (a + b)
       End Function
End Class
</script>
```

Before any code has had a chance to modify the input parameters, you should run checks to see if they fall within the valid bounds that you have specified. This enables you to inspect them for accuracy. If the check fails, you can throw an exception to the browser that gives you some helpful debugging information. If an input parameter is of a complex data type (for example, an ADO.NET OleDbDataReader), you might want to check one or more of its properties to verify that it contains the proper data. If your procedure is more complex and modifies the input parameters within the code, you might want to place these checkpoints in more than one place to verify that they are being properly calculated.

The output to a function can be tested in a similar fashion. You can test the bounds of the output values of your code and throw exceptions as appropriate. Listings 3.5 and 3.6 exemplify this sort of test.

Listing 3.5   **Validating the Output of a Method (C#)**

```
<%@ Page Language="C#" ClientTarget="DownLevel" %>

<%
foo objFoo = new foo();
int a = 8;
int b = 2;
int c = 0;

c = objFoo.CalcThis(a,b);
if(c < 10) throw new Exception("c=" + c.ToString() +
    " is too small.");

Response.Write(c.ToString());
%>
```

Listing 3.6   **Validating the Output of a Method (Visual Basic .NET)**

```
<%@ Page Language="VB" ClientTarget="DownLevel" %>

<%
Dim objFoo As New foo
Dim a As Integer = 8
Dim b As Integer = 2
Dim c As Integer = 0

c = objFoo.CalcThis(a,b)
If c < 10 Then Throw New Exception("c=" & CStr(c) & _
    " is too small.")

Response.Write(CStr(c))
%>
```

Don't worry if you are unfamiliar with using exceptions in this manner. We will be covering them in detail in Chapter 4, "Code Structure That Eases Debugging." They are extremely useful for flagging data integrity issues with the data that goes into and comes out of your processes.

> **Beyond the Basics**
>
> In Part II, "Debugging the New ASP.NET Features," we will introduce more advanced tools and methods for handling debugging tasks. These tools are the Trace object, the Visual Studio Runtime Debugging Environment, and the event log utility objects.

Simple Before Complex

Some common words of wisdom are that you must first learn to crawl before you learn to walk. Nowhere do these words ring more true than in the case of web application development. When building complex functionality, it is often better to start with a simple foundation and gradually build upon it. This technique can be used both when you are building new functionality and when you are debugging existing functionality that doesn't seem to be working properly. It is much easier to find the source of a problem when you are building in small steps rather than in large ones. Take the following scenario as an example. Imagine that you want to build a form that has a text field that must contain a value when the form is submitted. You want the form to be validated by a dynamically generated ASP.NET RequiredFieldValidator control.

The Basics

The first order of business is to get the form to display. That is done with the ASP.NET code shown in Listing 3.7.

Listing 3.7   **Displaying a Simple Form**

```
<%@ Page Language="C#" ClientTarget="DownLevel" %>


<form id="frm1" runat="server">
    <asp:TextBox id="text1" runat="server" />
    <br>
    <asp:Button id="button1" text="Click Me" runat="server" />
</form>
```

> **Notes About This Part of the Example**
>
> For simplicity, we have left out the form's ACTION attribute, so the form will post to itself. Also, even though the Language attribute of the Page directive indicates C# as the language, you have not done anything language-specific yet. As we add more complex code to the example, we will show implementations in both C# and Visual Basic .NET.

At this point, the form does little other than maintain form state by using the runat="server" attribute of the ASP.NET server controls. Although you eventually want to use a dynamically generated ASP.NET field validator control, you start out simply by creating one the traditional way. After adding an ASP.NET RequiredFieldValidator control, your code now looks like Listing 3.8.

Listing 3.8 **Adding a Static ASP.NET Validation Control**

```
<%@ Page Language="C#" ClientTarget="DownLevel" %>

<form id="frm1" runat="server">
    <asp:TextBox id="text1" runat="server" />
    <asp:RequiredFieldValidator id="valid1"
        ControlToValidate="text1"
        ErrorMessage="This field must contain a value!"
        runat="server" />
    <br>
    <asp:Button id="button1" text="Click Me" runat="server" />
</form>
```

Your form now displays an error message if a value is not placed in the text field before the form is submitted. This implementation is not your final intention (remember, you wanted the field validator to be created dynamically), but at least you have a checkpoint to know that you're on the right track to getting your form to work properly.

Adding Complexity

To dynamically create the field validator control, you need to implement the Page_Load event of your ASP.NET page. In this event, you create the field validator control and bind it to the form as shown in Listings 3.9 and 3.10.

Listing 3.9 **Dynamically Creating ASP.NET Validation Control (C#)**

```
<%@ Page Language="C#" ClientTarget="DownLevel" %>

<script language="C#" runat="server">
void Page_Load(Object sender, EventArgs E)
{
    if(IsPostBack)
    {
        RequiredFieldValidator valid1 = new
        RequiredFieldValidator();
            valid1.ID = "valid1";
```

continues

Listing 3.9   **Continued**

```
                valid1.ControlToValidate = "text1";
                valid1.ErrorMessage =
                    "This field must contain a value!";
                frm1.Controls.Add(valid1);
            }
    }
</script>


<form id="frm1" runat="server">
        <asp:TextBox id="text1" runat="server" />
        <br>
        <asp:Button id="button1" text="Click Me" runat="server" />
</form>
```

Listing 3.10   **Dynamically Creating ASP.NET Validation Control (Visual Basic .NET)**

```
<%@ Page Language="VB" ClientTarget="DownLevel" %>

<script language="VB" runat="server">
        Sub Page_Load(sender as Object, E as EventArgs)
            If (IsPostBack) Then
                    Dim valid1 As RequiredFieldValidator = _
                        New RequiredFieldValidator
                    valid1.ID = "valid1"
                    valid1.ControlToValidate = "text1"
                    valid1.ErrorMessage = _
                        "This field must contain a value!"
                    frm1.Controls.Add(valid1)
            End If
        End Sub
</script>
```

You have removed the ASP.NET validation control from the form definition and are now dynamically creating it in the `Page_Load` event. If you run this code, however, the validation does not take place. Why, you ask? Well, if you hadn't taken the previous steps and reached a checkpoint, you would have absolutely no idea what the problem was. You did, however, so you know that it is not a problem with the validation logic. It must be a problem with the way you have implemented it. A little snooping around leads you to the conclusion that the form is being validated before the `Page_Load` event is fired, so your dynamic validation control is being created after the fact. To correct this, you must call the `Validate()` method of the `Page` object to re-evaluate the form based on your new validation object.

That's not the only problem, however. Even after you call the `Validate` method, the error message is being rendered in the wrong place. It's showing up after the Submit button instead of after the text field to which it references. The reason for this is that when you use the `Add` method of the form's `Controls` collection, it appends the control to the end of the form. To insert the `RequiredFieldValidator` control after the text field, you must use the `AddAt` method of the form's `Controls` collection and specify a control index. With a little trial and error, you can determine that an index of two puts the error message where you want it. The final code looks like that shown in Listings 3.11 and 3.12.

Listing 3.11   **Fixing the Placement and Behavior of the Validation Control (C#)**

```csharp
<%@ Page Language="C#" ClientTarget="DownLevel" %>


<script language="C#" runat="server">
void Page_Load(Object sender, EventArgs E)
{
    if(IsPostBack)
    {
        RequiredFieldValidator valid1 = new
            RequiredFieldValidator();
        valid1.ID = "valid1";
        valid1.ControlToValidate = "text1";
        valid1.ErrorMessage =
            "This field must contain a value!";
        frm1.Controls.AddAt(2,valid1);
        Validate();
    }
}
</script>


<form id="frm1" runat="server">
    <asp:TextBox id="text1" runat="server" />
    <br>
    <asp:Button id="button1" text="Click Me" runat="server" />
</form>
```

Listing 3.12   **Fixing the Placement and Behavior of the Validation Control (Visual Basic .NET)**

```vbnet
<%@ Page Language="VB" ClientTarget="DownLevel" %>


<script language="VB" runat="server">
    Sub Page_Load(sender as Object, E as EventArgs)
```

continues

Listing 3.12   **Continued**

```
        If (IsPostBack) Then
            Dim valid1 As RequiredFieldValidator = _
                New RequiredFieldValidator
            valid1.ID = "valid1"
            valid1.ControlToValidate = "text1"
            valid1.ErrorMessage = _
                "This field must contain a value!"
            frm1.Controls.AddAt(2,valid1)
            Validate()
        End If
    End Sub
</script>
```

As you can see, starting out simple and gradually building complexity greatly reduces the amount of time that it takes to troubleshoot problems because you already know what parts definitely work. You can then dedicate your time to finding the problems with the parts that you are not certain of.

Turtle Makes the Wiser

Just about everyone has heard the tale of the tortoise and the hare, and the lesson to be learned from it. Many parallels exist between this timeless fable and the debugging process. When trying to solve what appears to be an unsolvable bug, it is hard to resist the temptation to quickly and randomly make changes with the hope that you will stumble upon the solution by accident.

Although this method occasionally works, it has a few drawbacks. First, swapping code and fiddling with application settings without any rhyme or reason is a colossal waste of time when you consider the odds against hitting the magic combination. Second, even if you do strike gold and fix the problem, it is unlikely that you will understand or remember how you did it. In your moment of triumph, this might not concern you much. However, most types of bugs can be tucked away for only so long before they rear their ugly heads again. And when they do, you'll be right back at square one when it comes to fixing them.

Plan Carefully

When you encounter a bug that looks like it is going to take more than a trivial amount of time to solve, you must make a plan of attack. Take a step back and ask yourself, "What is the most likely cause of the bug?" Jot down some ideas, as well as things you could add or change to test your theories. From these ideas, formulate a set of logical steps to find the bug. All the concepts already introduced in this chapter can be used to aid you in this effort.

Proceed with Caution

Armed with a debugging plan, you can now begin making modifications to both code and application settings. Be careful to make only one modification at a time. That way, you will know what worked if the bug suddenly disappears (which has happened to us on several occasions). Always document the modifications that you make either in the code, in a separate file, or even on a sheet of paper. That way, you can always take a few steps back before proceeding down a different route without having to reload your code from your backup files (you did create backup files before you started, didn't you?).

The key to the whole process is patience. The most complex bugs usually require a combination of changes to fix them, and there is always an element of luck involved with choosing the right debugging route first. It's definitely not all in the cards, however, because your luck will most definitely improve with experience. (If only our luck with poker could follow this same trend.) The best part is that if you stick to your debugging plan, you will have a road map to fix the problem the next time it occurs. If you get to the end of your plan before you resolve the bug, don't give up. Take another step back and follow the strategies outlined in this chapter again. Perhaps you are not looking in the right place after all.

Summary

This chapter introduced some proven strategies for tracking down and eliminating bugs in your code. These strategies, when applied together, form a solid debugging foundation. First, you divide a web application into logical segments (tier sandboxes) to narrow the problem scope and eliminate the tiers that are not contributing to the problem. Second, you divide the code in each tier into functional units that you can test individually for bugs. This is done through the logic test and by testing the code's input and output. This chapter also demonstrated how to break a complex piece of code into its simplest form, gradually building in complexity while continually verifying proper functionality. Finally, we discussed how to take a logical and systematic approach to creating and executing a debugging plan, emphasizing that results can be achieved faster by proceeding with caution.

In the next chapter, we introduce some guidelines for creating and structuring code that makes debugging a much easier task.

4

Code Structure That Eases Debugging

A S THE POPULAR SAYING GOES, "AN OUNCE of prevention is worth a pound of cure." This statement is quite true when it comes to software development, especially for the Internet. If you take the time to plan and build your web applications in a structured and organized way, you can accomplish two things. First, you reduce the number of bugs that are introduced into your code (namely, the ones caused when you complicate things to the point of absolute confusion). Second, when you do encounter bugs in your code, you will be able to find and eliminate them much more easily. This chapter is designed to help you create your code in an organized fashion, as well as give you a foundation on which to debug your web application after it is built.

Code Partitioning

ASP.NET offers better solutions for code partitioning than were offered with traditional ASP. In traditional ASP, your primary options were to put your partitioned code into include files, separate ASP files that you executed with `Server.Execute` or business object components. The extra overhead of having multiple copies of include files in memory (one for each file that uses it) made this solution undesirable. Using `Server.Execute` was somewhat helpful, but you could not pass the executed ASP file any additional query string parameters. Business object components were the only good alternative in traditional ASP. With ASP.NET, you can use include files (not rec-ommended) and business object components, as well as two new techniques to parti-tion code: code-behind classes and user controls.

Code-Behind Classes

You can use a code-behind class as an effective way of separating client-side HTML code from server-side event-processing code. Breaking up the code in this way makes it easier to track down problems because you don't have to sift through user-interface code to get to the business logic code. Also, if the user-interface code of your project is created by a different group of developers than your business logic code is, using code-behind classes prevents one group from accidentally stepping on the code of the other group. Listings 4.1, 4.2, and 4.2 demonstrate how easy code-behind classes are to implement.

> **Notes About the Code Partitioning Example**
>
> The example in the "Code Partitioning" section of this chapter builds upon itself and uses the pubs data-base that comes standard with SQL Server 2000.

Listing 4.1   **User-Interface Code for an Author Search**

```
<%@ Language="C#" Inherits="AuthorSearch" Src="listing42.cs" %>
<form id="frm_search" method="post" runat="server">
Search for an author:<br>
Name:
<asp:TextBox id="txt_name" runat="server" />
<asp:Button id="btn_name" text="Search" onClick="btn_name_click"
runat="server" />
<br>
<asp:Label id="lbl_author" name="lbl_author" runat="server" />
 </form>
```

Listing 4.2   **Code-Behind Class to Handle User Input**

```
using System;
using System.Web.UI;
using System.Web.UI.WebControls;

public class AuthorSearch : Page
{
        public Label lbl_author;
        public TextBox txt_name;
```

```
        public void btn_name_click(Object sender, EventArgs e)
        {
                lbl_author.Text = "You are searching for "
                      + txt_name.Text;
        }
}
```

Listing 4.3   **User-Interface Code for an Author Search**

```
Imports System
Imports System.Web.UI
Imports System.Web.UI.WebControls

Public Class AuthorSearch
Inherits Page
        Public lbl_author As Label
        Public txt_name As TextBox

        Public Sub btn_name_click(sender As Object, e As EventArgs)
            lbl_author.Text = "You are searching for " & _
                txt_name.Text
        End Sub
End Class
```

You can see that having all your user-interface code in one place and all your business logic code in another makes it much easier to comprehend and maintain. User controls, described next, add another dimension to code partitioning: reusability.

User Controls

Have you ever found a problem with a piece of your code and gotten completely flustered because, after you fixed it, you had to make the change in a hundred other places where you used the exact same code? In traditional ASP, common business logic functions were often encapsulated in include files or in components. Elements of the user-interface, however, were encapsulated much more rarely. This was typically the case because there was no convenient way to do it. ASP.NET introduces user controls to help ease the user-interface encapsulation nightmare and enable you to fix bugs once, having them seamlessly applied everywhere the code is used. This reusability greatly reduces the time it takes to test, maintain, and implement web applications.

Continuing with the previous example, suppose that you want to search for authors by state as well as by name. The code to create a drop-down box of state names is an ideal candidate for a user control as can be seen in Listing 4.4.

Listing 4.4   **Author Search User-Interface Code Implementing a User Control**

```
<%@ Language="C#" Inherits="AuthorSearch" Src="listing48.cs" %>
<%@ Register TagPrefix="ch04" TagName="StateList" src="listing45.ascx" %>


<form id="frm_search" method="post"
    runat="server">
Search for an author:<br>
Name:
<asp:TextBox id="txt_name" runat="server" />
<asp:Button id="btn_name" text="Search" onClick="btn_name_click"
    runat="server" />
<br>OR<br>
<ch04:StateList id="uc_statelist" runat="server" />
<asp:Button id="btn_state" text="Search" onClick="btn_state_click"
    runat="server" />
<br>
<asp:Label id="lbl_author" name="lbl_author" runat="server" />
</form>
```

At the top of Listing 4.4, you register a user control that contains a `DropDownList` server control populated with all the state abbreviations. Any page that needs to access a list of all the states can use the same control. Listings 4.5, 4.6, and 4.7 present the code for the user control and its code-behind class.

Listing 4.5   **User Control Code**

```
<%@ Language="C#" Inherits="Chapter4.StateList" %>


State:
<asp:DropDownList id="lst_state" runat="server">
    <asp:ListItem>AL</asp:ListItem>
    <asp:ListItem>AK</asp:ListItem>
    <asp:ListItem>WV</asp:ListItem>
    <!—Remaining states omitted for space reasons—>
    <asp:ListItem>WI</asp:ListItem>
    <asp:ListItem>WY</asp:ListItem>
    <asp:ListItem>DC</asp:ListItem>
</asp:DropDownList>
```

Listing 4.6   **Code-Behind Class for User Control**

```csharp
using System;
using System.Web.UI;
using System.Web.UI.WebControls;

namespace Chapter4
{
    public class StateList : UserControl
    {
        protected DropDownList lst_state;

        public string SelectedState
        {
            get {return lst_state.SelectedItem.ToString();}
        }
    }
}
```

Listing 4.7   **Code-Behind Class for User Control (Visual Basic .NET)**

```vbnet
Imports System
Imports System.Web.UI
Imports System.Web.UI.WebControls

Namespace Chapter4
    Public Class StateList
            Inherits UserControl

        Protected lst_state As DropDownList

        Public ReadOnly Property SelectedState() As String
            Get
                    Return lst_state.SelectedItem.ToString()
            End Get
        End Property
    End Class
End Namespace
```

To be able to reference your user control as its own Type (such as StateList), you must create a compiled assembly. You would use the following compile script to compile the C# version of the code in Listing 4.6:

```
csc /t:library /out:chapter4.dll /r:System.Web.dll listing46.cs
```

The Visual Basic code in Listing 4.7 can be compiled using the following compile script:

```
vbc /t:library /out:chapter4.dll /r:System.Web.dll listing47.vb
```

Make sure that you enter the entire compile script as one command line. After your assembly is compiled, you must be sure to move the chapter4.dll file to the bin subdirectory of your web application. You'll see how to reference the Chapter4 namespace in Listings 4.8 and 4.9.

You can now extend the code-behind class shown in Listings 4.2 and 4.3 to include code to reference your StateList user control. This is shown in Listings 4.8 and 4.9.

Listing 4.8   **Code–Behind Class Referencing the User Control**

```csharp
using System;
using System.Web.UI;
using System.Web.UI.WebControls;
using Chapter4;

public class AuthorSearch : Page
{
        protected Label lbl_author;
        protected TextBox txt_name;
        protected StateList uc_statelist;

        public void btn_name_click(Object sender, EventArgs e)
        {
                lbl_author.Text = "You are searching for " + txt_name.Text;
        }

        public void btn_state_click(Object sender, EventArgs e)
        {
                lbl_author.Text = "You are searching for authors in " +
                        uc_statelist.SelectedState;
        }
}
```

Listing 4.9   **Code-Behind Class Referencing the User Control (Visual Basic .NET)**

```
Imports System
Imports System.Web.UI
Imports System.Web.UI.WebControls
Imports Chapter4

Public Class AuthorSearch
     Inherits Page

     Protected lbl_author As Label
     Protected txt_name As TextBox
     Protected uc_statelist As StateList

     Public Sub btn_name_click(sender As Object, e As EventArgs)
          lbl_author.Text = "You are searching for " & txt_name.Text
     End Sub

     Public Sub btn_state_click(sender As Object, e As EventArgs)
          lbl_author.Text = "You are searching for authors in " & _
               uc_statelist.SelectedState
     End Sub
End Class
```

If you apply user controls in your web applications whenever you are going to use the same groups of user interface elements repeatedly, you will drastically reduce the amount of time required to make changes. You will also eliminate the risk of changing one implementation of the user interface and forgetting to change it in the other places where it is used. Less risk and less code equals fewer bugs. You'll get more thorough coverage of user controls as they pertain to debugging in Chapter 11, "Debugging User Controls."

Business Objects

Although user controls are great for reuse of user interface elements, they are not really meant for reuse of business logic. That is where traditional business objects come into play. Next you'll extend your AuthorSearch example to actually retrieve records from the authors table in the pubs database. To do that, you'll create a business object named AuthorLogic. It will implement a GetAuthorByName method and a GetAuthorByState method to encapsulate the stored procedure calls to retrieve authors from the database.

The GetAuthorByName method will accept an author name and a database connection string. The GetAuthorByState method will accept a state name (its abbreviation, to be exact) and a database connection string. Because you will be connecting to SQL

Server, you will use the System.Data.Sql namespace instead of the more generic System.Data.OleDb namespace. Listings 4.10 and 4.11 present the code for your business object.

Listing 4.10   *AuthorLogic* **Object Code**

```
using System;
using System.Data;
using System.Data.SQL;

namespace Chapter4
{
public class AuthorLogic
{
        public DataTable GetAuthorByName(string name, string connectString)
        {
            //construct stored procedure call
            string sql = "sp_get_author_by_name '" + name + "'";

            //create a dataset to hold results
            DataSet ds = new DataSet();

            //create connection to database, open it, and retrieve results
            SQLDataSetCommand cmd = new SQLDataSetCommand(sql,connectString);
            cmd.FillDataSet(ds,"DataTable");

            //return only the DataTable that contains your results
            return ds.Tables["DataTable"];
        }

        public DataTable GetAuthorByState(string state, string connectString)
        {
            //construct stored procedure call
            string sql = "sp_get_author_by_state '" + state + "'";

            //create a dataset to hold results
            DataSet ds = new DataSet();

            //create connection to database, open it, and retrieve results
            SQLDataSetCommand cmd = new SQLDataSetCommand(sql,connectString);
            cmd.FillDataSet(ds,"DataTable");
```

```
            //return only the DataTable that contains your results
            return ds.Tables["DataTable"];
        }
    }
}
```

Listing 4.11   *AuthorLogic* **Object Code (Visual Basic .NET)**

```
Imports System
Imports System.Data
Imports System.Data.SQL


Namespace Chapter4
Public Class AuthorLogic
    Public Function GetAuthorByName(name As String, _
        connectString As String) As DataTable

        'construct stored procedure call
        Dim sql AS String = "sp_get_author_by_name '" & name & "'"

        'create a dataset to hold results
        Dim ds As DataSet = New DataSet()

        'create connection to database, open it, and retrieve results
        Dim cmd As SQLDataSetCommand = _
            New SQLDataSetCommand(sql,connectString)
        cmd.FillDataSet(ds,"DataTable")

        'return only the DataTable that contains your results
        return ds.Tables("DataTable")
    End Function

    Public Function GetAuthorByState(state As String, _
        connectString As String) As DataTable

        'construct stored procedure call
        Dim sql As String = "sp_get_author_by_state '" & state & "'"

        'create a dataset to hold results
        Dim ds As DataSet = New DataSet()

        'create connection to database, open it, and retrieve results
```

continues

Listing 4.11 **Continued**

```
        Dim cmd As SQLDataSetCommand = _
            New SQLDataSetCommand(sql,connectString)
        cmd.FillDataSet(ds,"DataTable")

        'return only the DataTable that contains your results
        return ds.Tables("DataTable")
    End Function
End Class
End Namespace
```

You added your AuthorLogic class definition to your existing Chapter4 namespace (which already contains the code-behind class for your StateList user control). It doesn't matter that the code resides in separate files. You'll see when you recompile your assembly that you can specify multiple source code files.

Both methods in the AuthorLogic class are pretty straightforward. They accept arguments, construct stored procedure calls, make the calls, and return the results to the client.

Now that you have added to your Chapter4 namespace, you need to recompile your assembly. For the C# version, use this compile script:

```
csc /t:library /out:chapter4.dll /r:System.dll;System.Web.dll;System.Data.dll
➥listing46.cs listing410.cs
```

For the Visual Basic.net version, use this compile script:

```
vbc /t:library /out:chapter4.dll /r:System.dll,System.Web.dll,System.Data.dll
➥listing47.vb listing411.vb
```

Make sure that you enter the entire compile script on the same line. The lines are wrapped here because of space constraints.

Next, take a look at Listings 4.12 and 4.13 to see how we have modified the ASP.NET page and its code-behind class to use the AuthorLogic object.

Listing 4.12 **Author Search Page Using *AuthorLogic* Object**

```
<%@ Language="C#" Inherits="AuthorSearch" Src="listing414.cs" %>
<%@ Register TagPrefix="ch04" TagName="StateList" src="listing45.ascx" %>
<%@ Import Namespace="System.Data" %>

<form id="frm_search" method="post"
    runat="server">
Search for an author:<br>
Name:
```

```
<asp:TextBox id="txt_name" runat="server" />
<asp:Button id="btn_name" text="Search" onClick="btn_name_click"
     runat="server" />
<br>OR<br>
<ch04:StateList id="uc_statelist" runat="server" />
<asp:Button id="btn_state" text="Search" onClick="btn_state_click"
     runat="server" />
<br>
<asp:Label id="lbl_author" name="lbl_author" runat="server" />
<br /><br >
<asp:repeater id="authorList" runat="server">
    <template name="ItemTemplate">
        <%# ((DataRow)Container.DataItem)["au_fname"].ToString() %>
         
        <%# ((DataRow)Container.DataItem)["au_lname"].ToString() %>
        <br />
        <%# ((DataRow)Container.DataItem)["address"].ToString() %>
        <br />
        <%# ((DataRow)Container.DataItem)["city"].ToString() %>,
        <%# ((DataRow)Container.DataItem)["state"].ToString() %>
         
        <%# ((DataRow)Container.DataItem)["zip"].ToString() %>
        <hr />
    </template>
</asp:repeater>
</form>
```

Listing 4.13 **Author Search Page Using** *AuthorLogic* **Object (Visual Basic .NET)**

```
<%@ Language="VB" Inherits="AuthorSearch" Src="listing415.vb" %>
<%@ Register TagPrefix="ch04" TagName="StateList" src="listing45.ascx" %>
<%@ Import Namespace="System.Data" %>

<form id="frm_search" method="post"
     runat="server">
Search for an author:<br>
Name:
<asp:TextBox id="txt_name" runat="server" />
<asp:Button id="btn_name" text="Search" onClick="btn_name_click"
     runat="server" />
<br>OR<br>
<ch04:StateList id="uc_statelist" runat="server" />
```

continues

Listing 4.13   **Continued**

```
<asp:Button id="btn_state" text="Search" onClick="btn_state_click"
     runat="server" />
<br>
<asp:Label id="lbl_author" name="lbl_author" runat="server" />
<br /><br >
<asp:repeater id="authorList" runat="server">
     <template name="ItemTemplate">
          <%# CType(Container.DataItem,System.Data.DataRow)("au_fname") %>
           
          <%# CType(Container.DataItem,System.Data.DataRow)("au_lname") %>
          <br />
          <%# CType(Container.DataItem,System.Data.DataRow)("address") %>
          <br />
          <%# CType(Container.DataItem,System.Data.DataRow)("city") %>,
          <%# CType(Container.DataItem,System.Data.DataRow)("state") %>
           
          <%# CType(Container.DataItem,System.Data.DataRow)("zip") %>
          <hr />
     </template>
</asp:repeater>
</form>
```

These two listings look similar to Listing 4.4, with a few additions. For example, there is the addition of an @Import directive for the System.Data namespace. This enables you to reference the objects contained in the System.Data namespace without explicitly typing System.Data as a prefix to its members each time you want to use one. The code-behind class for your author search ASP.NET page binds the Repeater server control to the Rows collection of a DataTable, so you need to be able to cast its individual data items to DataRow objects.

Finally, take a look at how the code-behind class for your author search ASP.NET page uses the AuthorLogic object to get lists of authors and binds it to the Repeater server control. This can be seen in the listings 4.14 and 4.15.

Listing 4.14   **Code-Behind Class for Author Search Page That Uses *AuthorLogic* Object**

```
using System;
using System.Web.UI;
using System.Web.UI.WebControls;
using Chapter4;

public class AuthorSearch : Page
```

```
{
        protected Label lbl_author;
        protected TextBox txt_name;
        protected StateList uc_statelist;
        protected Repeater authorList;

        //normally, you would keep database connection info
        //in the global.asax file or in an XML configuration file
        private string connectString = "Password=;User ID=sa;" +
                "Initial Catalog=pubs;Data Source=localhost;";

        //declare your AuthorLogic business object
        private AuthorLogic al;

        public void btn_name_click(Object sender, EventArgs e)
        {
            lbl_author.Text = "You are searching for " + txt_name.Text;

            //create a new instance of your AuthorLogic business object
            al = new AuthorLogic();

            //assign the results of your search to the repeater control
            authorList.DataSource =
                    al.GetAuthorByName(txt_name.Text,connectString).Rows;
            authorList.DataBind();
        }

        public void btn_state_click(Object sender, EventArgs e)
        {
            lbl_author.Text = "You are searching for authors in " +
                    uc_statelist.SelectedState;

            //create a new instance of your AuthorLogic business object
            al = new AuthorLogic();

            //assign the results of your search to the repeater control
            authorList.DataSource =
                    al.GetAuthorByState(uc_statelist.SelectedState,
                    connectString).Rows;
            authorList.DataBind();
        }
}
```

Listing 4.15   **Code-Behind Class for Author Search Page That Uses** *AuthorLogic*
Object (Visual Basic .NET)

```
Imports System
Imports System.Web.UI
Imports System.Web.UI.WebControls
Imports Chapter4


Public Class AuthorSearch
     Inherits Page

     Protected lbl_author As Label
     Protected txt_name As TextBox
     Protected uc_statelist As StateList
     Protected authorList As Repeater

     'normally, you would keep database connection info
     'in the global.asax file or in an XML configuration file
     Private connectString As String = "Password=;User ID=sa;" & _
          "Initial Catalog=pubs;Data Source=localhost;"

     'declare your AuthorLogic business object
     Private al As AuthorLogic

     Public Sub btn_name_click(sender As Object, e As EventArgs)
          lbl_author.Text = "You are searching for " & txt_name.Text

          'create a new instance of your AuthorLogic business object
          al = new AuthorLogic()

          'assign the results of your search to the repeater control
          authorList.DataSource = _
               al.GetAuthorByName(txt_name.Text,connectString).Rows
          authorList.DataBind()
     End Sub

     Public Sub btn_state_click(sender As Object, e As EventArgs)
          lbl_author.Text = "You are searching for authors in " & _
               uc_statelist.SelectedState

          'create a new instance of your AuthorLogic business object
          al = new AuthorLogic()
```

```
                    'assign the results of your search to the repeater control
                    authorList.DataSource = _
                          al.GetAuthorByState(uc_statelist.SelectedState, _
                          connectString).Rows
                    authorList.DataBind()
             End Sub
      End Class
```

Although setting up all of this might seem like a bit of a hassle at first, the effort pales in comparison to the amount of work that you will do in the long run if you handle every page á la carte. With the introduction of the .NET framework, many sources will tell you that because ASP.NET pages are now compiled, it isn't necessary to use components. Don't listen to them. Compiled ASP.NET pages might buy you performance, but good design is what yields maintainability and, most importantly, robust, bug-free code.

Control-of-Flow Guidelines

A good way to keep yourself out of trouble when it comes to debugging and code maintenance is to employ good control-of-flow coding practices. This might seem like a no-brainer, but experience has shown that the concept definitely warrants reinforcement.

If Statements and *Case/Switch* Constructs

For simple decisions in your code that have two or fewer possible alternatives, If statements are ideal. They are a quick and easy way to guide the flow of your code. If you need to make a selection based on a long list of possible alternatives, however, If statements can get messy and intertwined. If you are choosing the path of execution based on the value of a single variable, we strongly recommend using a `Case` construct (`Switch` construct, in C#). Consider Listings 4.16 and 4.17 that use multiple If statements.

Listing 4.16   **Large *If* Statement Block**

```
public int Foo(int someVar)
{
      if(someVar==10 || someVar==20 || somevar==30)
            {//do something here}
      else if(someVar==15 || someVar==25 || someVar==35)
            {//do something here}
      else if(someVar==40 || someVar==50 || someVar==60)
            {//do something here}
```

continues

Listing 4.16   **Continued**

```
    else
        {//do something here}
}
```

Listing 4.17   **Large *If* Statement Block (Visual Basic .NET)**

```
Public Function Foo(someVar As Integer) As Integer
    If someVar = 10 Or someVar = 20 Or someVar = 30 Then
        'do something here
    ElseIf someVar = 15 Or someVar = 25 Or someVar = 35 Then
        'do something here
    ElseIf someVar = 40 Or someVar = 50 Or someVar = 60 Then
        'do something here
    Else
        'do something here
    End If
End Function
```

Although you can tell what is going on upon close examination of the code, it might not be apparent when you are scanning it for bugs. A more concise and organized way of accomplishing this task is to use a Case/Switch construct as shown in Listings 4.18 and 4.19.

Listing 4.18   **Switch Block (C#)**

```
public int Foo(int someVar)
{
    switch(someVar)
    {
        case 10: case 20: case 30:
            //do something here
            break;
        case 15: case 25: case 35:
            //do something here
            break;
        case 40: case 50: case 60:
            //do something here
            break;
        default:
            //do something here
```

```
                break;
        }
}
```

Listing 4.19   **Case Statement Block (Visual Basic .NET)**

```
Public Function Foo(someVar As Integer) As Integer
      Select Case someVar
            Case 10, 20, 30
                  'do something here
            Case 15, 25, 35
                  'do something here
            Case 40, 50, 60
                  'do something here
            Case Else
                  'do something here
      End Select
End Function
```

Function and Loop Exit Points

Some of the most elusive bugs in applications arise from improper use of function and loop exit points. As a general rule, a function or loop should have only one exit point. Why should this be so? If a function or loop has more than one exit point, then it is more difficult to track down which exit point your code is using when you are debugging. An exit point could be hidden in your code, leaving you scratching your head when you try to determine why your code is not working properly. Consider the following function that violates the single exit point rule (shown in Listings 4.20 and 4.21).

Listing 4.20   **Code with Multiple Exit Points**

```
public int Foo(int someVar)
{
      int i = 0;

      for(i=0;i<=100;i++)
      {
            //do something to someVar
            someVar = i;
```

continues

Listing 4.20   **Continued**

```
            //see whether you need to get out early
            if(someVar==50)
                    {break;}

            if((someVar * 2) % 10 == 0)
                    {break;}
        }

        if(i < 100)
                {return 1;}

        return 0;
    }
```

Listing 4.21   **Code with Multiple Exit Points (Visual Basic .NET)**

```
Public Function Foo(someVar As Integer) As Integer
        Dim i As Integer

        For i = 1 To 100
            'do something to someVar
            someVar = i

            'see whether you need to get out early
            If someVar = 50 Then
                    Exit For
            End If

            If (someVar * 2) Mod 10 = 0 Then
                    Exit For
            End If
        Next i

        If i < 100 Then
                'loop ended prematurely, so get out
                Return 1
        End If

        Return 0
End Function
```

You would need to set breakpoints and step through your code line by line to determine what is going on here. A more effective approach is to use status flags. Status flags can be included in loop definitions to determine when the loop should end. Status flags can also be used to set return codes at the single function exit point. Listings 4.22 and 4.23 demonstrate this concept.

Listing 4.22   **Code with a Single Exit Point**

```
public int Foo2(int someVar)
{
    int status = 0;

    for(int i=0;i<=100;i++)
    {
        //do something to someVar
        someVar = i;

        //see whether you need to get out early
        if(someVar==50)
            {status = 1;}

        if((someVar * 2) % 10 == 0)
            {status = 1;}

        //single place where loop can terminate early
        if(status==1) {break;}
    }

    return status;

}
```

Listing 4.23   **Code with Single Exit Point (Visual Basic .NET)**

```
Public Function Foo(someVar As Integer) As Integer
    Dim i As Integer = 0
    Dim status As Integer = 0

    For i = 1 To 100
        'do something to someVar
        someVar = i

        'see whether you need to get out early
        If someVar = 50 Then
```

continues

Listing 4.23   **Continued**

```
            status = 1
        End If


        If (someVar * 2) Mod 10 = 0 Then
            status = 1
        End If


        'single place where loop can terminate early
        If status = 1 Then Exit For
    Next i


    Return status
End Function
```

Structured Exception Handling

One of the greatest enhancements introduced with ASP.NET is structured exception handling. With structured exception handling, you can be more selective with error trapping. Rather than put a blanket On Error Resume Next statement in your code and constantly check for errors in the Err object, you can enclose blocks of code that are prone to errors and catch specific exceptions.

When to Use Structured Exception Handling

Structured exception handling can be an effective tool for catching and dealing with runtime errors. However, it should be used only when you are going to do something useful with the exception that is raised. For example, if you need to do any cleanup processing when an exception occurs, then structured exception handling is ideal. If you want to log the error and display it to the user, then you can implement a global exception handler with a custom error page (discussed later in this chapter in the section "Implementing the Application_Error Event Handler").

Effective Use of Structured Exception Handling

When using structured exception handling in ASP.NET, avoid using the generic Exception class. If you want to trap and clean up after a particular type of exception, then specify it. Later, we'll discuss using a global exception handler and a custom error page to catch generic exceptions. Listings 4.24 and 4.25 demonstrate catching specific exceptions.

Listing 4.24   **Trapping a Specific Exception Type**

```
<%@ Page Language="C#" %>
<%@ Import Namespace="System.IO" %>


<%
try
{
    StreamReader sr = new StreamReader(@"c:\bogusfile.txt");
}
catch(FileNotFoundException e)
{
    Response.Write(e.ToString());
}
%>
```

Listing 4.25   **Trapping a Specific Exception Type (Visual Basic .NET)**

```
<%@ Page Language="VB" %>
<%@ Import Namespace="System.IO" %>


<%
Try
    Dim sr As StreamReader = New StreamReader("c:\bogusfile.txt")
Catch e As FileNotFoundException
    Response.Write(e.ToString())
End Try
%>
```

Global Exception Handling

You can't debug a problem if you don't know that it exists. After you take your web application live, you are no longer the only one who is using it (hopefully), so you need an effective plan to track exceptions when they occur while *others* are surfing your site. A great way to do this is to implement an exception handler at the application level. This will allow you to consolidate the logging and notification parts of your exception handling in one convenient place. As you'll see from the code examples that follow, your global exception handler can handle both specific exceptions that you trap in your code and generic unhandled exceptions.

After your global exception handler has done its work, you'll want to redirect the users of your website to a friendly page that tells them that something has gone wrong, and then provide them with customer support information as well as a link back to your web application's home page.

Implementing the Application_Error Event Handler

The `HttpApplication` class in the System.Web namespace implements an `Error` event handler. This should not be confused with the `HttpApplicationState` class, which contains the definition for the `Application` object that you use in a typical ASP.NET page (see the .NET framework documentation for more detail on the differences between these two classes). You can implement this event handler in the global.asax file as shown in Listings 4.26 and 4.27.

Listing 4.26   *Application_Error* **Event Handler**

```
<%@ Application Language="C#" %>
<%@ Import Namespace="System.Diagnostics" %>

<script language="C#" runat="server">
void Application_Error(object sender, EventArgs e)
{
    //get reference to the source of the exception chain
    Exception ex = Server.GetLastError().GetBaseException();

    //log the details of the exception and page state to the
    //Windows 2000 Event Log
    EventLog.WriteEntry("Test Web",
        "MESSAGE: " + ex.Message +
        "\nSOURCE: " + ex.Source +
        "\nFORM: " + Request.Form.ToString() +
        "\nQUERYSTRING: " + Request.QueryString.ToString() +
        "\nTARGETSITE: " + ex.TargetSite +
        "\nSTACKTRACE: " + ex.StackTrace,
        EventLogEntryType.Error);

    //Insert optional email notification here...
}
</script>
```

Listing 4.27   *Application_Error* **Event Handler (Visual Basic .NET)**

```
<%@ Application Language="VB" %>
<%@ Import Namespace="System.Diagnostics" %>

<script language="VB" runat="server">
Sub Application_Error(sender As Object, e As EventArgs)
    'get reference to the source of the exception chain
    Dim ex As Exception = Server.GetLastError().GetBaseException()
```

```
    'log the details of the exception and page state to the
    'Windows 2000 Event Log
    EventLog.WriteEntry("Test Web", _
        "MESSAGE: " & ex.Message & _
        "\nSOURCE: " & ex.Source & _
        "\nFORM: " & Request.Form.ToString() & _
        "\nQUERYSTRING: " & Request.QueryString.ToString() & _
        "\nTARGETSITE: " & ex.TargetSite & _
        "\nSTACKTRACE: " & ex.StackTrace, _
        EventLogEntryType.Error)

    'Insert optional email notification here...
End Sub
</script>
```

First, you have to be sure to set a reference to the System.Diagnostics namespace. You'll use the EventLog class in this namespace to write exception details to the Windows 2000 event log. Inside the Application_Error event handler, you declare an Exception object and initialize it through a call to Server. GetLastError().GetBaseException().

The GetLastError() method of the Server object simply returns a reference to a generic HttpException. This is a wrapper that was placed around the original exception when it was passed from your ASP.NET page to the Application_Error event. To get access to the original exception, you need to call its GetBaseException() method. This will yield the original exception information, regardless of how many layers have been added to the exception tree.

Next, you make a call to the WriteEntry() method of the EventLog class. There are several overloaded signatures for this method. You can read more about how to leverage the Windows 2000 event log in Chapter 8, "Leveraging the Windows 2000 Event Log." The implementation that we chose to use here accepts three parameters. The first parameter is the source of the error. It appears in the Source field of the Windows 2000 event log viewer. The second parameter is the log data itself. You can see that we have added a lot of information to help track down what caused the exception, including the exception message, the exception source, the contents of the Form collection, the contents of the QueryString collection, the name of the method that generated the error (TargetSite), and a complete stack trace.

Note that the stack trace contains the name of the file that was the source of the exception. However, it strips off the contents of the query string—hence the need to specifically include it previously. The third and final parameter to the WriteEntry() method is an enumeration of type EventLogEntryType. We chose to use the Error element of the enumeration.

At the end of the event handler, we inserted a comment block where you can optionally put code to email the exception information to your IT support staff. Discussion of the different messaging paradigms in the .NET framework is beyond the scope of this book.

After the `Application_Error` event has completed its work, it automatically redirects the user of your web application to your custom error page (which you will set up in the next section). Optionally, however, you can use the `Server.ClearError()` method after you have logged the exception and redirect your user using the `Server.Execute()` method, specifying the page that you want to load in the user's browser.

The code that you have just implemented will capture all unhandled exceptions that occur in your web application. If you need to do some cleanup in the event of an exception and you implement structured exception handling inside your ASP.NET page, you can still leverage the global exception handler. Listings 4.28 and 4.29 present examples of how you would do it.

Listing 4.28   **Throwing a Handled Exception**

```
<%@ Page Language="C#" %>

<script language="C#" runat="server">
protected void button1_click(object sender, EventArgs e)
{
    try
    {
        //do some complex stuff

        //generate your fictional exception
        int x = 1;
        int y = 0;
        int z = x / y;
    }
    catch(DivideByZeroException ex)
    {
        //put cleanup code here
        throw(ex);
    }
}
</script>

<form runat="server">
    <asp:button id="button1" onclick="button1_click"
        text="click me" runat="server" />
</form>
```

Listing 4.29   **Throwing a Handled Exception (Visual Basic .NET)**

```
<%@ Page Language="VB" %>

<script language="VB" runat="server">
Protected Sub button1_click(sender As Object, e As EventArgs)
    Try
        'do some complex stuff

        'generate your fictional exception
        Dim x As Integer = 1
        Dim y As Integer = 0
        Dim z As Integer = x / y
    Catch ex As DivideByZeroException
        'put cleanup code here
        Throw(ex)
    End Try
End Sub
</script>

<form runat="server">
    <asp:button id="button1" onclick="button1_click"
        text="click me" runat="server" />
</form>
```

The code in these listings defines a web form with a text box and a button. When you click the button, it fires the button1_click event handler. In the event handler, you would do processing as usual. For the purposes of this demonstration, however, you intentionally generate a DivideByZeroException. This takes you to the catch block. Here, you can perform any page-specific cleanup code before calling throw(ex) to pass your exception to the global exception handler to be logged to the Windows 2000 event log.

When the global exception handler is finished logging the error, the defaultredirect attribute that you set in your config.web file (discussed in the next section) takes over, and you are redirected to the error.aspx page to display your friendly message to the user of your web application.

Setting Up the Custom Error Page

The first step in setting up a custom error page is to modify your config.web file to route the users of your web application to a friendly error page if an exception occurs. It helps to boost users' confidence in your site when it can recover gracefully from the unexpected. Add the code in Listing 4.30 to the config.web file of your web application.

Listing 4.30   **Adding the *<customerrors>* Tag to Your Config.web File**

```
<configuration>
    <customerrors mode="On" defaultredirect="error.aspx" />
</configuration>
```

Note that your config.web file might already have a <customerrors> tag, so you might only need to modify the existing one. The mode attribute of the <customerrors> tag has three settings: On, Off, and RemoteOnly. If the mode is On, users will always be redirected to the custom error page specified by the defaultredirect attribute if an unhandled exception occurs. If the mode is Off, the details of any exception that occurs will be shown to the user in the browser. The RemoteOnly mode is a hybrid of the two other modes. If you are browsing your web application while sitting at the web server itself, it behaves like the Off mode. All other browsers of the site will get the behavior of the On mode. If no defaultredirect attribute is set, a default ASP.NET "friendly, yet not so friendly" message will be displayed to the user when exceptions occur.

Next, you need to build the custom error page (error.aspx) referenced in the config.web file. This is just an ordinary ASP.NET page that includes helpful information for the user of your web application if an error occurs. An extremely simple example is the one in Listing 4.31.

Listing 4.31   **Simple Custom Error Page**

```
<html>
<head>
<title>My web application: Error page</title>
</head>
<body>
An unexpected error occurred in the application. Please contact customer
service at (800)555-5555. Or, you can click <a href="home.aspx">here</a>
to go back to the homepage. Thank you for your patience.
</body>
</html>
```

Summary

This chapter covered a tremendous amount of ground. It started off with a discussion of code partitioning and how it helps to reduce bugs that are caused by failure to update repetitive code. The introduction of code-behind classes helps you to better separate your user interface logic from your business logic. Leveraging user controls enables you to reuse pieces of user interface code much more efficiently than using include files in traditional ASP web applications. ASP.NET continues to support and encourage the use of business objects to encapsulate frequently used business logic in your web applications

Next, the chapter moved on to control-of-flow guidelines to help you prevent bugs from happening in the first place. We covered how Switch and Case constructs are often superior to multiple If statements. The importance of a single exit point to both functions and loops was also stressed. This was followed with a discussion of when and how to use structured exception handling in your ASP.NET web applications.

We rounded out the chapter with a discussion on how to implement a global exception handler to log both unhandled exceptions in your ASP.NET web applications and handled exceptions that you still want to be logged. In this discussion, you were introduced to the <customerrors> tag in the config.web file, and you learned how it is used to specify a custom error page that the user will be redirected to in the event of an error.

The next chapter discusses conditional compiling and shows how it enables you to toggle between debug and production code quickly and easily.

II

ASP.NET Debugging Tools

5 Conditional Compiling

6 Tracing

7 Visual Studio .NET Debugging Environment

8 Leveraging the Windows 2000 Event Log

5

Conditional Compiling

CONDITIONAL COMPILING IS ARGUABLY ONE OF the greatest debugging tools available to any programmer. This chapter discusses what conditional compiling is, tells how it works, and shows what it can provide for you in terms of debugging your ASP.NET applications.

What Is Conditional Compiling?

Conditional compiling is a very basic concept that enables you to do some pretty powerful things. Basically, conditional compiling enables you to compile parts of your code based on a certain condition defined at compile time. Generally, this is used if you have a debugging function that you do not want to include in your release build. Or, you might have a function that you want two versions of: one for your debugging and one for a release. The debug version might be littered with output statements or other code that would be too slow to execute in a release environment. With conditional compiling, you could create two versions of the function and flip the switch on which one should be compiled in your program, depending on its environment.

In the .NET framework, there are two ways to accomplish this type of conditional compilation. One method uses function attributes to tag the function as conditionally compiled. The second method involves using preprocessing directives to tell the compiler at compile time which functions to include and which functions to remove.

Conditional Compiling with Function Attributes

First take a look at conditional compiling using attributes. Listing 5.1 is a program listing in C# that uses conditional compiling via function attributes.

Listing 5.1 **Conditionally Compiled Code (C#)**

```csharp
using System;
using System.Diagnostics;

namespace WebApplication7
{
    public class WebForm1 : System.Web.UI.Page
    {
        public WebForm1()
        {
            Page.Init += new System.EventHandler(Page_Init);
        }

        protected void Page_Load(object sender, EventArgs e)
        {
                CondClass cc = new CondClass();g
                cc.IAmHere();
                Response.Write("Am I here?   " + cc.AmIHere());
            }

            protected void Page_Init(object sender, EventArgs e)
        •   {
                InitializeComponent();
            }

            private void InitializeComponent()
            {
                this.Load += new System.EventHandler
            ➥ (this.Page_Load);
            }
        }
    }

    public class CondClass
    {
        String str;

        [Conditional("DEBUG")]
        public void IAmHere()
```

```
    {
        str = "I am here!";
    }

    public String AmIHere()
    {
        return str;
    }
}
```

Listing 5.2 is the same program written Visual Basic .NET.

Listing 5.2   **Conditionally Compiled Code (Visual Basic .NET)**

```
Imports System
Imports System.Diagnostics

Public Class WebForm1
        Inherits System.Web.UI.Page

        Dim WithEvents WebForm1 As System.Web.UI.Page

        Sub New()
                WebForm1 = Me
        End Sub

        Private Sub InitializeComponent()

        End Sub

        Protected Sub WebForm1_Load(ByVal Sender As System.Object, ByVal
        ➥ e As System.EventArgs)
                Dim cc As CondClass = New CondClass()
                cc.IAmHere()
                Response.Write("Am I here?    " + cc.AmIHere())
        End Sub

        Protected Sub WebForm1_Init(ByVal Sender As System.Object, ByVal
        ➥ e As System.EventArgs)
                InitializeComponent()
                End Sub

        End Class
```

continues

Listing 5.2 **Continued**

```
Public Class CondClass
        Dim str As String


        <Conditional("DEBUG")>
        Public Sub IAmHere()
                str = "I am here!"
        End Sub

        Public Function AmIHere() As String
                AmIHere = str
        End Function
End Class
```

Now you'll examine what is going on in these code snippets. The first thing that you will need to do in either language is to "import" the System.Diagnostics namespaces. In Visual Basic .NET, you use the Imports keyword; in C#, you use the using keyword.

In each of these pieces of code, we have created a class named CondClass that contains a string and two functions: IAmHere and AmIHere. Calling IAmHere sets the string in the class to "I am here!". Otherwise, that particular string is empty. You will notice that, in both code snippets, the Conditional attribute is used with the IAmHere function. Notice the different placement, depending on the language you are using. The condition in which this function will be compiled is whether DEBUG is defined in the project properties. In a debug build, this is always the case. In a release build, this is never the case.

In the WebForm1_Load/Page_Load method, you will notice that an instance of your CondClass object is instantiated, and then both the IAmHere and AmIHere methods are called. Then a Response.Write is called to see if the string in the object has been set by the call to IAmHere.

If you're compiling in debug mode, the symbol DEBUG has been defined by the default settings of the project, so the string will be set and the output will show "Am I here? I am here!". If you compile in release mode, you will see only the "Am I here?" string—the IAmHere function will not be called because it has not been compiled into the application due to the Conditional failing.

If you are compiling from the command line, you will need to define the DEBUG symbol yourself. This can be done with the /d switch. In this case, it would look like /d:DEBUG. Note that you can use any symbol that you choose instead of DEBUG.

If you are compiling using the Visual Studio .NET IDE, you can change between RELEASE and DEBUG builds with the Project Properties dialog box. You can access this from the Build menu under Configuration Manager.

Conditional Compiling with Preprocessor Directives

Now you'll take a look at the second way to achieve conditional compiling through preprocessor directives. Listings 5.3 and 5.4 show the same program in C# and Visual Basic .NET, respectively.

Listing 5.3   **Conditional Compiling with Preprocessor Directives (C#)**

```
#define MYDEBUG

using System;

namespace WebApplication7
{
    public class WebForm1 : System.Web.UI.Page
    {
        public WebForm1()
        {
            Page.Init += new System.EventHandler(Page_Init);
        }

        protected void Page_Load(object sender, EventArgs e)
        {
            CondClass cc = new CondClass();

            cc.IAmHere();

            Response.Write("Am I here?  " + cc.AmIHere());
        }

    protected void Page_Init(object sender, EventArgs e)
    {
        InitializeComponent();
    }

    private void InitializeComponent()
    {
        this.Load += new System.EventHandler (this.Page_Load);
    }
    }
}

public class CondClass
{
```

continues

Listing 5.3 **Continued**

```
        String str;

        public void IAmHere()
        {
#if MYDEBUG
            str = "I am here!";
#endif
        }

        public String AmIHere()
        {
            return str;
        }
}
```

Listing 5.4 **Conditional Compiling with Preprocessor Directives (Visual Basic .NET)**

```
#Const MYDEBUG = 1

Public Class WebForm1
    Inherits System.Web.UI.Page


    Dim WithEvents WebForm1 As System.Web.UI.Page

    Sub New()
        WebForm1 = Me
    End Sub

    Private Sub InitializeComponent()

    End Sub


    Protected Sub WebForm1_Load(ByVal Sender As System.Object, ByVal e
➥ As System.EventArgs)
        Dim cc As CondClass = New CondClass()

        cc.IAmHere()

        Response.Write("Am I here?  " + cc.AmIHere())
```

```
    End Sub

    Protected Sub WebForm1_Init(ByVal Sender As System.Object, ByVal e As
    ➥System.EventArgs)
        InitializeComponent()
    End Sub

End Class

Public Class CondClass
    Dim str As String

    Public Sub IAmHere()

#If MYDEBUG Then
    str = "I am here!"
#End If

    End Sub

    Public Function AmIHere() As String
        AmIHere = str
    End Function

End Class
```

The same class with the same functionality is provided. However, this version of the code works a bit differently. First, we'll discuss what preprocessor directives are.

Simply put, preprocessor directives are commands embedded in your code that are interpreted by the compiler at compilation time and that will influence its behavior as it compiles your code. In this instance, you are using the `#If...Then...#End If`/`#if...#endif` and the `#Const/#define` directives.

`#Const` in Visual Basic .NET and `#define` in C# define conditional compiler constants. These can be thought of as variable constants in either Visual Basic .NET or C#, but these compiler constants are known to the compiler only. They cannot be referenced in your program like a Visual Basic .NET or a C# variable constant. In both versions, you will see that a constant known as MYDEBUG is defined using each language's method, as described. In Visual Basic .NET, the `#Const` declaration must come before any namespace imports or any program code for it to be valid. You can see these used in the previous examples. In the Visual Basic .NET listing, the line looks like `#Const MYDEBUG`. In the C# example, it is written as `#define MYDEBUG`.

These constants are used in conjunction with the #If...Then...#End If directives in Visual Basic .NET and the #if...#endif directives in C#. In either case, these tags are wrapped around the statements that you want to be included only if the constant that you choose has been defined. In the previous sample, these tags were put around the contents of the IAmHere function. If you keep the constant in place at the top of your code, then the contents of what is in between the tags will be compiled in, and you will get the "Am I here? I am here!" output. If you remove the constant, the function's internals will not be compiled in, and you will get only the "Am I here?" output because the internal string in the class will not be set during the IAmHere call. Listing 5.5 shows the appropriate lines in C#.

Listing 5.5   **Usage of #if...#endif (C#)**

```
    public void IAmHere()
    {
#if MYDEBUG
        str = "I am here!";
#endif
    }
```

Listing 5.8 demonstrates the same concept in Visual Basic .NET.

Listing 5.6   **Usage of #If...Then...#End If (Visual Basic .NET)**

```
    Public Sub IAmHere()
#If MYDEBUG Then
        str = "I am here!"
#End If
    End Sub
```

If you are using C#, you may also use operators to test whether an item has been defined. You can use the following operators to evaluate multiple symbols: == (equality), != (inequality), && (and), and || (or). You can group symbols and operators with parentheses.

Other Preprocessor Directives

A few other preprocessor directives are available in C# that are not found in Visual Basic .NET. This section discusses these additional directives, tells how they work, and shows what they can provide for you.

#undef

#undef is the exact opposite of #define. It removes the definition of a preprocessor constant. Listing 5.7 shows an example of how it is used.

Listing 5.7   Using *#undef*

```
#define MYDEBUG

public void MyFunction()
{
#if MYDEBUG
    Response.Write("Hello");
#endif

#undef MYDEBUG

#if MYDEBUG
    Response.Write("You won't see me!");
#endif
}
```

If you called the MyFunction function, you would get an output of Hello but not You won't see me!. Because MYDEBUG has been defined, the first Response.Write will be compiled in and executed. However, immediately afterward, the MYDEBUG symbol is undefined, so the second #if check will fail; the second Response.Write will not be compiled into the program and, therefore, will not be executed.

This can be useful if you need to temporarily remove a line or two inside a debugging function. You could simply #undef the symbol for the lines that you want to execute and then again #define the symbol where you want to restart the execution of the function.

#warning and #error

#warning and #error are very similar, so they are demonstrated together here. These two directives enable you to display a message to the user in the output window as the program is compiling. This message can have either a warning status or an error status. Listing 5.8 shows an example of each.

Listing 5.8   *#warning* **and** *#error* **Example**

```
#define MYDEBUG

#if MYDEBUG && !DEBUG
#error Both MYDEBUG and RELEASE are defined!!
#elif MYDEBUG
#warning WARNING - MYDEBUG is defined!
#endif
```

In this example, if you were in a debug build with MYDEBUG defined, you would simply see a warning telling you that MYDEBUG was defined while compiling your program. This is just a handy hint. However, if you switched your build configuration to a release build and built the program, you would get a compiler error with the text stated because both MYDEBUG and RELEASE were defined and DEBUG was not. This would be very useful to ensure that you do not compile any of your own debugging code into your release application.

Summary

Conditional compiling is extremely easy to implement, with tremendously powerful results. This chapter looked at two different ways to accomplish a similar task: through preprocessor directives and via function attributes. The key difference here is that by using the Conditional function attribute, the debug code is compiled into the application; however, it is never executed. By using the preprocessor directives of this section, the code is never compiled into the application—therefore, it could never be executed.

Next, you looked at some other preprocessor compiler directives and how they can provide additional information to aid you in debugging your ASP.NET applications.

By adding some conditional compiling to your code, you will be able to add a robust debugging interface to your application and immediately remove it from the production-level output at the proverbial flip of a switch.

In the next chapter, you will start to look at the built-in .NET tracing facilities and how they can help you explore what is happening inside your application as it is running, both in a debug and a production environment.

6

Tracing

ONE OF THE MOST COMMON WAYS to debug traditional ASP web applications is to use trusty calls to `Response.Write`. This enables you to create checkpoints in your code to view the contents of variables in the browser. This approach had several drawbacks, however. The output created by calls to `Response.Write` appears wherever the call is made in the code. It sometimes becomes a chore trying to interpret your debugging information because it is strewn all over the page in the browser. The formatting of your page is also affected.

When you are finished debugging your web application using calls to `Response.Write`, you are then faced with the daunting task of stripping out all this debug code. Because you are using the same type of code both to debug and to create valid output, you must carefully scan each of your ASP pages to make sure that you remove all the `Response.Write` calls that pertain to debugging. When your ASP pages get to be hundreds of lines long, this can be a real pain.

To address this issue, ASP.NET implements the `TraceContext` class. The `TraceContext` class solves all these issues and offers many more features. Let's take a look at some of the ways that the `TraceContext` class can help you debug your ASP.NET web applications more effectively.

Configuration

To use tracing in your ASP.NET web application, you need to enable it. This can be done at either the page level or the application level.

Page-Level Configuration

Enabling tracing at the page level entails adding the `Trace` attribute to the `@Page` directive, like this:

```
<%@ Page Language="C#" Trace="true" %>
```

If the `Trace` attribute has a value of `true`, tracing information will be displayed at the bottom of your ASP.NET page after the entire page has been rendered. Alternatively, you can include the `TraceMode` attribute. The value that you assign to this attribute determines the display order of the trace results. The possible values are `SortByTime` and `SortByCategory`. `SortByTime` is the default if you do not specify the `TraceMode` attribute.

Application-Level Configuration

Several tracing options are available at the application level. These settings are specified using the `<trace>` XML element in the `<system.web>` section of the web.config file. The attributes available to you are shown in Table 6.1.

Table 6.1 **Tracing Options**

`enabled`	Is `true` if tracing is enabled for the application; otherwise, is `false`. The default is `false`.
`pageOutput`	Is `true` if trace information should be displayed both on an application's pages and in the .axd trace utility; otherwise, is `false`. The default is `false`. Note that pages that have tracing enabled on them are not affected by this setting.
`requestLimit`	Specifies the number of trace requests to store on the server. The default is 10.
`traceMode`	Indicates whether trace information should be displayed in the order it was processed, `SortByTime`, or alphabetically by user-defined category, `SortByCategory`. `SortByTime` is the default.
`localOnly`	Is true if the trace viewer (trace.axd) is available only on the host Web server; otherwise, is false. The default is true.

An example of a trace entry in the web.config file might look like Listing 6.1.

Listing 6.1   **Application-Level Trace Configuration in the web.config File**

```
<configuration>
    <system.web>
        <trace enabled="true" pageOutput="false" requestLimit="20"
            traceMode="SortByTime" localOnly="true" />
    </system.web>
</configuration>
```

Even though this example uses all the available attributes, none of them is required. Also note that page-level configuration settings overrule application-level settings. For instance, if tracing is disabled at the application level but is enabled at the page level, trace information will still be displayed in the browser.

The `requestLimit` attribute sets a limit on how many page requests are kept in the trace log. This prevents the logs from getting too large.

Setting the `localOnly` attribute to `true` enables you to view trace information if you are logged into the server locally, but remote users will not see anything. That way, you can enable tracing to debug a problem, and the users of your website will never be the wiser.

Trace Output

Now that you've heard so much about configuring ASP.NET tracing, what exactly does it provide? Essentially, the trace output generated by the `TraceContext` object and displayed at the bottom of your rendered ASP.NET page contains several sections. Each of these sections is outlined here, along with explanations. Because the total output is too large to be viewed in one screenshot, a screenshot is included for each individual section of the trace output. Later in the chapter, when we discuss writing messages to the trace output, you'll get a chance to see what several sections put together look like.

Request Details

The Request Details section contains six pieces of information, outlined in Table 6.2.

Table 6.2 **Request Details**

Item	Description
Session Id	Unique identifier for your session on the server
Time of request	The time (accurate to the second) that the page request was made
Request encoding	The encoding of the request—for example, Unicode (UTF − 8)
Request type	GET or POST
Status code	The status code for the request—for example, 200
Response encoding	The encoding of the response—for example, Unicode (UTF − 8)

You can see it all put together in Figure 6.1.

Request Details			
Session Id:	pgihh345eog4lp55zbq1nuae	Request Type:	GET
Time of Request:	7/7/2001 11:05:12 PM	Status Code:	200
Request Encoding:	Unicode (UTF-8)	Response Encoding:	Unicode (UTF-8)

Figure 6.1   Request Details section of trace output.

Trace Information

The Trace Information section contains the various trace messages and warnings that both you and the ASP.NET engine add to the trace output. By default, the ASP.NET engine adds messages for when any events begin or end, as with `PreRender` and `SaveViewState`. The fields displayed for each item are Category, Message, time interval from the beginning of page processing, and time interval from the last trace output item. The order in which the contents of the Trace Information section appear is determined by either the `TraceMode` attribute of the `@Page` directive or the `TraceMode` property of the `TraceContext` class. Figure 6.2 shows an example of the Trace Information section.

Trace Information			
Category	Message	From First(s)	From Last(s)
	Custom message		
	Custom warning	0.000083	0.000083
aspx.page	Begin PreRender	0.005187	0.005104
aspx.page	End PreRender	0.005275	0.000088
aspx.page	Begin SaveViewState	0.005498	0.000223
aspx.page	End SaveViewState	0.005588	0.000090
aspx.page	Begin Render	0.005668	0.000080
aspx.page	End Render	0.063119	0.057451

Figure 6.2   Trace Information section of trace output.

Control Tree

The Control Tree section lists all the elements on your ASP.NET page in a hierarchical fashion. This enables you to get a feeling for which controls contain other controls, helping you to decipher control scope and ownership issues. The fields displayed for each item are Control Id, Type, Render Size Bytes, and Viewstate Size Bytes. Figure 6.3 shows an example of the Control Tree section.

Control Tree			
Control Id	Type	Render Size Bytes (including children)	Viewstate Size Bytes (excluding children)
__PAGE	ASP.test_vb_aspx	371	20
ctrl1	System.Web.UI.LiteralControl	47	0
ctrl0	System.Web.UI.HtmlControls.HtmlForm	312	0
ctrl2	System.Web.UI.LiteralControl	5	0
textbox1	System.Web.UI.WebControls.TextBox	77	0
ctrl3	System.Web.UI.LiteralControl	6	0
button1	System.Web.UI.WebControls.Button	68	0
ctrl4	System.Web.UI.LiteralControl	12	0

Figure 6.3   Control Tree section of trace output.

Cookies Collection

The Cookies Collection section lists all the cookies that are associated with your ASP.NET web application. The fields displayed for each item are Name, Value, and Size. Figure 6.4 shows an example of the Cookies Collection section.

Cookies Collection		
Name	**Value**	**Size**
ASP.NET_SessionId	olezi155mb5v4r45m4b53q45	42
TestCookie	Chocolate Chip	25

Figure 6.4 Cookies Collection section of trace output.

Headers Collection

The Headers Collection section lists all the HTTP headers that are passed to your ASP.NET page. The fields displayed for each item are Name and Value. Figure 6.5 shows an example of the Headers Collection section.

Headers Collection	
Name	**Value**
Connection	Keep-Alive
Accept	*/*
Accept-Encoding	gzip, deflate
Accept-Language	en-us
Host	localhost:8080
User-Agent	Mozilla/4.0 (compatible; MSIE 6.0b; Windows NT 5.0; .NET CLR 1.0.2914)

Figure 6.5 Headers Collection section of trace output.

Form Collection

The Form Collection section is displayed only if your ASP.NET page includes a web form and you have already submitted it back to the server. It contains two important pieces of information. First, it displays the page's VIEWSTATE. This is the condensed representation of the state of each of the controls on the web form. Below the VIEWSTATE item is a listing of each control in the Form Collection section, along with its value. The fields displayed for each item are Name and Value. Figure 6.6 shows an example of the Form Collection section.

Form Collection	
Name	**Value**
__VIEWSTATE	dDwxNTQ0MTc5NDg0Ozs+
textbox1	Jonathan Goodyear
button1	click me

Figure 6.6 Form Collection section of trace output.

Querystring Collection

The Querystring Collection section is displayed only if your ASP.NET page has Querystring parameters passed to it. The fields displayed for each item are Name and Value. Figure 6.7 shows an example of the Querystring Collection section.

Querystring Collection	
Name	**Value**
trace	1

Figure 6.7 Querystring Collection section of trace output.

Server Variables

The Server Variables section contains a listing of all the server variables associated with your ASP.NET page. A few examples are `PATH_INFO`, `REMOTE_HOST`, and `SCRIPT_NAME`. The fields displayed for each item are Name and Value. Figure 6.8 shows an example of the Server Variables section (truncated because of the large number of elements in the collection).

Server Variables	
Name	**Value**
ALL_HTTP	HTTP_CONNECTION:Keep-Alive HTTP_ACCEPT:image/gif, image/x-xbitmap, image/jpeg, image/pjpeg, application/vnd.ms-powerpoint, application/vnd.ms-excel, application/msword, */* HTTP_ACCEPT_ENCODING:gzip, deflate HTTP_ACCEPT_LANGUAGE:en-us HTTP_COOKIE:TestCookie=Chocolate Chip HTTP_HOST:localhost:8080 HTTP_USER_AGENT:Mozilla/4.0 (compatible; MSIE 6.0b; Windows NT 5.0; .NET CLR 1.0.2914)
ALL_RAW	Connection: Keep-Alive Accept: image/gif, image/x-xbitmap, image/jpeg, image/pjpeg, application/vnd.ms-powerpoint, application/vnd.ms-excel, application/msword, */* Accept-Encoding: gzip, deflate Accept-Language: en-us Cookie: TestCookie=Chocolate Chip Host: localhost:8080 User-Agent: Mozilla/4.0 (compatible; MSIE 6.0b; Windows NT 5.0; .NET CLR 1.0.2914)
APPL_MD_PATH	/LM/W3SVC/1/ROOT
APPL_PHYSICAL_PATH	d:\devwebs\default\
AUTH_TYPE	
AUTH_USER	
AUTH_PASSWORD	
LOGON_USER	
REMOTE_USER	
CERT_COOKIE	
CERT_FLAGS	
CERT_ISSUER	
CERT_KEYSIZE	
CERT_SECRETKEYSIZE	
CERT_SERIALNUMBER	
CERT_SERVER_ISSUER	
CERT_SERVER_SUBJECT	

Figure 6.8 Server Variables section of trace output.

Setting Trace Messages

The `TraceContext` class has a fairly simple interface, with only one constructor, two properties, and two methods. Of course, these are in addition to the standard properties and methods inherited from the `Object` class. An instance of the `TraceContext` class is available to your ASP.NET pages through the `Trace` property of the `Page` object, so you will need the constructor only if you want to enable tracing in your .NET components (discussed later in this chapter).

TraceContext **Properties**

The IsEnabled property works the same way as the Trace attribute of the @Page directive. The nice part about having this property available to you is that, unlike the @Page
directive, it can be dynamically assigned. For instance, you can specify tracing through a
Querystring parameter, as shown in Listings 6.2 and 6.3.

Listing 6.2   **Setting the *IsEnabled* Property Dynamically (C#)**

```
<%@ Page Language="C#" %>

<script language="C#" runat="server">
    protected void Page_Load(object Sender, EventArgs e)
    {
        bool traceFlag = Request.QueryString["trace"] != null
            ? true : false;
        Trace.IsEnabled = traceFlag;
    }
</script>
```

Listing 6.3   **Setting the *IsEnabled* Property Dynamically (Visual Basic .NET)**

```
<%@ Page Language="Visual Basic" %>

<script language="Visual Basic" runat="server">
    Protected Sub Page_Load(Sender As Object, e As EventArgs)
        Dim traceFlag As Boolean = IIF(Request.QueryString("trace") _
            <> Nothing, True, False)
        Trace.IsEnabled = traceFlag
    End Sub
</script>
```

These listings set the IsEnabled property of the Trace object dynamically, based on the
presence of the trace Querystring variable. Notice that no Trace attribute is assigned
to the @Page directive. It is interesting to note that even if you specify a Trace attribute
and set it to false, the IsEnabled property value still dictates whether trace information was displayed to the page.

The real power of using the IsEnabled property is that when you set it to false, the
trace information not only isn't displayed, but it also isn't even compiled. This means
that you can leave your tracing code in your ASP.NET application when you move it
to production. As long as the IsEnabled property is set to false, you will not suffer any
performance penalty.

The `TraceMode` property works exactly like the `TraceMode` attribute of the `@Page` directive. The same behaviors and advantages that apply to the `IsEnabled` property also exist for the `TraceMode` property.

TraceContext **Methods**

Only one thing (besides their names) differentiates the two methods of the `TraceContext` class, `Write` and `Warn`: The output generated by the `Write` method is black, while the output generated by the `Warn` method is red. For this reason, we will be discussing only the `Write` method. Just realize that everything said about the `Write` method can also be applied to the `Warn` method. There are three overloaded versions of the `Write` and `Warn` methods. The first version accepts a trace message. The second version accepts a trace message and a category. The third version accepts a trace message, a category, and an instance of an `Exception` class. Each of these is covered in more detail next.

TraceContext. Write (string)

The first of the overloaded `Write` methods of the `TraceContext` class accepts a single-string parameter. This string contains the message that is displayed in the Message field of the Trace Information section of the trace output (as seen in Figure 6.2). Listings 6.4 and 6.5 demonstrate its use.

Listing 6.4 **Implementing *TraceContext. Write (string)* (C#)**

```
<%@ Page Language="C#" Trace="true" %>

<script language="C#" runat="server">
    protected void Page_Load(object Sender, EventArgs e)
    {
        Trace.Write("I'm tracing now");
    }
</script>
```

Listing 6.5 **Implementing *TraceContext. Write (string)* (Visual Basic .NET)**

```
<%@ Page Language="Visual Basic" Trace="true" %>

<script language="Visual Basic" runat="server">
    Protected Sub Page_Load(Sender As Object, e As EventArgs)
        Trace.Write("I'm tracing now")
    End Sub
</script>
```

Figure 6.9 shows what the trace output for the previous code looks like.

Request Details			
Session Id:	gmsxqg45y4ypz2aqyfz2ne55	Request Type:	GET
Time of Request:	7/8/2001 12:08:41 PM	Status Code:	200
Request Encoding:	Unicode (UTF-8)	Response Encoding:	Unicode (UTF-8)

Trace Information			
Category	Message	From First(s)	From Last(s)
aspx.page	Begin Init		
aspx.page	End Init	0.000077	0.000077
	I'm tracing now	0.000996	0.000919
aspx.page	Begin PreRender	0.001121	0.000125
aspx.page	End PreRender	0.001208	0.000086
aspx.page	Begin SaveViewState	0.001413	0.000205
aspx.page	End SaveViewState	0.001499	0.000086
aspx.page	Begin Render	0.001581	0.000081
aspx.page	End Render	0.001885	0.000304

Control Tree			
Control Id	Type	Render Size Bytes (including children)	Viewstate Size Bytes (excluding children)
__PAGE	ASP.test_vb_aspx	0	0

Figure 6.9   Viewing a trace message in the trace output.

Notice the message "I'm tracing now" that appears as the third line item in the Trace Information section. No category was specified, so it is blank. The next overloaded version of the `Write`/`Warn` method includes the category parameter.

TraceContext.Write (string, string)

The second overloaded `Write` method of the `TraceContext` class takes two string parameters. The first parameter is the category of the trace item. It appears in the Category field of the Trace Information section of the trace output. The second parameter is the message that will be displayed in the Message field, and it is the same as the single-string parameter in the first overloaded `Write` method.

This is probably the most likely version of the `Write` method that you will use when debugging your ASP.NET pages. You can assign categories to your trace items, leveraging the `TraceMode` attribute of the `@Page` directive or the `TraceMode` property of the `TraceContext` class to sort the Trace Information section results. As previously described, this is done using the `SortByCategory` member of the `TraceMode` enumeration.

Listings 6.6 and 6.7 demonstrate the use of this version of the `Write` method.

Listing 6.6   **Implementing** *TraceContext.Write (string, string)* **(C#)**

```
<%@ Page Language="C#" Trace="true" %>

<script language="C#" runat="server">
    protected void Page_Load(object Sender, EventArgs e)
    {
        Trace.TraceMode = TraceMode.SortByCategory;
```

```
            Trace.Write("Category 1", "Category 1 data");
            Trace.Write("Category 2", "Category 2 data");
            Trace.Write("Category 1", "More Category 1 data");
    }
</script>
```

Listing 6.7   **Implementing** *TraceContext.Write (string, string)* (**Visual Basic .NET**)

```
<%@ Page Language="Visual Basic" Trace="true" %>

<script language="Visual Basic" runat="server">
    Protected Sub Page_Load(Sender As Object, e As EventArgs)
        Trace.TraceMode = TraceMode.SortByCategory
        Trace.Write("Category 1", "Category 1 data")
        Trace.Write("Category 2", "Category 2 data")
        Trace.Write("Category 1", "More Category 1 data")
    End Sub
</script>
```

Figure 6.10 shows the trace output for the previous code.

Request Details

Session Id:	1wgiph3gz2rdegz1c1xvzoiq	Request Type:	GET
Time of Request:	7/8/2001 4:20:45 PM	Status Code:	200
Request Encoding:	Unicode (UTF-8)	Response Encoding:	Unicode (UTF-8)

Trace Information

Category	Message	From First(s)	From Last(s)
aspx.page	Begin Init		
aspx.page	End Init	0.000155	0.000155
aspx.page	Begin PreRender	0.003154	0.000097
aspx.page	End PreRender	0.003250	0.000096
aspx.page	Begin SaveViewState	0.003469	0.000219
aspx.page	End SaveViewState	0.003568	0.000099
aspx.page	Begin Render	0.003662	0.000094
aspx.page	End Render	0.003970	0.000308
Category 1	Category 1 data	0.002762	0.002606
Category 1	More Category 1 data	0.003057	0.000098
Category 2	Category 2 data	0.002958	0.000197

Control Tree

Control Id	Type	Render Size Bytes (including children)	Viewstate Size Bytes (excluding children)
__PAGE	ASP.test_vb_aspx	0	0

Figure 6.10   Viewing a trace message with a category in the trace output.

Notice that the trace items are sorted by category so that both of the category 1 items appear together, instead of being separated by the category 2 item (which was the order in which the code made the calls to the Write method). Also, the previous code uses the TraceMode property of the Trace object to set the sort order. You could alternatively have used the TraceMode attribute of the @Page directive.

TraceContext. Write (string, string, Exception)

The third overloaded version of the Write method takes three parameters. The first two parameters match up with the two parameters of the previous overloaded method call. For the third parameter, you should pass in an object instance of the Exception class or an object instance of a class that inherits from the Exception class. You would most likely use this method call when writing trace output in conjunction with structured exception handling. Listings 6.8 and 6.9 demonstrate this concept by intentionally causing an exception in a Try block that adds to the trace information in the Catch block.

Listing 6.8   **Implementing** *TraceContext. Write (string, string, Exception)* **(C#)**

```csharp
<%@ Page Language="C#" Trace="true" %>

<script language="C#" runat="server">
    protected void Page_Load(object Sender, EventArgs e)
    {
        int x = 1;
        int y = 0;

        try
        {
            int z = x / y;
        }
        catch(DivideByZeroException ex)
        {
            Trace.Write("Errors","Testing the limits of infinity?",ex);
        }
    }
</script>
```

Listing 6.9   **Implementing** *TraceContext. Write (string, string, Exception)* **(Visual Basic .NET)**

```vbnet
<%@ Page Language="Visual Basic" Trace="true" %>

<script language="Visual Basic" runat="server">
    Protected Sub Page_Load(Sender As Object, e As EventArgs)
        Dim x As Integer = 1
        Dim y As Integer = 0

        Try
```

```
                    Dim z As Integer = x / y
                Catch ex As OverflowException
                    Trace.Write("Errors","Testing the limits of
                    ➥infinity?",ex)
                End Try
            End Sub
    </script>
```

Figure 6.11 shows the trace output for the C# version of this code.

Request Details			
Session Id:	2m1kcw550mgjqy45siwmmqzs	**Request Type:**	GET
Time of Request:	7/8/2001 5:05:08 PM	**Status Code:**	200
Request Encoding:	Unicode (UTF-8)	**Response Encoding:**	Unicode (UTF-8)

Trace Information			
Category	**Message**	**From First(s)**	**From Last(s)**
aspx.page	Begin Init		
aspx.page	End Init	0.000080	0.000080
Errors	Testing the limits of infinity? Attempted to divide by zero. at ASP.test_cs_aspx.Page_Load(Object Sender, EventArgs e)	0.000410	0.000330
aspx.page	Begin PreRender	0.000783	0.000373
aspx.page	End PreRender	0.000870	0.000087
aspx.page	Begin SaveViewState	0.001066	0.000196
aspx.page	End SaveViewState	0.001154	0.000088
aspx.page	Begin Render	0.001235	0.000080
aspx.page	End Render	0.001524	0.000290

Control Tree			
Control Id	**Type**	**Render Size Bytes (including children)**	**Viewstate Size Bytes (excluding children)**
__PAGE	ASP.test_cs_aspx	0	0

Figure 6.11 Viewing a trace message with a category and
exception information in the trace output.

In addition to the message that you specify in the call to the Write method, you get
the message from the exception that was thrown, as well as the name of the procedure
where the exception occurred. You can see valuable debugging information associated
with the error that was thrown alongside your own custom comments, making it easier to combine the two into a solution to the bug.

Trace Viewer

In the "Application-Level Configuration" section at the beginning of the chapter, we
discussed the various attributes of the <trace> XML element in the web.config file.
You'll recall that the requestLimit attribute sets how many page requests to keep in
the trace log. So, now that you have all that data stored in the trace log, what do you
do with it? Another fine question! The answer is to use the Trace Viewer to analyze it.

Accessing the Trace Viewer

The Trace Viewer is accessed via a special URL. In any directory of your web application, you can access it by navigating to trace.axd. You'll notice that there is no trace.axd file anywhere. Instead, any request for this file is intercepted by an HttpHandler that is set up in either the machine.config file or your web application's web.config file. An entry within the <httpHandlers> XML element looks like Listing 6.10.

Listing 6.10   *HttpHandlers* **Section of the machine.config File**

```
<httpHandlers>
        ...other handler entries...
        <add verb="*" path="trace.axd"
                type="System.Web.Handlers.TraceHandler,
                System.Web, Version=1.0.2411.0, Culture=neutral,
                PublicKeyToken=b03f5f7f11d50a3a" />
        ...other handler entries...
</httpHandlers>
```

With this HttpHandler entry in place, all that is left to do to use the Trace Viewer is make sure that the enabled attribute of the <trace> XML element in your web.config file is set to true.

Using the Trace Viewer

The Trace Viewer uses a fairly simple interface, consisting of two different pages. When you first navigate to the trace.axd file, you are presented with the Application Trace screen. It contains a list of page requests for which trace information has been tracked.

Three items are present in the header of this page. The first is a link to clear the current trace log. Clicking this link resets tracing, clearing all page requests from the screen. The second item in the header is the physical directory of the ASP.NET web application. The third header item is a counter that tells you how many more requests can be tracked before the requestLimit is reached. After that point, trace information is not stored for anymore page requests until the trace information is cleared by clicking the Clear Current Trace link.

The fields displayed for each page request on the Application Trace screen are No., Time of Request, File, Status Code, and Verb. In addition, a link next to each item in the list shows the details for that specific page request. Figure 6.12 shows an example of the Application Trace screen of the Trace Viewer.

Application Trace

[clear current trace]
Physical Directory: d:\devwebs\default\

Requests to this Application				Remaining: 3
No. **Time of Request**	**File**	**Status Code**	**Verb**	
1 7/8/2001 7:16:01 PM	chapter6/test_cs.aspx	200	GET	View Details
2 7/8/2001 7:16:11 PM	chapter6/test_cs.aspx	200	GET	View Details
3 7/8/2001 7:16:17 PM	chapter6/test_vb.aspx	200	GET	View Details
4 7/8/2001 7:16:19 PM	chapter6/test_vb.aspx	200	GET	View Details
5 7/8/2001 7:16:24 PM	chapter6/test_cs.aspx	200	GET	View Details
6 7/8/2001 7:16:29 PM	chapter6/test_vb.aspx	200	GET	View Details
7 7/8/2001 7:16:33 PM	chapter6/test_cs.aspx	200	GET	View Details

Figure 6.12 Application Trace page of the Trace Viewer.

When you click one of the View Details links on the Application Trace screen, you are taken to the Request Details screen. On this page you will see is an exact representation of the trace information that would be displayed at the end of the particular ASP.NET page if tracing had been enabled on it. The only difference is the large Request Details caption at the top of the page. Several examples of this screen have been shown in previous figures in this chapter, so there is no need to present it again.

Tracing via Components

The Page object in your ASP.NET pages contains an instance of the TraceContext class, making it easy to write trace information from your ASP.NET page. But what if you want to write trace information from within a component? Luckily, the .NET Framework makes this task equally easy. Let's take a look at how this would be done. First, you need to build your simple component. Listings 6.11 and 6.12 present the component.

Listing 6.11   **Component That Leverages ASP.NET Tracing (C#)**

```csharp
using System;
using System.Web;

namespace Chapter6
{
    public class TestClass
    {
        public void DoStuff()
        {
            HttpContext.Current.Trace.Write
                ("Component", "I'm inside the component");
        }
    }
}
```

Listing 6.12   **Component That leverages ASP.NET Tracing (Visual Basic .NET)**

```
Imports System
Imports System.Web

Namespace Chapter6
    Public Class TestClass
        Public Sub DoStuff()
            HttpContext.Current.Trace.Write _
                ("Component", "I'm inside the component")
        End Sub
    End Class
End Namespace
```

Next, compile your component using one of the following compile scripts. The first is for C#, and the second is for Visual Basic .NET.

```
csc /t:library /out:Chapter6.dll /r:System.Web.dll Chapter6.cs
```

or

```
vbc /t:library /out:Chapter6.dll /r:System.Web.dll Chapter6.vb
```

Finally, you can see that this works by using it in an ASP.NET page.

Listing 6.13   **Using Trace-Enabled Component in an ASP.NET Page (C#)**

```
<%@ Page Language="C#" Trace="true" %>
<%@ Import Namespace="Chapter6" %>

<script language="C#" runat="server">
    protected void Page_Load(object Sender, EventArgs e)
    {
        TestClass tc = new TestClass();
        tc.DoStuff();
    }
</script>
```

Listing 6.14   **Using Trace-Enabled Component in an ASP.NET Page (Visual Basic .NET)**

```
<%@ Page Language="Visual Basic" Trace="true" %>
<%@ Import Namespace="Chapter6" %>

<script language="Visual Basic" runat="server">
```

```
        Protected Sub Page_Load(Sender As Object, e As EventArgs)
                Dim tc As TestClass = New TestClass()
                tc.DoStuff()
        End Sub
</script>
```

When you run this code, you'll get results like those shown in Figure 6.13.

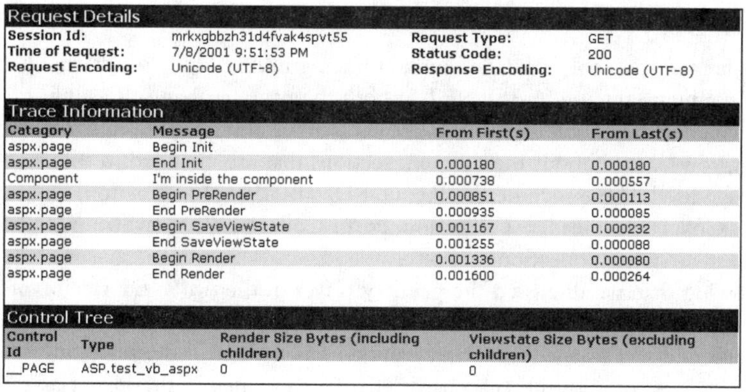

Request Details

Session Id:	mrkxgbbzh31d4fvak4spvt55	**Request Type:**	GET
Time of Request:	7/8/2001 9:51:53 PM	**Status Code:**	200
Request Encoding:	Unicode (UTF-8)	**Response Encoding:**	Unicode (UTF-8)

Trace Information

Category	Message	From First(s)	From Last(s)
aspx.page	Begin Init		
aspx.page	End Init	0.000180	0.000180
Component	I'm inside the component	0.000738	0.000557
aspx.page	Begin PreRender	0.000851	0.000113
aspx.page	End PreRender	0.000935	0.000085
aspx.page	Begin SaveViewState	0.001167	0.000232
aspx.page	End SaveViewState	0.001255	0.000088
aspx.page	Begin Render	0.001336	0.000080
aspx.page	End Render	0.001600	0.000264

Control Tree

Control Id	Type	Render Size Bytes (including children)	Viewstate Size Bytes (excluding children)
__PAGE	ASP.test_vb_aspx	0	0

Figure 6.13 Viewing trace information written to the trace output from within a component.

Inside the Trace Information section, you'll see the trace message "I'm inside the component," with a category of Component that was added from within the component. This can be a powerful tool for finding bugs in your ASP.NET web applications.

Tips for Using Trace Information

Now that you have all this trace information sitting in front of you, how do you use it to your best advantage? Well, that really depends. Most of the trace information presented (such as cookies, headers, and server variables) was available to you in traditional ASP. It just wasn't neatly packaged like it is in the Trace Viewer. You can use that information just as you previously did.

The true power of ASP.NET tracing is in the Trace Information section. It enables you to see when each part of your ASP.NET page is processing and determine how long it takes to process. This can be crucial to the process of finding performance bottlenecks in your code. It can also help you solve mysteries about why certain code is not processing correctly. Often, the code isn't being executed in the same order that you thought it was. Or, maybe the code is being executed multiple times by accident. These nuances, which were tough to discover in traditional ASP, become fairly obvious when observing the contents of the Trace Information section of the trace output.

Application-level tracing, if used properly, can greatly reduce the amount of time and effort expended on debugging your ASP.NET web applications. For instance, you could turn on tracing but set the pageOutput attribute of the <trace> XML element in the web.config file to false. Then you could let some of the potential users of your web application try it out. You can record lots of information about what they are doing and what is going wrong with their experience, all behind the scenes. This can help you to determine which particular scenarios cause errors.

Summary

In this chapter, you took a detailed look at tracing in ASP.NET. You started by learning how to configure tracing in ASP.NET, at both the page level and the application level. This entailed adding attributes to the @Page directive and to the web.config file.

Next, you learned about the different sections that are included in the trace output at the page level. These include the Request Details, Trace Information, Control Tree, Cookies Collection, Headers Collection, Form Collection, QueryString Collection, and Server Variables Collection sections.

Following that, we discussed the primary player in the ASP.NET tracing process: the TraceContext class. You learned about its two properties, IsEnabled and TraceMode, and you learned how they can be used to control the trace output of your ASP.NET pages through the TraceContext object instance in the Page class's Trace property.

The TraceContext class's two methods, Write and Warn, were discussed next. Each of the three overloaded Write methods was explained and was correlated to the similar Warn method, which differs only in name and output appearance. We deferred the discussion of the constructor to the section on tracing via components, later in the chapter.

Then you learned how to both configure and use the Trace Viewer, as well as how it is accessed via an HttpHandler that intercepts requests for the trace.axd file.

Tracing in an ASP.NET web application is not just limited to ASP.NET pages. We also discussed how to leverage ASP.NET tracing from within components that your ASP.NET pages call. The chapter wrapped up with a few tips and techniques for utilizing ASP.NET tracing to its fullest potential.

In the next chapter, you'll get a thorough introduction to debugger in the Visual Studio .NET IDE.

7

Visual Studio .NET Debugging Environment

THE ASP SCRIPT DEBUGGER THAT IS INTEGRATED with the new Visual Studio .NET IDE is, without a doubt, one of the greatest enhancements to debugging from the previous versions of ASP. Unlike trying to debug traditional ASP pages in Visual Interdev, this actually works right out of the box!

In this chapter, you will be looking at all the features available for debugging in the Visual Studio .NET IDE, how to use them, and where each one is applicable for the problem you might be trying to conquer. This will all be accomplished by building a project from scratch in the IDE, so we recommend creating the project on your own as it is done in this chapter.

Introduction to Features

Let's start out by taking a look at the most important features of the Visual Studio .NET IDE debugger. You will take a detailed look at all of these as the chapter progresses. Many of these features have existed in the Visual Studio 6.0 IDEs; however, not all were previously available when debugging traditional ASP pages in Visual InterDev.

Call Stack

The call stack enables you to display the list of functions currently called. As the name implies, this can be imagined simply as a stack. (As functions are called from within function, which, in turn, are called from within functions, a stack is created.) With the call stack viewer, you can look at this stack and jump forward and backward into the stack to debug at any point in the chain. Figure 7.1 shows the call stack in action.

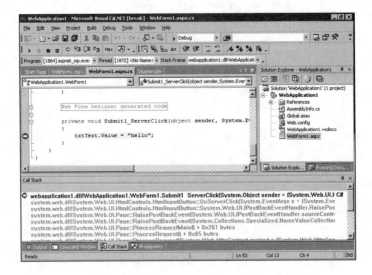

Figure 7.1   The call stack window.

Command Window

If you have used the Visual Basic IDE previously, the command window will be quite familiar to you. The command window enables you to execute program statements separately from the running program. For example, if you want to set a variable equal to a new value, or if you want to print the value of a variable, or even if you want to create an object and call some methods on it, you can do it from this window. Figure 7.2 shows how the command window can be used.

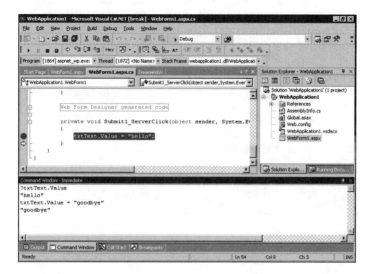

Figure 7.2   The command window.

Breakpoints

Breakpoints enable you to stop the execution of a program at a defined point either in all instances or based on a certain set of criteria. The easiest way to set a breakpoint is to click in the gray left margin next to the line where you want to stop. The IDE drops a red "dot" in the margin; when you start the program in debug mode, it stops at that specified position. By popping up the breakpoint window from the debugging windows at the bottom of the screen, you can see all breakpoints currently set in the system. Figure 7.3 shows an example of the breakpoint window.

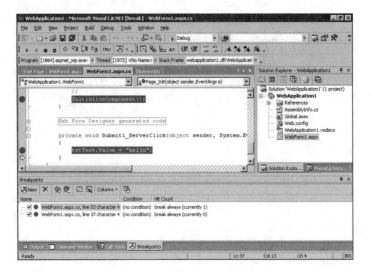

Figure 7.3   The breakpoint window.

Watch Window

The watch window can be used to watch the contents of a variable or series of variables. This window also enables you to change the value of a variable, which can be quite useful in debugging applications. You can see an example of the watch window in Figure 7.4.

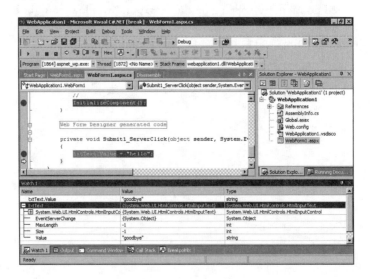

Figure 7.4   The watch window.

Tracing

Tracing simply enables you to write out a series of text messages as the program is executing so that you can see what is happening at any point during the program's life cycle. This can be very useful in creating a log of events that can be inspected later to ensure that the program is operating as you expect in all aspects. Figure 7.5 shows an output from a `Debug.Trace` statement in the output window.

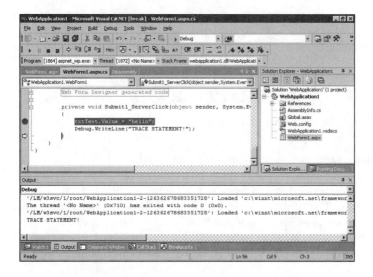

Figure 7.5   Tracing and the output window.

Attaching to Processes

At some point you might need to attach to a process running somewhere on the computer and debug it from within the ASP.NET page. This could be the ASP.NET process, aspnet_wp.exe, or another running service, or any other program running on the server. This can be accomplished quite easily.

Under the Debug menu you will find the Processes selection. Clicking this brings up the dialog box in Figure 7.6.

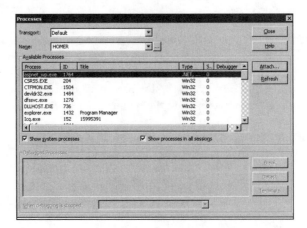

Figure 7.6   Attaching to a running process.

By default, you will see only the processes that you have started in some way. If you click the Show System Processes check box, you have access to everything that is running on the current machine. Click the process to be debugged, and then click the Attach button. Now, if that process hits a breakpoint or any other type of debugger event, that event pops up in the Visual Studio .NET IDE. You can also force the program to break by clicking the Break button at the bottom of the window. At any time, you can stop debugging the process by clicking the Detach button. Terminate kills the process altogether.

After clicking the Attach button, you are given a choice of what type of debugging you want to do on the process you've selected. Figure 7.7 shows an example of this dialog box.

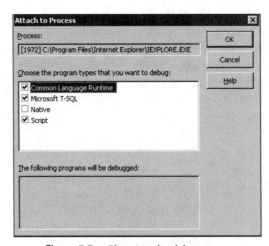

Figure 7.7   Choosing the debug type.

If you are attaching to a .NET process written using the Common Language Runtime (CLR), choose the Common Language Runtime option from the dialog box. If you'll be breaking into a process that uses Microsoft Transact SQL language, check Microsoft T-SQL as your debug type. Native enables you to debug a standard Win32 application. This enables you to debug a Win32 program at an assembly language level. Finally, the Script type gives you the capability to debug standard Visual BasicScript and JavaScript. This is especially useful for debugging an instance of Internet Explorer.

Setting It All Up

There really isn't a whole lot to mention here. It is extremely simple to use the Visual Studio .NET IDE for debugging ASP.NET pages. In most cases, it will be a plug-and-play affair. The default debug build of any ASP.NET project will have everything set up for you to begin. However, even though that probably will be the case, we will discuss what is absolutely required for the debugging to work, just in case something goes wrong.

Take a look at the web.config file contained in your project. This is an XML file that contains specific configuration information for your ASP.NET project. One line in this file will look similar to the following:

```
<compilation defaultLanguage="vb" debug="true" />
```

The `defaultLanguage` parameter will be based on the default language of your ASP.NET project. But what we are concerned about here is the `debug` parameter. If you are running in a debugging environment and want to be able to access the spiffy features of the Visual Studio .NET IDE, this `debug` parameter must be set to `true`, as it is in the previous line. If it is set to `false`, none of the features will work. This is what you want for a release build of your project.

Inline Debugging of ASP.NET Pages

This is so very easy—you're going to be extremely happy about this. If you've ever debugged a program using Visual Studio 6.0 (Visual Basic, Visual C++, and so on) you will feel right at home with what you are about to learn about Visual Studio .NET. Let's discuss these great features using a sample project mentioned earlier in the chapter. As usual, both Visual Basic .NET and C# versions of the code will be provided for you to see.

This sample project will consist of an ASP.NET page and a Visual Basic .NET/C# component so that you can see how easily the two interact and how they can be debugged simultaneously. The project itself will simply ask the user for a valid email address and then send a form letter to that address. Start out by creating the project. We called ours Chap5Visual Basic for the Visual Basic .NET version and Chap5CS for the C# version.

The first thing to do is create the ASP.NET page that the user will see. Listing 7.1 contains the main ASP.NET page that contains the input form on which the user can enter the email address where the mail will be sent. Here the page name is left as WebForm1, the default name provided when the project was created.

Listing 7.1 **ASP.NET Page for Debugging Example**

```
<%@ Page Language="vb" AutoEventWireup="false"
➥Codebehind="WebForm1.aspx.vb" Inherits="Chap7VB.WebForm1"%>
<html>
    <HEAD>
        <title>Email Test Page</title>
    </HEAD>
    <body MS_POSITIONING="GridLayout">
        <form id="Form1" method="post" runat="server">
            Please enter the email address to send to:
            <br>
            <input type="text" id="txtEmail" runat="server"
            ➥NAME="txtEmail">
            <br>
            <input type="submit" id="btnSubmit" value="Send Email"
            ➥runat="server" NAME="btnSubmit">
        </form>
    </body>
</html>
```

This page would work in a Visual Basic .NET project. To have it work in a C# project, change the first line to the following:

```
<%@ Page language="c#" Codebehind="WebForm1.aspx.cs" AutoEventWireup="false"
➥Inherits="Chap7CS.WebForm1" %>
```

This is a very simple page. It consists of two elements: a text box for the email address and a Submit button to send the form to the server. Now you will create the server-side code for this project. It will be contained in two parts: First, you will look at the code-behind file that is associated with this file. Here you will verify that you have a valid email address. Second, you will create a Visual Basic .NET/C# component that will actually send the email. Listing 7.2 contains the code-behind file for the C# project, and Listing 7.3 contains the code-behind file for the Visual Basic .NET project.

Listing 7.2 **Listing for Debugging Example (C#)**

```csharp
using System;

namespace Chap7CS
{
    public class WebForm1 : System.Web.UI.Page
    {
        protected System.Web.UI.HtmlControls.HtmlInputText txtEmail;
        protected System.Web.UI.HtmlControls.HtmlInputButton btnSubmit;

        public WebForm1()
        {
            Page.Init += new System.EventHandler(Page_Init);
        }

        private void Page_Init(object sender, EventArgs e)
        {
            InitializeComponent();
        }

        private void InitializeComponent()
        {
                this.btnSubmit.ServerClick += new
                ➥System.EventHandler(this.btnSubmit_ServerClick);
        }

        private void btnSubmit_ServerClick(object sender,
        ➥System.EventArgs e)
        {
            if(txtEmail.Value.IndexOf("@") == -1 ||
                txtEmail.Value.IndexOf(".") == -1)
                Response.Write("The supplied email address is not
                ➥valid.");
        }
    }
}
```

Listing 7.3 **Listing for Debugging Example (Visual Basic .NET)**

```
Public Class WebForm1
        Inherits System.Web.UI.Page
        Protected WithEvents txtEmail As
        ➥System.Web.UI.HtmlControls.HtmlInputText
        Protected WithEvents btnSubmit As
        ➥System.Web.UI.HtmlControls.HtmlInputButton

    Private Sub btnSubmit_ServerClick(ByVal sender As System.Object, ByVal e
    ➥As System.EventArgs) Handles btnSubmit.ServerClick
        If txtEmail.Value.IndexOf("@") = -1 Or _
            txtEmail.Value.IndexOf(".") = -1 Then
            Response.Write("The supplied email address is not valid.")
        End If
    End Sub
End Class
```

These examples are also extremely simple, but they demonstrate the features of the
Visual Studio .NET IDE quite effectively.

In this example, you are listening to the `ServerClick` event of the Submit button,
named `btnSubmit`. When the user clicks the Submit button, this event is fired. At this
point, you can inspect what is in the text box on the form. If it does not contain an @
symbol or a ., it cannot be a valid email address and you then report this back to the
user with a `Response.Write` of an error message.

Next you will look at how the previously mentioned debugging tools can aid you
in tracking down a problem in this simple page.

Setting a Breakpoint

Let's start out by setting a breakpoint on the `ServerClick` event of the Submit button.
This is the `btnSubmit_ServerClick` function in either piece of code. To set a breakpoint, simply move the mouse cursor to the gray left margin in the code editor
window, and click. This drops a red dot into the margin, signifying that a breakpoint
has been set at that specific line. Figure 7.8 shows exactly where to set this breakpoint
and what the margin will look like after clicking.

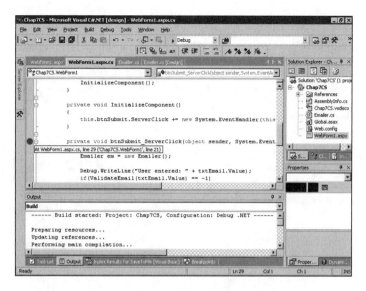

Figure 7.8   Setting the breakpoint in the example program.

Now go ahead and run the program. When Internet Explorer appears, enter some gibberish into the text box that does not contain either an @ symbol or a .. Now click the Submit button. When this occurs, the Visual Studio .NET IDE should pop up with
the breakpoint line highlighted in yellow. The execution of your program has paused, and now you can use some of the other debugging features. You will look at the watch window next.

Watch Window

At the bottom of your screen, you will see a debugging window with some tabs below it. Click the one labeled Watch 1. If this tab is not available, you will find the same entry under the Debug menu as part of the Windows suboption. Figure 7.9 shows the menu entry.

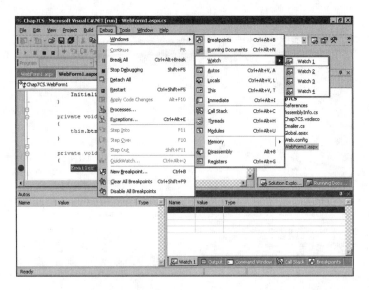

Figure 7.9   The watch window option under the Debug menu.

The watch window enables you to type in a specific variable name, control name, or other object and then see what value it contains and what type it is. For now, type in txtEmail. You will see that you can expand this entry into all the control's properties to see what they each contain. To save space, you might want to see only the Value property—in that case, you could enter txtEmail.Value as your watch name.

With the txtEmail control expanded, you can see that the Value property contains whatever you entered in the control on the client side. This can be extremely useful when debugging all types of controls to see what values they contain. It is always useful to start here when debugging almost any problem to make sure that the data isn't to blame. For example, you might be chasing after a problem only to find that the Value property is empty for some reason or that it does not contain the data that you think it does.

The other thing that you can do with the watch window is change the value of a variable. If you click the property value in the Value column in the watch window, you can enter a new value as you see fit. This might be helpful if you want to test a certain case in your logic that might be difficult to hit. For example, if an error is supposed to occur if a value equals −1, at this point you could change the value to −1 and continue execution to make sure that the code path is operating properly.

That's about it for the watch window. This is a feature that you will use quite a bit in your debugging. Remember that you can enter any variable or any object into the window and view any or all of its specific properties. Also note that you can change the values of any of these properties at any time.

The Command Window

If you have used Visual Basic, this will be a familiar sight. The command window was called the immediate window in Visual Basic, but its features are identical. This window enables you to issue commands to debug or evaluate expressions on the fly.

To display the window, either click the Command Window tab located at the bottom of your screen, or choose Windows, Immediate from the Debug menu at the top of your screen. Figure 7.10 shows where you can find the option under the Debug menu.

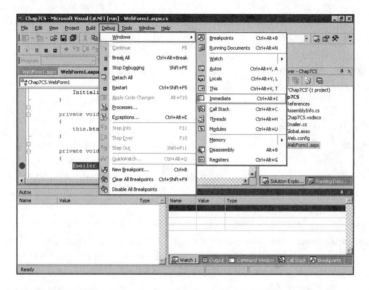

Figure 7.10   The immediate window option under the Debug menu.

To view the contents of a variable or object, just type its name into the command window. For example, typing `txtEmail.Value` while at the breakpoint displays the contents of the text box upon submission to the server.

Similar to the watch window, you can change the value of variables or object properties. To change the value of the form text box, you could enter `txtEmail.Value = "newvalue"`, which would set the string to `"newvalue"`.

What makes the command window a bit more exciting than the watch window is its capability to execute functions. For example, if you want to execute the `ValidateEmail` function in your code listing at any time, you could do it right from the command window: Just click in the window and call the function with the appropriate parameter. For example, if you type `ValidateEmail("test@myhost.com")`, you will see that it returns `0`. If you type `ValidateEmail("asdfasdf")`, it returns −1. So, you can test any function that you write right here without having the executing program call it explicitly—a great debugging aid.

Tracing

Tracing is a very simple method of debugging problems. Tracing can be used to print text statements during the execution of your code. This can be used as a log to see exactly what is happening at any point in your code. As you can see in the previous examples, in the `ServerClick` function of the Submit button, you are calling `Debug.WriteLine` with the value of the form's text box. This call spits out the value of the text box to the debug stream. The easiest place to see the debug stream is in the output window at the bottom of the Visual Studio .NET IDE.

This window can be displayed by either clicking the Output tab or choosing Output under the View menu and then choosing Other Windows. This window shows you all the debug statements that you have inserted into your code, as well as anything else that gets written to the debug stream by any other components that might be associated with the running project. Keep this in mind if you see a flood of messages that you didn't write into your code.

Execution Control

Before we start talking about the call stack, let's take a brief journey into the execution control features of the debugger. These features enable you to control exactly what is executed in your program—and in what order. They can also be used to trace deeply into certain portions of the code or skip over them, if that level of detail is unnecessary.

All these features can be found under the Debug menu at the top of your screen. All are also associated with keyboard shortcuts that vary depending on how you have configured Visual Studio .NET. The keyboard shortcuts are the easiest method of using these features because they enable you to move through many lines of code in a very quick fashion. We recommend learning the keyboard shortcuts and using them while debugging your own code.

The three options are Step Into, Step Over, and Step Out. Step Into enables you to step one level deeper into the code at the current point of execution or, at the very least, move to the next statement. If you are about to call a function in your code, using Step Into continues execution at the first line of the called function.

Step Over does the opposite of Step Into. If you are about to call a function, using Step Over at this point does just that—it steps over execution of the function to the very next line of the function that you are currently executing. Now keep in mind that this does not mean that it will not execute the function—it just will not allow you to dig into it. It executes the function and moves on to the next line. This is quite useful when you know that a function or block of code is working correctly and you do not want to spend the time hitting every single line.

Step Out enables you to jump out of the current function that you are debugging and go one level up. Again, similar to the Step Over feature, this does not skip the execution of the remaining lines of code; they just execute behind your back, and your debugging cursor moves to the next line in the previous function you were in.

So how do you know which function you were previously in? That leads to the next debugging feature, the call stack.

Call Stack

The call stack shows the current function you are in and all functions that preceded it. When you call a function from a function from a function from a function, you have a call stack that is four levels deep, with the current function on the top. You can view the call stack window by clicking the Call Stack tab at the bottom of your screen or by choosing Call Stack from the Debug menu under Windows.

Continuing the previous example, stop execution again on the btnSubmit_ServerClick function and then trace into the ValidateEmail function. Now you have called a function from a function. Take a look at the call stack window. The top two levels should show you the ValidateEmail function, followed by the btnSubmit_ServerClick function. You will also see quite a few other functions that are called by the ASP.NET system processes.

Now go ahead and double-click the btnSubmit_ServerClick function. A green highlight appears over the point in the function that you currently are in. In this case, the call to ValidateEmail is highlighted because this is the exact position that you are currently at in that function.

This feature can be of use when you are debugging code that might not be all your own. If you are many levels deep into a function stack, you might need to know where you came from. By using this, you can trace back to the calling stack and see exactly who called you and with what information. After you have traced back to the call stack, you can use the watch window or the command window to inspect the local variables from the previous functions. This can be handy when you want to find where certain data values are coming from if they are wrong.

Feature Summary

That about wraps up the baseline features of the Visual Studio .NET IDE. Next you will look at how to add a C# or Visual Basic .NET component to your project and debug that simultaneously with your ASP.NET pages. The process is extremely streamlined and quite
seamless, as you will soon see.

Inline Debugging of Components

If you tried debugging Visual Basic components within an ASP page in the previous version of Visual Studio, you will remember that it can be a pain to deal with. You need the Visual Interdev IDE open for debugging the ASP page, and you need the separate Visual Basic IDE open to debug the components at the same time.

The new Visual Studio .NET IDE makes this process remarkably simpler. You can add the component to your ASP.NET project, and debugging of that component can be done within the same IDE in sequence with your ASP.NET code. Let's look at how this is done. To do this, you will add a component to the previous project that actually sends out the email to the address provided.

Adding the Component

You will now add the component to the ASP.NET application. Just right-click your mouse on the project name (Chap5VB or Chap5CS, if you've named them what we called them) and choose Add Component under the Add submenu. Here, choose either a Visual Basic .NET component class or a C# component class, depending on which type of project you are currently doing. Name the component Emailer, for lack of a better name. Figure 7.11 shows the menu option to choose after right-clicking the project name.

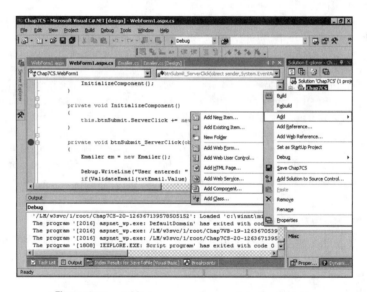

Figure 7.11   Adding a new component to the project.

Now that you have added the component, it needs some code. Listing 7.4 is the C# version of the emailer, and Listing 7.5 is the Visual Basic .NET version. Reference whichever one is applicable for your project.

Listing 7.4 **Code for Emailer Component (C#)**

```csharp
using System.Web.Mail;

namespace Chap7CS
{
    public class Emailer : System.ComponentModel.Component
    {
        private System.ComponentModel.Container components = null;

        public Emailer(System.ComponentModel.IContainer container)
        {
            container.Add(this);
            InitializeComponent();
        }

        public Emailer()
        {
            InitializeComponent();
        }

        private void InitializeComponent()
        {
            components = new System.ComponentModel.Container();
        }

        public void SendFormEmail(string toAddr)
        {
            MailMessage mm = new MailMessage();

            mm.To = toAddr;
            mm.From = "admin@domain.com";
            mm.Body = "This is a test message.  Exciting, isn't it?";
            mm.Subject = "Chapter 7 Test Message";
            SmtpMail.SmtpServer = "smtp.domain.com";
            SmtpMail.Send(mm);
        }
    }
}
```

Listing 7.5   **Code for Emailer Component (Visual Basic .NET)**

```vb
Imports System.Web.Mail

Public Class Emailer
    Inherits System.ComponentModel.Component

    Public Sub New(ByVal Container As System.ComponentModel.IContainer)
        MyClass.New()

        Container.Add(Me)
    End Sub

    Public Sub New()
        MyBase.New()

        InitializeComponent()
    End Sub

    Private components As System.ComponentModel.Container

    <System.Diagnostics.DebuggerStepThrough()> Private Sub
    ➥InitializeComponent()
      components = New System.ComponentModel.Container()
    End Sub

    Public Sub SendFormEmail(ByVal toAddr As String)
        Dim mm As MailMessage = New MailMessage()

        mm.To = toAddr
        mm.From = "admin@domain.com"
        mm.Body = "This is a test message.  Exciting, isn't it?"
        mm.Subject = "Chapter 7 Test Message"
        SmtpMail.SmtpServer = "smtp.domain.com"
        SmtpMail.Send(mm)
    End Sub
End Class
```

The code here is pretty simple. Each version contains a function called `SendFormEmail` that takes the email address to send to as a parameter. Then you use the `MailMessage` and `SmtpMail` objects from the `System.Web.Mail` assembly to form the email message and send it out using a valid SMTP server. To get this to work in your environment, be sure to replace the `SmtpMail.SmtpServer` value with the SMTP server of your local network.

You will need to modify your `btnSubmit_ServerClick` function to create an instance of this component and call the `SendFormEmail` method to make it happen. Listing 7.6 gives the code for the modified `btnSubmit_ServerClick` in C#, and Listing 7.7 gives the same code in Visual Basic .NET.

Listing 7.6   **Modified Code for** *btnSubmit_ServerClick* **(C#)**

```csharp
private void btnSubmit_ServerClick(object sender, System.EventArgs e)
{
    Emailer em = new Emailer();

    Debug.WriteLine("User entered: " + txtEmail.Value);
    if(ValidateEmail(txtEmail.Value) == -1)
        Response.Write("The supplied email address is not valid.");
    else
    {
        em.SendFormEmail(txtEmail.Value);
        Response.Write("The email was sent successfully.");
    }
}
```

Listing 7.7   **Modified Code for** *btnSubmit_ServerClick* **(Visual Basic .NET)**

```vbnet
Private Sub btnSubmit_ServerClick(ByVal sender As System.Object, ByVal e _
As System.EventArgs) Handles btnSubmit.ServerClick
    Dim em As Emailer = New Emailer()

    If txtEmail.Value.IndexOf("@") = -1 Or _
        txtEmail.Value.IndexOf(".") = -1 Then
        Response.Write("The supplied email address is not valid.")
    Else
        em.SendFormEmail(txtEmail.Value)
        Response.Write("The email was sent successfully.")
    End If
End Sub
```

Debugging the Component

Now we get to the cool part. You can debug this component while you debug the ASP.NET page and its respective code-behind file. To prove this, set a breakpoint on the `btnSubmit_ServerClick` in the code-behind file and then start the program.

When Internet Explorer appears, enter a valid email address in the appropriate box, and click the Submit button. Immediately, the breakpoint on the `btnSubmit_ServerClick` function should fire and the program is paused on that line. Now step to the point where the current function is about to call the `Emailer.SendFormEmail` function. At this position, do a Step Into. You will see that the source code to the Emailer component appears with the code pointer at the top of the `SendFormEmail` function.

From here, you can use all the techniques mentioned earlier to inspect variables, set trace statements, modify variable values, and so on. It couldn't be easier! Say goodbye to multiple programs being open simultaneously and other configuration issues that make your life difficult.

Remote Debugging

Every time we have a discussion with someone regarding debugging ASP pages, we always ask if that person has ever tried to set up ASP debugging on the local machine. The response usually is "yes." We then follow up with the question of if that person has ever gotten it to work. The number who answer "yes" to that question is much lower. Finally, we ask if that person has ever gotten ASP debugging to work remotely. We have yet to find someone who has gotten it to work properly and consistently.

With ASP.NET and Visual Studio .NET, that all changes. It finally works. And it couldn't possibly be easier to install, configure, and use.

Installation

When you install Visual Studio .NET on your server, all you need to do is install both Remote Debugging options listed under the Server Components option during the install
procedure.

Setup

To configure remote debugging, the only thing you need to do is place your user account into the newly created Debugger Users group both on the client machine and on the server machine. This can be done using the standard user configuration tools that are part of whichever Windows operating system you are using.

Using It

This is the easiest part of all. To use the new remote debugging features, simply create a project on your client computer that points to the project running on the server. This can be done by choosing Open Project from the Web from the File menu. Just type in the name of the server where the project resides, and you will be presented with a list of projects currently residing on that server. Choose the appropriate one.

If you are not connecting to an existing project, you can create a brand new project on the server, and remote debugging will still take place.

Next, set a breakpoint on the line where you want to stop, or simply start the application running. It will connect to the server and bring up an Internet Explorer window, as usual. The big difference here is that the application is running entirely on the server. When you hit your breakpoint, you are hitting it on the server, in the server's memory space. The same goes for components and anything else that you might be debugging. Everything that can be debugged in Visual Studio .NET locally can now be debugged remotely on any server where the remote debugging options have been installed.

And that's it! It's almost completely automatic. I wish it was this easy in Visual Studio 6.0—it's a huge time saver and a powerful tool.

Summary

In this chapter, you looked at many of the debugging features found in the new Visual Studio .NET IDE. You should now be familiar with things such as the watch window, the command window, breakpoints, variable inspection, and variable modification as applied both to debugging ASP.NET pages and Visual Basic .NET and C# components. With these concepts in mind, you are prepared to start debugging your own projects, and you are prepared for what is explained in the remainder of this book.

In the next chapter, we discuss how you can use the Windows NT and Windows 2000 Event Log to aid in tracking down troublesome code in your projects.

8

Leveraging the Windows 2000 Event Log

WHILE YOU ARE DEVELOPING A WEB APPLICATION, if something goes wrong and you receive a page error, you get feedback right on the screen. You can then use that information to track down the source of the error and fix it. After you put your web application into production, however, you are not always there when a problem occurs. Without a way to track these errors, they could go unnoticed for days or even weeks. A great solution to this problem is to leverage the Windows 2000 Event Log. This chapter explains what the Windows 2000 Event Log is and tells how to implement it in your web applications. We'll also define expected and unexpected events, and tell how to handle both types. The chapter concludes with an exercise in building a web-based event log viewer.

The Windows 2000 Event Log Defined

The Windows 2000 Event Log is the system by which Windows 2000 tracks events that happen on the server. The event log tracks three types of events: security events, system events, and application events. The last category, application events, is what this chapter focuses on. The application event log is designed for notifications concerning non–system-level applications on the server. Most often, these are custom applications from third-party vendors.

Web Applications Can Use the Event Log

Web applications can also leverage the application event log. Previous versions of ASP did not offer an easy way to write information to the application event log—you had to build a Visual Basic component that would enable this functionality. This, coupled with the fact that there was no structured error handling in traditional ASP applications, meant that you had to either use the On Error Resume Next statement or direct all of your page errors to a centralized error page for processing—not very elegant at all.

ASP.NET offers full support for manipulating the Windows 2000 Event Log. This includes creating custom application logs that are specific to your web application. This helps you stay organized if you are hosting multiple web applications on the same server. The structured error handling that Microsoft's .NET Framework provides is ideal for capturing and logging application events. Global events also can be used to capture error information if errors occur in your web application.

The System.Diagnostics Event Log Interface

The event log interface in the System.Diagnostics namespace is very feature-complete; this namespace is the one discussed and used in all the code examples in this chapter. Despite its extra features, the EventLog object in the System.Diagnostics namespace is quite easy to manipulate and use. To write a message to the Windows 2000 Event Log, simply call the static WriteEntry method of the EventLog class as illustrated in Listings 8.1 and 8.2.

Listing 8.1   **Writing to the Event Log Using the *EventLog* object in System.Diagnostics (C#)**

```
<%@ Page Language="C#" %>
<%@ Import Namespace="System.Diagnostics" %>


<%

    EventLog.WriteEntry("EventTest",
        "I'm a little teapot, short and stout.");
    Response.Write("Done!");
%>
```

Listing 8.2   **Writing to the Event Log Using the *EventLog* object in System.Diagnostics (Visual Basic .NET)**

```
<%@ Page Language="VB" %>
<%@ Import Namespace="System.Diagnostics" %>


<%
```

```
EventLog.WriteEntry("EventTest", _
    "I'm a little teapot, short and stout.")
Response.Write("Done!")
%>
```

Figure 8.1 shows how the event that you just logged would look when viewed in the Windows 2000 Event Log Viewer.

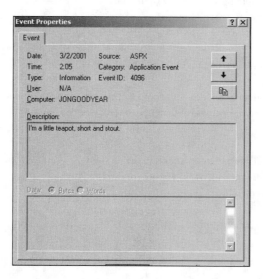

Figure 8.1   Double-clicking an event in the Windows 2000
Event Log Viewer displays its details in a property page dialog box.

Notice that you can specify a source EventTest for the event that appears in the Source field of the Windows 2000 Event Log Viewer. The EventLog object gives you a great deal of power and control over the Windows 2000 Event Log. It also enables you to create custom event logs and to control event logs on other machines on your network (discussed next), among other things.

Custom Event Logs

One of the neat things that the EventLog object enables you to do is create custom event logs and write to them on the fly. To do this, however, you must first check to see whether the log that you want to write to already exists or whether you need to create it. As you'll see in Listings 8.3 and 8.4, only a few extra lines of code are needed.

Listing 8.3   **Creating a Custom Event Log and Logging an Entry in It (C#)**

```
<%@ Page Language="C#" %>
<%@ Import Namespace="System.Diagnostics" %>


<%

    EventLog el = new EventLog();

    el.MachineName = "."; //local computer
    el.Source = "Test Source";
    el.Log = "Test Log";

    if (!EventLog.SourceExists(el.Source))
    {
        //Event source doesn't exist, so create a new one
        EventLog.CreateEventSource(el.Source,el.Log);
    }

    el.WriteEntry("Just look at me
➥now!",EventLogEntryType.Information,12);
    el.Close();

    Response.Write("Done!");
%>
```

Listing 8.4   **Creating a Custom Event Log and Logging an Entry in It
(Visual Basic .NET)**

```
<%@ Page Language="VB" %>
<%@ Import Namespace="System.Diagnostics" %>


<%

    Dim el As EventLog = New EventLog()

    el.MachineName = "." 'local computer
    el.Source = "Test Source"
    el.Log = "Test Log"

    If Not EventLog.SourceExists(el.Source) Then
        'Event source doesn't exist, so create a new one
        EventLog.CreateEventSource(el.Source,el.Log)
    End If

    el.WriteEntry("Just look at me now!",EventLogEntryType.Information, _
```

```
            12
        el.Close()

        Response.Write("Done!")
    %>
```

You should note a few interesting things about the code just shown. First, contrary to the previous examples so far, you actually create an instance of the EventLog object here rather than using Static methods of the EventLog class. Next, you set a few properties of the EventLog instance. You then feed the Source property of your EventLog instance into the Static SourceExists method of the EventLog class. If a Boolean false value is returned from the method (meaning that the source does not exist in the Windows 2000 Event Log), then you can call the CreateEventSource static method to create it. You then can call the WriteEntry method of your EventLog instance to write an entry to your custom event log.

The WriteEntry method has several overloaded method signatures, but the one that is used here takes three parameters. The first parameter is the actual message that you want to write to your custom event log. The second parameter is a typed Enum (short for enumeration). The possible values for the EventLogEntryType are as follows:

Error

FailureAudit

Information

SuccessAudit

Warning

You should use the Error value when something has definitely gone wrong with your web application. Use the Information value when something happens in your web application that might not be a problem but that you just want to know about it. Use the Warning value when something bad is about to happen or when something (or somebody) is trying to do something that is not supposed allowed. The other two values, FailureAudit and SuccessAudit, are used for logging to the security log and will not be discussed here.

The final parameter to the WriteEntry method is the event ID. This parameter is a Short datatype and can contain any numerical value that you want to pass in. It is just another way to logically separate unique event types. Remember that you already specified the machine name, source, and log to for your EventLog object instance, so these values take part in the WriteEntry method as well. A final important thing to remember is that you must call the Close method of your EventLog object to release the read and write memory handles to the event log. Figure 8.2 shows the custom event log that you just created.

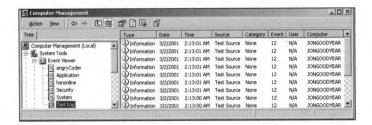

Figure 8.2   You can organize your debugging
efforts by separating events into different logs.

Notice in the figure that you just created a new custom event log named Test Log in
the Windows 2000 Event Log Viewer tree node under System Tools. You can also see
the `Test Source` value in the Source field and the value `12` in the Event field. If you
double-clicked on this event, you would see a figure similar to Figure 8.1 that shows
your new message in the Description box.

Handling Different Types Of Events

Generally, you log entries to the Windows 2000 Event Log when something significant happens in your web application. These "events" fall into two categories: expected
events and unexpected events.

Expected Events

Expected events are things that are not completely out of the ordinary, but you want
to make a record of the fact that they did happen. Generally, you determine whether
an expected event happened by using a logic structure. Items can be logged to the
proper event log (or not logged at all), depending on the outcome of the logic structure. Listings 8.5 and 8.6 provide examples.

Listing 8.5   **Logging Expected Events with Logic Structures (C#)**

```
<%@ Page Language="C#" %>
<%@ Import Namespace="System.Diagnostics" %>

<script language="C#" runat="server">
      //build a generic function for logging, to prevent redundant code
      void LogStuff(string message, EventLogEntryType eventType,
          short eventID)
      {
          EventLog el = new EventLog();
```

```
            el.MachineName = "."; //local computer
            el.Source = "Test Source";
            el.Log = "Test Log";

            if (!EventLog.SourceExists(el.Source))
            {
                    //Event source doesn't exist, so create a new one
                    EventLog.CreateEventSource(el.Source,el.Log);
            }

            el.WriteEntry(message,eventType,eventID);
            el.Close();
    }
</script>

<%
    //grab the "second" portion of the time
    int second = DateTime.Now.Second;

    //write to a different log, depending on the value
    if(second % 2 == 0)
    {
        LogStuff("The value is even: " + second.ToString(),
            EventLogEntryType.Information, 1);
    }
    else if(second == 7)
    {
        LogStuff("Beware of superstitions: " + second.ToString(),
            EventLogEntryType.Warning, 2);
    }
    else
    {
        LogStuff("The value is odd: " + second.ToString(),
            EventLogEntryType.Information, 3);
    }

    Response.Write("Done!");
%>
```

Listing 8.6   **Logging Expected Events with Logic Structures (Visual Basic .NET)**

```vb
<%@ Page Language="VB" %>
<%@ Import Namespace="System.Diagnostics" %>

<script language="VB" runat="server">
    'build a generic function for logging, to prevent redundant code
    Sub LogStuff(message As String, eventType As EventLogEntryType, _
        eventID as Short)

        Dim el As EventLog = New EventLog()

        el.MachineName = "." 'local computer
        el.Source = "Test Source"
        el.Log = "Test Log"

        If Not EventLog.SourceExists(el.Source) Then
            'Event source doesn't exist, so create a new one
            EventLog.CreateEventSource(el.Source,el.Log)
        End If

        el.WriteEntry(message,eventType,eventID)
        el.Close()
    End Sub
</script>

<%
    'grab the "second" portion of the time
    Dim second As Integer = DateTime.Now.Second

    'write to a different log, depending on the value
    If second Mod 2 = 0 Then
        LogStuff("The value is even: " & second.ToString(), _
            EventLogEntryType.Information, 1)
    ElseIf second = 7 Then
        LogStuff("Beware of superstitions: " & second.ToString(), _
            EventLogEntryType.Warning, 2)
    Else
        LogStuff("The value is odd: " & second.ToString(), _
            EventLogEntryType.Information, 3)
    End If

    Response.Write("Done!")
%>
```

The example starts by defining a `LogStuff` function. Because several different types of log entries can be made on the page, it makes sense to consolidate the logic into a utility function. In your own web applications, you might also want to encapsulate this logic into a lightweight utility component. For now, a utility function will suffice.

The example itself is not very complex. You retrieve the "second" portion of the current time and write an entry to the custom event log based on the value that you obtain. Notice that each call to `LogStuff` feeds in a different value for the event ID (the last parameter). You can use the sorting capabilities of the Windows 2000 Event Log Viewer to group similar events for analysis. Also, the `EventLogEntryType` parameter is set to `Warning` when the number 7 (often considered lucky by superstitious people) comes up.

Unexpected Events

Unexpected events happen when errors occur in your web application. Microsoft's .NET Framework provides structured error handling to capture and handle these errors. Structured error handling also presents the perfect place to log these errors to the Windows 2000 Event Log. The examples provided in Listings 8.7 and 8.8 will help clarify.

Listing 8.7 **Logging Unexpected Events with Structured Error Handling (C#)**

```
<%@ Page Language="C#" %>
<%@ Import Namespace="System.Diagnostics" %>

<script language="C#" runat="server">
        //build a generic function for logging, to prevent redundant code
        void LogStuff(string message, EventLogEntryType eventType,
                short eventID)
        {
                //code truncated - see example 8.7
        }
</script>

<%
        int value1 = 10;
        int value2 = 0;
        int value3 = 0;

        try
        {
                value3 = value1 / value2;
        }
```

continues

Listing 8.7   **Continued**

```
catch (DivideByZeroException e)
{
        //log the error to the event log
        LogStuff(e.Message, EventLogEntryType.Error, 1);
}

Response.Write("Done!");
%>
```

Listing 8.8   **Logging Unexpected Events with Structured Error Handling (Visual Basic .NET)**

```
<%@ Page Language="VB" %>
<%@ Import Namespace="System.Diagnostics" %>

<script language="VB" runat="server">
    'build a generic function for logging, to prevent redundant code
    Sub LogStuff(message As String, eventType As EventLogEntryType, _
        'code truncated - see example 8.8
    End Sub
</script>

<%
    Dim value1 As Integer = 10
    Dim value2 As Integer = 0
    Dim value3 As Integer = 0

    Try
        value3 = value1 / value2
    Catch e As OverflowException
        'log the error to the event log
        LogStuff(e.Message, EventLogEntryType.Error, 1)
    End Try

    Response.Write("Done!")
%>
```

You start off by declaring three integer variables. Next, you open a structured error handling "try" block. You then intentionally manufacture a `DivideByZeroException` (`OverflowException`, in Visual Basic) by dividing `value1` by `value2` (which translates to `10 / 0`). The "catch" block intercepts the exception because it was defined as the proper type. Had the error not been of `DivideByZeroException` (`OverflowException`, in Visual Basic), a normal runtime error would have occurred on the page. To prevent this, you can declare another catch block underneath it for the generic `Exception` class. That way, specific exceptions will be caught, but if a strange exception occurs, then you're still covered.

Access Event Log Data via the Web

Now that you have all this information stored in the Windows 2000 Event Log, how do you view it? Well, if you're sitting at the machine or have access to another machine on the same network, then you can use the Windows 2000 Event Log Viewer. If you're not on the network, then you have to come up with something else. Assuming that you have a secure directory on your website (you wouldn't want to make your logs public), you can build a web-based viewer to check your web server's event log. This is because the `EventLog` class in the System.Diagnostics namespace exposes a complete interface for the manipulation of your event logs. You'll build a small event log viewer here if you follow along with Listings 8.9 and 8.10.

Listing 8.9   **Web-Based Event Log Viewer (C#)**

```
<%@ Page Language="C#" %>
<%@ Import Namespace="System.Diagnostics" %>

<script language="C#" runat="server">
    protected void Page_Load(object sender, EventArgs e)
    {
        if (!IsPostBack)
        {
            EventLog[] elArray = EventLog.GetEventLogs(".");
            logs.DataSource = elArray;
            logs.DataTextField = "Log";
            logs.DataValueField = "Log";
            logs.DataBind();
        }
    }

    protected void getMessages_Click(object sender, EventArgs e)
    {
        GetLogEntries();
    }
```

continues

Listing 8.9 **Continued**

```
protected void clearLog_Click(object sender, EventArgs e)
{
     EventLog el = new EventLog();
     el.MachineName = ".";
     el.Log = logs.SelectedItem.ToString();
     el.Clear();
     el.Close();

     GetLogEntries();
}

protected void GetLogEntries()
{
     EventLog el = new EventLog();
     el.MachineName = ".";
     el.Log = logs.SelectedItem.ToString();

     messages.DataSource = el.Entries;
     messages.DataBind();
     el.Close();
}

protected string GetEventTypeDesc(EventLogEntryType elet)
{
     switch(elet)
     {
          case EventLogEntryType.Error:
               return "Error";
               break;
          case EventLogEntryType.Warning:
               return "Warning";
               break;
          case EventLogEntryType.Information:
               return "Information";
               break;
          case EventLogEntryType.SuccessAudit:
               return "Success Audit";
               break;
          default: //EventLogEntryType.FailureAudit
               return "Failure Audit";
```

```
                            break;
                }
        }
</script>

<html>
<head>
<title>Event Log Viewer</title>
</head>
<body>

<form runat="server">
    <asp:dropdownlist id="logs" runat="server" />
    <asp:button id="getMessages" text="Get Log Entries"
        onclick="getMessages_Click" runat="server" />
    <asp:button id="clearLog" text="Clear Log Entries"
        onclick="clearLog_Click" runat="server" />
</form>

<asp:repeater id="messages" runat="server">
        <HeaderTemplate>
            <table border="1" cellspacing="0" cellpadding="2">
                <tr>
                        <th>Type</th>
                        <th>Date/Time</th>
                        <th>Source</th>
                        <th>Category</th>
                        <th>Event</th>
                        <th>User</th>
                        <th>Computer</th>
                        <th>Message</th>
                </tr>
        </Headertemplate>
        <ItemTemplate>
            <tr>
                <td>
                    <%#GetEventTypeDesc(
                    ((EventLogEntry)Container.DataItem).EntryType)%>
                </td>
                <td>
                    <%#((EventLogEntry)Container.DataItem)
                    .TimeGenerated.ToString("G",null)%>
```

continues

Listing 8.9   **Continued**

```
            </td>
            <td>
                <%#((EventLogEntry)Container.DataItem).Source%>
            </td>
            <td>
                <%#((EventLogEntry)Container.DataItem).Category%>
            </td>
            <td>
                <%#((EventLogEntry)Container.DataItem).EventID%>
            </td>
            <td>
                <%#((EventLogEntry)Container.DataItem).UserName%>
            </td>
            <td>
                <%#((EventLogEntry)Container.DataItem).MachineName%>
            </td>
            <td>
                <%#((EventLogEntry)Container.DataItem).Message%>
            </td>
        </tr>
    </Itemtemplate>
    <FooterTemplate">
            </table>
    </Footertemplate>
</asp:repeater>
</body>
</html>
```

Listing 8.10   **Web-based Event Log Viewer (Visual Basic .NET)**

```
<%@ Page Language="VB" %>
<%@ Import Namespace="System.Diagnostics" %>

<script language="VB" runat="server">
    Protected Sub Page_Load(sender As Object, e As EventArgs)
        If Not IsPostBack Then
            Dim elArray() As EventLog = EventLog.GetEventLogs(".")
            With logs
                .DataSource = elArray
                .DataTextField = "Log"
```

```
                        .DataValueField = "Log"
                        .DataBind()
                End With
        End If
End Sub


Protected Sub getMessages_Click(sender As Object, e As EventArgs)
        GetLogEntries()
End Sub


Protected Sub clearLog_Click(sender As Object, e As EventArgs)
        Dim el As EventLog = New EventLog()
        el.MachineName = "."
        el.Log = logs.SelectedItem.ToString()
        el.Clear()
        el.Close()

        GetLogEntries()
End Sub


Protected Sub GetLogEntries()
        Dim el As EventLog = New EventLog()
        With el
                .MachineName = "."
                .Log = logs.SelectedItem.ToString()
        End With

        messages.DataSource = el.Entries
        messages.DataBind()
End Sub


Protected Function GetEventTypeDesc(elet As EventLogEntryType) _
        As String
        Select Case elet
                Case EventLogEntryType.Error
                        return "Error"
                Case EventLogEntryType.Warning
                        return "Warning"
                Case EventLogEntryType.Information
                        return "Information"
                Case EventLogEntryType.SuccessAudit
                        return "Success Audit"
```

continues

Listing 8.10 **Continued**

```
                    Case Else 'EventLogEntryType.FailureAudit
                        return "Failure Audit"
            End Select
        End Function
</script>

<html>
<head>
<title>Event Log Viewer</title>
</head>
<body>

<form runat="server">
    <asp:dropdownlist id="logs" runat="server" />
    <asp:button id="getMessages" text="Get Log Entries"
        onclick="getMessages_Click" runat="server" />
    <asp:button id="clearLog" text="Clear Log Entries"
        onclick="clearLog_Click" runat="server" />
</form>

<asp:repeater id="messages" runat="server">
    <HeaderTemplate>
        <table border="1" cellspacing="0" cellpadding="2">
            <tr>
                <th>Type</th>
                <th>Date/Time</th>
                <th>Source</th>
                <th>Category</th>
                <th>Event</th>
                <th>User</th>
                <th>Computer</th>
                <th>Message</th>
            </tr>
    </Headertemplate>
    <ItemTemplate>
        <tr>
            <td>
                <%#GetEventTypeDesc(Container.DataItem.EntryType)%>
            </td>
            <td>
```

```
                    <%#Container.DataItem.TimeGenerated.ToString("G")%>
            </td>
            <td>
                    <%#Container.DataItem.Source%>
            </td>
            <td>
                    <%#Container.DataItem.Category%>
            </td>
            <td>
                    <%#Container.DataItem.EventID%>
            </td>
            <td>
                    <%#Container.DataItem.UserName%>
            </td>
            <td>
                    <%#Container.DataItem.MachineName%>
            </td>
            <td>
                    <%#Container.DataItem.Message%>
            </td>
        </tr>
    </Itemtemplate>
    <FooterTemplate>
            </table>
    </Footertemplate>
</asp:repeater>
</body>
</html>
```

In this sample, when the page first loads, you build and display an ASP.NET
`DropDownList` server control that contains the names of all the event logs on the local
server. This list is obtained by calling the Static `GetEventLogs` method of the `EventLog`
class and passing in the . wildcard character that stands for local server. Alternatively,
you could specify another machine on the network. The `GetEventLogs` method returns
an array of `EventLog` objects that you bind to the `DropDownList` server control.

If you select one of the event logs from the `DropDownList` control and click the Get
Log Entries button, the `getMessages_Click` server event is fired. This event calls the
`GetLogEntries` function that you define. The `GetLogEntries` function gets a list of
event log entries for the selected event log. It then binds this collection of
`EventLogEntry` objects to the messages `Repeater` server control. The messages
`Repeater` displays the properties of each `EventLogEntry` object in an HTML table. The
function then calls the `Close` method of the `EventLog` object instance.

continues

A Clear Log Entries button also calls the `clearLog_Click` event. Inside this event, you establish a connection to the event log that was selected in the `DropDownList` server control and call the `Clear` method of the `EventLog` object instance. You then call the `Close` method. Finally, you call the `GetLogEntries` function to refresh the `Repeater` server control. The web-based Event Log Viewer with some sample results will look similar to Figure 8.3.

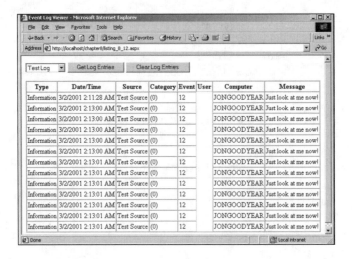

Figure 8.3   You can programmatically re-create the Windows 2000 Event Log in the form of an ASP.NET page.

Summary

In this chapter, you learned that Microsoft's .NET Framework exposes an interface for managing the Windows 2000 Event Log. This interface is located in the System.Diagnostics namespace. The `EventLog` class in the System.Diagnostics namespace offers a rich interface for both reading and writing to the Windows 2000 Event Log. This includes setting up custom event logs and manipulating all the properties of an event.

You also learned that there are two different types of events: expected events and unexpected events. Expected events are identified using logic structures and are logged according to the rules outlining their importance. Unexpected events are trapped and handled via structured error handling. Specific exceptions can be trapped and logged, as can generic exceptions.

The chapter concluded by showing you how to build a web-based Event Log Viewer that enables you to select an event log from a `DropDownList` server control and click a button to display all the events in that event log. Another button clears all the log entries from the selected event log in the `DropDownList` server control.

In the next chapter, you move on to Part III, "Debugging the New ASP.NET Features," and start off with a discussion on debugging ASP.NET server controls.

Debugging the New ASP.NET Features

9 Debugging Server-Side Controls

10 Debugging Data-Bound Controls

11 Debugging User Controls

12 Caching Issues and Debugging

9

Debugging Server-Side Controls

ASP.NET SERVER CONTROLS PROVIDE AN ENORMOUS amount of power to you as a programmer in developing truly object-oriented web-based applications. In the simplest terms, a server control is a control that is executed on the server and that provides some type of output to the user. These generally are used to create brand-new types of user-interface controls that are not currently available in ASP.NET.

If you have been using ASP.NET, you will be familiar with the `<asp:></asp>` style tags that have been introduced into the language. These tags that you insert into your HTML page are really server-side controls that implement either a standard HTML control or a custom control that is only part of ASP.NET, such as a data grid. In the traditional ASP paradigm, this can be thought of as an include file that contains the HTML or JavaScript required to implement a new type of control. Now, however, you are actually building a real compiled component that is executed entirely on the server.

This chapter focuses on creating a server-side ASP.NET control, including navigating some common pitfalls in developing a control like this and properly debugging it both as it is being written and after it has been completed. The demonstration project used in this chapter is an extremely simple tab control.

Creating the Project

If you plan to follow along step by step with this chapter, we recommend following some naming conventions to make compiling and debugging easier. As always, both C# and Visual Basic .NET code will be provided for this project.

You'll start by creating the project. First, create a standard ASP.NET application in the language of your choice. Name it either Chapter9CS for C# or Chapter9VB for Visual Basic .NET. Next, right-click the project name in the Solution window and choose Add and then New Component. In the dialog box that appears, choose Web Custom Control and name this component SimpleTabControl.cs or SimpleTabControl.vb, depending on the language you have chosen for this example.

Now you can start coding the basic tab control framework. First, you will create the very basic input and output routines of the tab control. Listing 9.1 contains the C# version of the code, while Listing 9.2 contains the Visual Basic .NET version. Listings 9.3 and 9.4 contain the code of one of the ASP.NET pages that you will be using to test the control for the C# and Visual Basic .NET projects, respectively. Finally, Listing 9.5 is a listing of the code-behind file that will be used for the C# ASP.NET pages, and Listing 9.6 contains the same code in Visual Basic .NET. You will want to create three separate ASP.NET pages, each with the same code. The only difference between the pages is having the proper code-behind file referenced from each page, as well as having each code-behind file with a unique class in it. This will be explained a bit more as we explain the example in the pages ahead.

Listing 9.1   **Tab Control (C#—SimpleTabControl.cs)**

```
using System;
using System.Web.UI;

namespace Chapter9CS
{
public class SimpleTabControl : System.Web.UI.WebControls.WebControl,
➡IPostBackEventHandler
    {
        private string[] aPages;
        private string[] aNames;

        public string CurPage
        {
            get { return (string)ViewState["curPage"]; }
            set { ViewState["curPage"] = value; }
        }

        public string Names
        {
```

```csharp
    get { return (string)ViewState["names"]; }
    set { ViewState["names"] = value; aNames = value.Split('~');
            ViewState["aNames"] = aNames; }
}

public string Pages
{
    get { return (string)ViewState["pages"]; }
    set { ViewState["pages"] = value; aPages = value.Split('~');
            ViewState["aPages"] = aPages; }
}

public string ActiveColor
{
    get { return (string)ViewState["activeColor"]; }
    set { ViewState["activeColor"] = value; }
}

public string InactiveColor
{
    get { return (string)ViewState["inactiveColor"]; }
    set { ViewState["inactiveColor"] = value; }
}

public string RedirPage
{
    get { return (string)ViewState["redirPage"]; }
    set { ViewState["redirPage"] = value; }
}

public void RaisePostBackEvent(string eventArgument)
{
    ViewState["curPage"] = eventArgument;
    ViewState["redirPage"] =
    ➥aPages[Convert.ToInt32(eventArgument)];
}

// Override for outputting text to the browser
protected override void Render(HtmlTextWriter output)
{
    int i;
```

continues

Listing 9.1 **Continued**

```
            if(aPages.GetUpperBound(0) != aNames.GetUpperBound(0))
            {
                // toss the error here
            }
            else
            {
                output.Write("<table width='100%' border><tr>");

                for(i = 0; i <= aNames.GetUpperBound(0); i++)
                {
                    output.Write("<td bgcolor=\"");
                    if(i.ToString() == (string)ViewState["curPage"])
                        output.Write(ViewState["activeColor"]);
                    else
                        output.Write(ViewState["inactiveColor"]);

                    output.Write("\"><a id=\"" + aPages[i] + "\"
                    ➥ href=\"javascript:" +
                    ➥ Page.GetPostBackEventReference(this,
                    ➥ i.ToString()) + "\">" + aNames[i]
                    ➥+ "</td>\n");
                }
                output.Write("</tr></table>");
            }
        }
    }
}
```

Listing 9.2 **Tab Control (Visual Basic .NET—SimpleTabControl.vb)**

```
Imports System.ComponentModel
Imports System.Web.UI

Public Class SimpleTabControl
    Inherits System.Web.UI.WebControls.WebControl
    Implements IPostBackEventHandler

    Dim aPages() As String
    Dim aNames() As String

    Property CurPage() As String
        Get
```

```
            CurPage = ViewState("curPage")
        End Get
        Set(ByVal Value As String)
            ViewState("curPage") = Value
        End Set
    End Property


    Property Names() As String
        Get
            Names = ViewState("names")
        End Get
        Set(ByVal Value As String)
            ViewState("names") = Value
            aNames = Value.Split("~")
            ViewState("aNames") = aNames
        End Set
    End Property


    Property Pages() As String
        Get
            Pages = ViewState("Pages")
        End Get
        Set(ByVal Value As String)
            ViewState("pages") = Value
            aPages = Value.Split("~")
            ViewState("aPages") = aPages
        End Set
    End Property


    Property ActiveColor() As String
        Get
            ActiveColor = ViewState("activeColor")
        End Get
        Set(ByVal Value As String)
            ViewState("activeColor") = Value
        End Set
    End Property


    Property InactiveColor() As String
        Get
            InactiveColor = ViewState("inactiveColor")
        End Get
```

continues

Listing 9.2   **Continued**

```
        Set(ByVal Value As String)
            ViewState("inactiveColor") = Value
        End Set
    End Property

    Property RedirPage() As String
        Get
            RedirPage = ViewState("redirPage")
        End Get
        Set(ByVal Value As String)
            ViewState("redirPage") = Value
        End Set
    End Property

Sub RaisePostBackEvent(ByVal eventArgument As String) Implements
➥IPostBackEventHandler.RaisePostBackEvent
  ViewState("curPage") = eventArgument
  ViewState("redirPage") = aPages(Convert.ToInt32(eventArgument))
End Sub

Protected Overrides Sub Render(ByVal output As
➥System.Web.UI.HtmlTextWriter)
        Dim i As Integer

        If aNames.GetUpperBound(0) <> aPages.GetUpperBound(0) Then
            'error
        Else
            output.Write("<table width='100%' border><tr>")

            For i = 0 To aNames.GetUpperBound(0)
                output.Write("<td bgColor='")
                If i.ToString() = ViewState("curPage") Then
                    output.Write(ViewState("activeColor"))
                Else
                    output.Write(ViewState("inactiveColor"))
                End If

                output.Write("'><a id='" & aPages(i) & "'
                ➥href=""javascript:" &
                ➥Page.GetPostBackEventReference(Me, i.ToString()) +
                ➥""">" & aNames(i) & "</td>" & vbCrLf)
            Next
```

```
        output.Write("</tr></table>")
      End If
   End Sub
End Class
```

Listing 9.3 **Test ASP.NET Page (C#)**

```
<%@ Register TagPrefix="Tab" Namespace="Chapter9CS" Assembly =
➥"Chapter9CS" %>
<%@ Page language="c#" Codebehind="Page1.aspx.cs" AutoEventWireup="false"
➥Inherits="Chapter9CS.Page1" %>
<!DOCTYPE HTML PUBLIC "-//W3C//DTD HTML 4.0 Transitional//EN" >
<HTML>
  <HEAD>
    <title>Chapter 9 - C#</title>
  </HEAD>
  <body>
    <form id="Form1" method="post" runat="server">
<Tab:SimpleTabControl pages="page1.aspx~page2.aspx~page3.aspx"
➥names="Page 1~Page 2~Page 3"
➥activeColor="#ff0000" inactiveColor="#0000ff" name="tab" id="tab"
➥runat="server"/>
    </form>
    This is PAGE 1.
  </body>
</HTML>
```

Listing 9.4 **Test ASP.NET Page (Visual Basic .NET)**

```
<%@ Register TagPrefix="Tab" Namespace="Chapter9Visual Basic" Assembly =
➥"Chapter9Visual Basic" %>
<%@ Page language="vb" Codebehind="Page1.aspx.vb" AutoEventWireup="false"
➥Inherits="Chapter9Visual Basic.Page1" %>
<!DOCTYPE HTML PUBLIC "-//W3C//DTD HTML 4.0 Transitional//EN" >
<HTML>
  <HEAD>
    <title>Chapter 9 - Visual Basic</title>
  </HEAD>
  <body>
    <form id="Form1" method="post" runat="server">
<Tab:SimpleTabControl pages="page1.aspx~page2.aspx~page3.aspx"
```

continues

Listing 9.4 **Continued**

```
    names="Page 1~Page 2~Page 3"
➥activeColor="#ff0000" inactiveColor="#0000ff" name="tab"
➥id="tab" runat="server"/>
        </form>
        This is PAGE 1.
      </body>
    </HTML>
```

Listing 9.5 **Code-Behind File (C#)**

```
using System;

namespace Chapter9CS
{
    public class Page1 : System.Web.UI.Page
    {
        protected Chapter9CS.SimpleTabControl tab;

        public Page1()
        {
            Page.Init += new System.EventHandler(Page_Init);
        }

        private void Page_Load(object sender, System.EventArgs e)
        {
            if(IsPostBack)
                tab.CurPage = Request.QueryString.Get("curpage");
            else
                tab.CurPage = "0";
        }

        private void Page_Init(object sender, EventArgs e)
        {
            InitializeComponent();
        }

        private void InitializeComponent()
        {
                this.Load += new ystem.EventHandler(this.Page_Load);
            ➥this.PreRender += new System.EventHandler
            ➥(this.Page_PreRender);
```

```
        }

        private void Page_PreRender(object sender, System.EventArgs e)
        {
            if(IsPostBack)
                Response.Redirect(tab.RedirPage + "?curpage=" +
                ➥tab.CurPage );
        }
    }
}
```

Listing 9.6 **Code-Behind File (Visual Basic .NET)**

```
Public Class Page1
    Inherits System.Web.UI.Page

    Protected tab As Chapter9Visual Basic.SimpleTabControl

    Private Sub Page_Load(ByVal sender As System.Object, ByVal e As
    ➥System.EventArgs) Handles MyBase.Load
        If IsPostBack Then
            tab.CurPage = Request.QueryString.Get("curpage")
        Else
            tab.CurPage = "0"
        End If
    End Sub

    Private Sub Page_PreRender(ByVal sender As System.Object, ByVal e As
    ➥System.EventArgs) Handles MyBase.PreRender
        If IsPostBack Then
            Response.Redirect(tab.RedirPage & "?curpage=" & tab.CurPage)
        End If
    End Sub
End Class
```

Every server control must inherit from the System.Web.UI.WebControls.Control
namespace. Ours is no different. You will also notice several properties that we have
created. These properties become attributes that can be set in the ASP.NET page after
the control has been put in place. For example, the standard HTML text box has an
attribute named `value` that can be used to set the default text that appears in the text
box when the page is loaded.

In the tab control are several properties: `Pages`, `Names`, `ActiveColor`, `InactiveColor`, `CurPage`, and `RedirPage`. `Pages` will contain a delimited list of ASP.NET pages that each tab will take the browser to. The `Names` property contains a delimited list of the name to display to the user. `ActiveColor` and `InactiveColor` store the background colors of the active and inactive tabs, respectively. Finally, the `CurPage` and `RedirPage` properties keep track of the current page and the page to move to based on which tab the user clicked. All these properties are stored in the ViewState dictionary, which provides a way to store state information between page requests of the same page, but only through form submissions.

In the namespace inherited from System.Web.UI.WebControls.Control, you need to override the Render method. This is the function that sends the output down to the browser. Typically, this is where you will output your HTML. In this function, you render a table with the links provided in the `Pages` and `Names` properties specified in the HTML tag.

The other thing to notice is that the `RaisePostBackEvent` method is implemented from the `IPostBackEventHandler` interface. This is done so that you can create clickable links that generate form submissions instead of just regular links. This method is called whenever one of these special links is clicked; it enables you to handle the click in a special way. In this example, you're simply grabbing the special parameter on your links: the index into the `Page` array that you will be redirecting to.

Now take a look at the ASP.NET page. To use the server control on the page, it is necessary to add the `Register` directive at the top of the page and specify what the tag name will be (`Tab`), what the namespace is (Chapter9VB or Chapter9CS) and, finally, the assembly that it is located inside (Chapter9VB or Chapter9CS).

With that directive in place, you can reference the server control using the following syntax:

```
<tab:SimpleTabControl/>
```

That creates an instance of the example tab control. Looking at the full page listed earlier, you will notice that the properties are specified on the tab control as HTML attributes. In the example, you have the attributes shown in Table 9.1.

Table 9.1 **Tag Attributes and Values for the Example**

Tag Attribute	Value
Pages	`page1.aspx~page2.aspx~page3.aspx`
Names	`Page 1~Page 2~Page 3`
activeColor	`#ff0000`
inactiveColor	`#0000ff`

Both `Pages` and `Names` contain a ~~delimited list of parameters. They must match in length of elements. Pages contains the pages to redirect to when the `Name` link is clicked. When writing this example, be sure to create ASP.NET pages named page1.aspx, page2.aspx, and page3.aspx. All three will have their own code-behind files and will contain the same code across all three pages, except for the name of the class contained in the Chapter9XX namespace. For example, Page1.aspx would contain a `Page1` class, while Page2.aspx would contain a `Page2` class.

That should be enough background information to understand the example. A detailed discussion of server-side controls is really outside the scope of this book, but a general understanding is required so that you can understand the example provided.

Debugging the Control

Now that you have created the control, let's discuss some of the common pitfalls and problems that you can fall into when creating a server-side control.

ViewState

The ViewState dictionary is a name/value pair that enables you to store state information across page requests. It can be thought of as a ScriptingDictionary from VB6. One of the important things to understand about the ViewState dictionary is that it simply is a hash table, just like the ScriptingDictionary. One very important difference, however, is that the ScriptingDictionary was not case-sensitive in terms of the key name used; the ViewState dictionary is.

For example, the following code would not work as you expect it to:

```
ViewState["MyKey"] = "Hello";
Response.Write(ViewState["mykey"]);
```

The string `"Hello"` is stored into a key named `MyKey`. When referencing this value any subsequent time, you must refer to it as `MyKey`, not `mykey` or `myKey` or any other variation. The key is case-sensitive and must be referred to in the same case each time.

Here's something else to keep in mind about the ViewState dictionary: It can't be used across pages via standard links. The ViewState dictionary gets turned into an encoded, hidden form variable on any page. Go ahead and choose View Source from Internet Explorer on any ASP.NET page, and you will see a hidden form field called `__VIEWSTATE` with a long, encrypted value assigned to it similar to that in Listing 9.7. This is the output from the tab control test page.

Listing 9.7 **Sample Output Showing __VIEWSTATE**

```
<!DOCTYPE HTML PUBLIC "-//W3C//DTD HTML 4.0 Transitional//EN" >
<HTML>
  <HEAD>
    <title>Chapter 9 - Visual Basic</title>
  </HEAD>
  <body>
    <form name="Form1" method="post" action="page1.aspx" id="Form1">
<input type="hidden" name="__VIEWSTATE"
```

continues

Listing 9.7 **Continued**

```
value="dDwtMTg5MTU0NDI2Njt0PDtsPGk8MT47PjtsPHQ8O2w8aTwxPjs+O2w8dDxwPHA8bD
xjdXJQYWdlOz47bDwwOz4+Oz47Oz47Pj47Pg==" />

<table width='100%' border><tr><td bgColor='#ff0000'><a id='page1.aspx'
➥href="javascript:__doPostBack('tab','0')">Page 1</td>
<td bgColor='#0000ff'><a id='page2.aspx'
➥href="javascript:__doPostBack('tab','1')">Page 2</td>
<td bgColor='#0000ff'><a id='page3.aspx'
➥href="javascript:__doPostBack('tab','2')">Page 3</td>
</tr></table>

<input type="hidden" name="__EVENTTARGET" value="" />
<input type="hidden" name="__EVENTARGUMENT" value="" />
<script language="javascript">
<!--
    function __doPostBack(eventTarget, eventArgument) {
        var theform = document.Form1;
        theform.__EVENTTARGET.value = eventTarget;
        theform.__EVENTARGUMENT.value = eventArgument;
        theform.submit();
    }
// -->
</script>
</form>
    This is PAGE 1.
  </body>
</HTML>
```

On every form submission, this element is sent to the server, where it is decoded and thrown into the ViewState dictionary. This is how ASP.NET resets default values in text boxes, list boxes, and other elements. In this case, it is how you keep track of our pages, their names, the page you are on, and the page you are moving to.

So, if you are creating some state information using the ViewState dictionary and are expecting to be able to use these values on a new page through a standard <a href></a> link, you will be very disappointed. These will be accessible only through a form submission to the same page. That is why, in this example, the page that you are on is passed via a query string variable because it can't be tracked the ViewState dictionary. The __VIEWSTATE form variable is not sent to the next page.

Declaring the Control in the Code-Behind File

In the ASP.NET page listed earlier, the tab control is declared in the actual page with the server control tag (<tab:SimpleTabControl.../>). However, this is not enough to reference the control from your code-behind file. To do this, it is necessary to have a declaration of the tab control in your code-behind file. In C#, this would look like this:

```
protected Chapter9CS.SimpleTabControl tab;
```

In Visual Basic .NET, it would be this:

```
Protected tab as Chapter9Visual Basic.SimpleTabControl
```

The critical thing to remember about the declaration here is that the variable name (tab, in this case) must match the name that you assigned to the control in its name and id parameters on the corresponding ASP.NET page.

If you do not remember to declare your controls in the code-behind file, you will not be able to reference the tab control directly, and your code will either not compile or not run as you had anticipated. Generally, you will see an error message similar to the following when trying to build your application:

```
The type or namespace name 'tab' could not be found (are you missing a using
directive or an assembly reference?)
```

If you see a similar error in your future projects, be sure that you have added a declaration of your control in your code-behind file.

Registration of Control on ASP.NET Page

At the top of any ASP.NET page that uses a server control, you must use the Register directive to register that specific control for use in that page. This looks like the following line:

```
<%@ Register TagPrefix="Tab" Namespace="Chapter9CS" Assembly="Chapter9CS" %>
```

In this line, you need to specify the TagPrefix, which is the name that will be used to reference the control. In the example, the name Tab is used, so when adding the control to the page, you would write this:

```
<tab:SimpleTabControl.../>
```

The other things to specify are the namespace that contains the control, as well as the assembly where the control is located. If these are incorrect, your page will not be displayed. Instead, you will see an error message because the ASP.NET parser will not be capable of finding the control to include in the page. If you forget either of these attributes, the parser will tell you which one is missing. Just add it in, as appropriate, and your control should work fine on that specific page.

runat=server

As with all server-side controls, it is absolutely essential to include the `runat=server` attribute on the control for it to work properly. We cannot stress enough how important this is. We stress this so much simply because the error message(s) that you will see state nothing about this being the problem. What you will most likely see is a message regarding a reference to the control, or a property or method on the control being `null`. The message will usually be the following:

```
Value null was found where an instance of an object was required.
```

If you see an error resembling this, the first thing to check is to be sure that you've placed the `runat=server` attribute on the server-side control.

Debugging in Visual Studio .NET

If you are using Visual Studio .NET, consider yourself lucky. You will have unprecedented power in debugging your server-side controls in this IDE. You can set breakpoints on any line in the server-side code or any references to it in your code-behind file. Then, when execution reaches any of these points, your code will break and you can inspect exactly what is happening and see if it is what you expect.

As discussed in Chapter 7, "Visual Studio .NET Debugging Environment," the Visual Studio .NET IDE provides a lot of flexibility when debugging your code. Figure 9.1 shows a debugging session from the C# project, inspecting the contents of the `curPage` entry in the ViewState dictionary in the Command window. You can also see the Autos window in the lower-left pane, with a few of the variables that the debugger has automatically decided to add for inspection.

Here in the IDE, you can also trace the order of events to make sure that they are being called in the order that you think they are being called, or to see if they are even being called at all. For example, if you forgot to use the `overrides` keyword when overriding the `Render` function on your server control, the function would never be called because it isn't the "proper" `Render` function. Within the IDE, you can set a breakpoint on the `Render` function and see if execution breaks at this spot that it is supposed to.

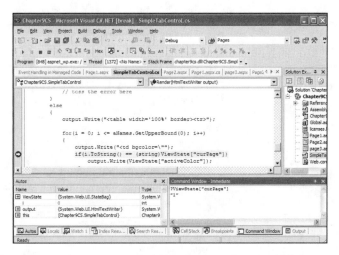

Figure 9.1 Debugging an ASP.NET server control in Visual Studio .NET.

Summary

This chapter discussed the issues that can arise when creating a server-side control in ASP.NET. This includes looking at the most common problems that developers can face when developing controls of this type. We also looked at solutions to these problems and ways to avoid them from the start.

The next chapter takes a look at data-bound controls and some common strategies for debugging them in the .NET environment.

10

Debugging Data-Bound Controls

I N THIS CHAPTER, WE WILL LOOK AT the issues that surround debugging data binding. Microsoft has included a list of new controls, such as the data grid and data list controls. These controls have the capability to bind data elements or data sources to them. This chapter looks at various areas such as templates, data grids, and namespace issues.

Data-Bound Controls

You can bind data to a limited number of controls, but we will focus on some of the more common controls, including the data grid, the data list, and a few others. Let's start out by taking a closer look at these data-bound controls and where you might have problems.

The Data Grid Control

The data grid control is a great new addition to the tool box. This control enables you to create a spreadsheet-like page of data and then manipulate the data as you need to. Listings 10.1 and 10.2 show a simple data grid control in C# and Visual Basic .NET. Then we'll identify some areas where you might need to implement some debugging techniques.

Listing 10.1 **Simple Data Grid Control (C#)**

```
private void Page_Load(object sender, System.EventArgs e)
            {
      // Put user code to initialize the page here
SqlConnection conn = new SqlConnection("server=(local);
➡database=northwind;Trusted_Connection=yes");
                  conn.Open();

                  SqlDataAdapter da = new SqlDataAdapter("Select * from
                  ➡products",conn);
                  DataSet ds = new DataSet();
                  da.Fill(ds,"products");
                  DataGrid1.AlternatingItemStyle.BackColor =
      Color.AliceBlue;
                  DataGrid1.HeaderStyle.BackColor = Color.Beige;
                  DataGrid1.Font.Bold = true;
                  DataGrid1.DataSource = ds;
                  DataGrid1.DataBind();
                  conn.Close();
            }
```

Listing 10.2 **Simple Data Grid Control (Visual Basic .NET)**

```
Private Sub Page_Load(ByVal sender As System.Object, ByVal e As
System.EventArgs) Handles MyBase.Load

Dim conn = New
SqlConnection("server=(local);database=northwind;Trusted_Connection=yes")
         conn.Open()

         Dim da As SqlDataAdapter = New SqlDataAdapter()
         da.SelectCommand = New SqlCommand("Select * from products",
         ➡conn)
         Dim ds = New DataSet()
         da.Fill(ds, "products")
         DataGrid1.AlternatingItemStyle.BackColor = Color.AliceBlue
         DataGrid1.HeaderStyle.BackColor = Color.Beige
         DataGrid1.Font.Bold = True
         DataGrid1.DataSource = ds
         DataGrid1.DataBind()
         conn.Close()
```

This is a pretty simple example. It just makes a call to the database to get a list of products and then displays them in the data grid.

Data Grid Paging

When you start getting into some of the other capabilities of the data grid, you will undoubtedly come across the paging feature that is built into the control. It is very easy to run into problems if you are not familiar with the workings of the data grid control. If you look at the following code line, you will see that it is very simple to turn on the paging feature on the data grid control:

```
<asp:datagrid id=DataGrid1 runat="server" AllowPaging="True"></asp:datagrid>
```

If you try to use the code as it appears here, you will notice buttons for Next and Previous at the bottom of the data grid, but they don't seem to do anything.

A few things need to happen to really get the paging feature to work. You will also need to implement the OnPageIndexChanged handler, as shown in this next example:

```
<asp:datagrid id=DataGrid1 runat="server"
OnPageIndexChanged="GridChange" AllowPaging="True"></asp:datagrid>
```

After you have changed the aspx code to include the OnPageIndexChanged attribute to point to a handler function such as GridChange, you can add the required code to handle the paging functionality. If you stop to look at what is happening here, you are just telling the data grid to call the GridChange function when the OnPageIndexChanged event is fired. You can put any additional code that you want in the GridChange function, but for the paging feature to work, a few things need to be done.

Take a look at what you need to do to make the paging feature work. Listings 10.3 and 10.4 show you how to implement the last piece of the data grid paging feature.

Listing 10.3 **Grid Paging Event Handler (C#)**

```csharp
public void GridChange(Object sender, DataGridPageChangedEventArgs e)
    {

        // Set CurrentPageIndex to the page the user clicked.
        DataGrid1.CurrentPageIndex = e.NewPageIndex;

SqlConnection conn = new SqlConnection("server=(local);database=north
➥wind;Trusted_Connection=yes");
        conn.Open();

        SqlDataAdapter da = new SqlDataAdapter("Select * from
➥products",conn);
        DataSet ds = new DataSet();
        da.Fill(ds,"products");
```

Listing 10.3 **Continued**

```
    // Rebind the data.
    DataGrid1.DataSource = ds;
    DataGrid1.DataBind();


}
```

Listing 10.4 **Grid Paging Event Handler (Visual Basic .NET)**

```
Public Function GridChange(ByVal sender As Object, ByVal e As
DataGridPageChangedEventArgs)


    ' Set CurrentPageIndex to the page the user clicked.
    DataGrid1.CurrentPageIndex = e.NewPageIndex

Dim conn As New
SqlConnection("server=(local);database=northwind;Trusted_Connection=yes")
    conn.Open()

    Dim da As New SqlDataAdapter("Select * from products", conn)
    Dim ds As New DataSet()
    da.Fill(ds, "products")

    ' Rebind the data.
    DataGrid1.DataSource = ds
    DataGrid1.DataBind()

End Function
```

You might notice that the key piece to this involves assigning the NewPageIndex value to the data grid's CurrentPageIndex property. After you have done this, the data grid will display only the set of data that resides on that new index page value.

You might come across the error shown in Figure 10.1 telling you that the function you provided to handle the events is not accessible because of its protection level. Don't worry—this is a simple fix.

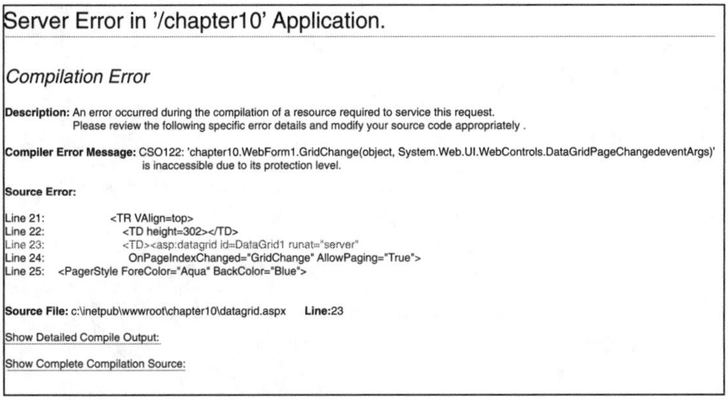

Figure 10.1 Protection-level compilation error listing.

You will see this error if your code does not declare the event-handling function as public. If you look at the following examples, you will see that the method is declared with the `public` keyword. When you don't define your method or variables, they might be set to private. Any method or property that is defined as private is accessible only to the context of its class or object. Setting the method or property to public grants external classes or objects access to that resource. This might differ in each language, so if you need to expose a method or property, be sure to use the `public` keyword, to avoid guesswork. Listings 10.5 and 10.6 provide examples of the proper way to create an event handler for paging through a data grid in both C# and Visual Basic .NET.

Listing 10.5 **Correct Method Definition (C#)**

```csharp
public void GridChange(Object sender, DataGridPageChangedEventArgs e)
    {

    // Set CurrentPageIndex to the page the user clicked.
    DataGrid1.CurrentPageIndex = e.NewPageIndex;

SqlConnection conn = new SqlConnection("server=(local);database=north
➥wind;Trusted_Connection=yes");
    conn.Open();

    SqlDataAdapter da = new SqlDataAdapter("Select * from
    ➥products",conn);
    DataSet ds = new DataSet();
    da.Fill(ds,"products");

    // Rebind the data to the datasource
```

Listing 10.5   **Continued**

```
    DataGrid1.DataSource = ds;
    DataGrid1.DataBind();


}
```

Listing 10.6   **Correct Method Definition (Visual Basic .NET)**

```
Public Sub GridChange(ByVal sender As Object, ByVal e As
DataGridPageChangedEventArgs)

    ' Set CurrentPageIndex to the page the user clicked.
    DataGrid1.CurrentPageIndex = e.NewPageIndex

Dim conn As New
SqlConnection("server=(local);database=northwind;Trusted_Connection=yes")
    conn.Open()

    Dim da As New SqlDataAdapter("Select * from products", conn)
    Dim ds As New DataSet()
    da.Fill(ds, "products")

    ' Rebind the data.
    DataGrid1.DataSource = ds
    DataGrid1.DataBind()
End Sub
```

Debugging Templates

Templates provide a more flexible way of displaying the data. Most likely, if you will be doing anything with data, you will probably be using templates to get the job done. In this section, we look at some problem areas that you may stumble over and how to work around them.

Working with Data List <*ItemTemplate*>

When you are working with templates you can easily run into problems that won't be caught by the compiler. This is because some aspx code is not validated or is syntactically correct but, at run time, is not valid. When you understand the basics of templates, though, they can be a very powerful tool in developing your site. So let's get started and take a look at some problems that you might run into.

When you start trying to customize your data list, you will run into the
`DataBinder`. Take a look at Listing 10.7 to see how the DataBinder is used in place of
a recordset.

Listing 10.7   **aspx Code**

```
<asp:DataList id=DataList1 runat="server" Width="218px" Height="125px">
<ItemTemplate>
<%# DataBinder.Eval(Container.DataItem, "stingvalue") %>
</ItemTemplate>
</asp:DataList>
```

When you include the `<ItemTemplate>` tag in your aspx page, whatever you put
between the tags is what is going to be displayed on the page; don't assume that all
the other data fields will just magically appear.

If you look at the error shown in Figure 10.2, you will notice that the error
occurred at Line 18. There you are trying to read a value from the data container
named stringvalue, but the line does not tell you what the problem is. If you look at
the stack trace, you will notice that it is telling us that the property name stringvalue
does not exist. That's because, in the products table, there is no column called
stringvalue.

Figure 10.2   Invalid property in `DataRowError` listing.

Namespace Issues

You might not think much about namespaces now, but when you start creating large applications or start to reuse your code from other projects, namespace will become an issue. So before you just blow off the namespace description, think hard about what it really means and then give it an appropriate name. Let's look at an example of where you might run into problems.

When you do run into namespace problems, the first thing you will probably see is the error message shown in Figure 10.3.

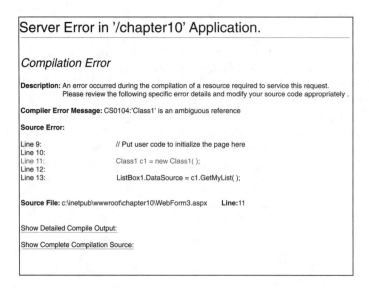

Figure 10.3   Ambiguous reference error message.

As the message indicates, there is an ambiguous reference. In other words, there are two classes called Class1 and the compiler does not know which to use.

This is where namespaces come into play. First, you'll take a look at how we arrived at this point; then you'll see what you need to do to fix the problem. If you want to use these snippets of code, you need to start with an existing web project or windows application. Then you can add the following snippets to your project to see how they react. Listings 10.8–10.11 illustrate the problem and show how namespaces enter into its solution.

Listing 10.8 *MySpace.Class1* **(C#)**

```csharp
namespace MySpace
{

    public class Class1
    {
        public Class1()
        {
        }
        public string[] GetMyList()
        {
            string[] mylist = new string[4];

            mylist[0]="cars";
            mylist[1]="trucks";
            mylist[2]="planes";
            mylist[3]="boats";

            return mylist;
        }
    }
}
```

Listing 10.9 *MySpace.Class1* **(Visual Basic .NET)**

```vbnet
Namespace MySpace

    Public Class Class1

        Public Function GetMyList() As String()

            Dim mylist As String()

            mylist(0) = "cars"
            mylist(1) = "trucks"
            mylist(2) = "planes"
            mylist(3) = "boats"

            Return mylist
        End Function

    End Class
End Namespace
```

Listing 10.10 *YourSpace.Class1* (C#)

```csharp
namespace YourSpace
{
    public class Class1
    {
        public Class1()
        {
        }
        public string[] GetMyList()
        {
            string[] mylist = new string[4];

            mylist[0]="eggs";
            mylist[1]="bacon";
            mylist[2]="milk";
            mylist[3]="bread";
            return mylist;
        }
    }
}
```

Listing 10.11 *YourSpace.Class1* **(Visual Basic .NET)**

```vbnet
Namespace YourSpace

    Public Class Class1

        Public Function GetMyList() As String()

            Dim mylist As String()

            mylist(0) = "cars"
            mylist(1) = "trucks"
            mylist(2) = "planes"
            mylist(3) = "boats"

            Return mylist
        End Function

    End Class
End Namespace
```

As you can see from these listings, both classes have the same name and the same methods. The only thing that differentiates them is their namespace. Now take a look at how we were trying to implement these classes in the web page (see Listing 10.12).

Listing 10.12 **aspx Code for Implementing the Classes (C#-Incorrect Method)**

```
<%@ Import Namespace="MySpace" %>
<%@ Import Namespace="YourSpace" %>

<script language="C#" runat=server>

private void Page_Load(object sender, System.EventArgs e)
            {
                    // Put user code to initialize the page here

                    Class1 c1 = new Class1();//Ambiguous Reference

                    ListBox1.DataSource  = c1.GetMyList();
                    ListBox1.DataSource  = c1.GetMyList();


                    ListBox1.DataBind();
                    ListBox2.DataBind();


            }
</script>
<HTML>
  <HEAD>
  </HEAD>
  <body MS_POSITIONING="GridLayout">

  <form id="WebForm3" method="post" runat="server">
  <asp:ListBox id=ListBox1  runat="server"></asp:ListBox>
  <asp:ListBox id=ListBox2  runat="server"></asp:ListBox>

  </form>

  </body>
</HTML>
```

As you can see, the namespaces have been included at the beginning of the file so that the compiler can identify the classes. What you need to do is preface the class with the namespace that it belongs to; then the compiler knows definitively what you want to do. Take a look at the code in Listing 10.13 to see the correct implementation for these classes.

Listing 10.13 **aspx Code for Correct Implementation of the Classes (C#–Correct Method)**

```
<%@ Import Namespace="MySpace" %>
<%@ Import Namespace="YourSpace" %>

<script language="C#" runat=server>

private void Page_Load(object sender, System.EventArgs e)
          {

                    MySpace.Class1 c1 = new MySpace.Class1();
                    YourSpace.Class1 c2 = new YourSpace.Class1();

                    ListBox1.DataSource  = c1.GetMyList();
                    ListBox1.DataSource  = c2.GetMyList();


                    ListBox1.DataBind();
                    ListBox2.DataBind();


          }
</script>
```

As you can see here, you need to identify which namespace you are using if there are naming conflicts like those with Class1.

Next you take a look at XML bindings and some hurdles that you might run into.

XML Binding

XML is a fundamental part of the .NET architecture. If you look at how data is handled in the Data namespace, you will see that it all revolves around XML. So if you are not familiar with XML basics, pick up some reading material on XML, such as Steve Holzner's *Inside XML* (New Riders Publishing, 2001).

Figure 10.4 shows an example of a problem that you might run into. However, the system does not throw an exception or give you any indication that there is a problem.

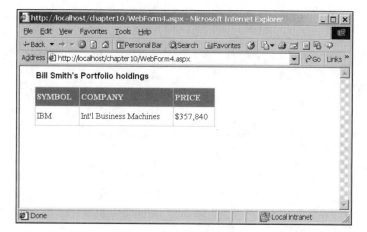

Figure 10.4   aspx output.

Everything looks fine on the page, but it seems to be missing a few records. Take a look at the example code in Listings 10.14 and 10.15 and XML file in Listings 10.16 and see if you can identify the problem.

Listing 10.14   **Using XML as a Data Source (C#)**

```csharp
private void Page_Load(object sender, System.EventArgs e)
        {
                // Put user code to initialize the page here
                DataSet ds = new DataSet();
                ds.ReadXml("c:\\portfolio.xml");
                DataGrid1.DataSource = ds;
                DataGrid1.DataBind();
        }
```

Listing 10.15   **Using XML as a Data Source (Visual Basic .NET)**

```vb
Private Sub Page_Load(ByVal sender As System.Object, ByVal e As
System.EventArgs) Handles MyBase.Load
        'Put user code to initialize the page here

        Dim ds As New DataSet()
        ds.ReadXml("c:\\portfolio.xml")
        DataGrid1.DataSource = ds
        DataGrid1.DataBind()

    End Sub
```

Listing 10.16   **portfolio.xml File**

```
<PRODUCT>
<SYMBOL>IBM</SYMBOL><COMPANY>Int'l Business Machines</COMPANY><PRICE>
$357,840 </PRICE>
</PRODUCT>


<PRODUCT>
<SYMBOL>WEINX</SYMBOL><COMPANY> AIM Weingarten Fund A</COMPANY><PRICE>
$318,150</PRICE>
</PRODUCT>


<PRODUCT>
<SYMBOL>CSTGX</SYMBOL>            <COMPANY>AIM Constellation Fund A</COM-
PANY><PRICE> $256,603</PRICE>
</PRODUCT>


<PRODUCT>
<SYMBOL>KGGAX</SYMBOL>            <COMPANY>Kemper Aggressive Growth A </COM-
PANY><PRICE>$121,600</PRICE>
</PRODUCT>


<PRODUCT>
<SYMBOL>SONE</SYMBOL>            <COMPANY>S1 Corporation
</COMPANY><PRICE>$111,960</PRICE>
</PRODUCT>
```

As you can see, it is very simple to load an XML file into a dataset and assign it to the data grid's data source property. Microsoft has done a nice job of implementing XML and data-bound controls together.

At first sight, this may look well formed, but there is one small problem. You are missing the root element! One way to make sure that your file is well formed is to look at it with IE 5.x. If it can't parse the file, it will tell you what the problem is. Figure 10.5 shows what happens when we tried to look at the file with IE.

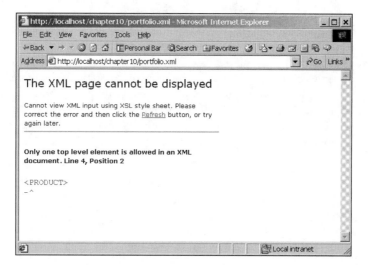

Figure 10.5 IE XML view.

If you simply add an element called PRODUCTS at the beginning and end of the file encompassing all the XML text, you will create a root element, as shown in Listing 10.17.

Listing 10.17 **XML File Corrected**

```
<PRODUCTS>
<PRODUCT>
<SYMBOL>IBM</SYMBOL><COMPANY>Int'l Business Machines</COMPANY><PRICE>
$357,840 </PRICE>
</PRODUCT>

<PRODUCT>
<SYMBOL>WEINX</SYMBOL><COMPANY> AIM Weingarten Fund A</COMPANY><PRICE>
$318,150</PRICE>
</PRODUCT>
</PRODUCTS>
```

Now that you have everything set up correctly, you will get a list of records displayed on your web page the way you intended to. Keep in mind that this XML file could be formatted in a number of ways to store just about any type of data you need.

Summary

This chapter looked at some key elements that play a vital part in data-bound controls. These components will make up the base foundation as you move forward in building new data-driven web sites. You looked here at how to use some of the more useful features of the data grid control, such as event handling and paging. You also learned how to use the data list and customize it with the item template tags. And don't forget to use namespaces when you are using classes with the same names. This will alleviate ambiguous names that will give you compiler errors.

11

Debugging User Controls

IN PREVIOUS VERSIONS OF ASP, IF YOU wanted to encapsulate sections of user interface code, you had limited options. You could use an include file, but there was no way to customize each "instance" of the code section. You could package the user interface code into a COM object and call one of its methods to display it, but that meant that you had to recompile the COM object each time you wanted to make a change. You could use a library of functions in script file includes, but this approach wasted a lot of web server resources because, most of the time, your page uses only a small subsection of the code in each include file.

In ASP.NET, User Controls solve this dilemma. User Controls are designed to give you the best of all worlds: encapsulation, optimized memory usage, compiled code, and the capability to make changes on the fly. With any aspect of programming, however, difficulties can emerge; this chapter deals with these difficulties. To make sure that we cover everything, the examples in this chapter follow the creation of a User Control and an ASP.NET page that consumes it from start to finish. Along the way, we'll expose some of the nuances, technicalities, and omissions that crop up with User Controls.

User Control Basics

To get started, let's build a simple User Control, MyControl.ascx, and an ASP.NET page that consumes it, MyPage.aspx.

MyControl

Most of the time, User Controls will contain dynamic elements, but that's not always the case. For instance, you might create a User Control to display copyright information at the bottom of each page in your web application. Likewise, the User Control MyControl will start off with just static content. Right now, you'll be concerned with the issues surrounding the basic plumbing of User Controls, as you can see in Listing 11.1.

Listing 11.1   *MyControl*—**Basics**

```
<%@ Control Language="C#" %>


This is MyControl.
```

MyPage

Now that you have a simple User Control built, you can implement it in an ASP.NET page. First, Listing 11.2 shows the correct implementation code.

Listing 11.2   *MyPage*—**Basics**

```
<%@ Page Language="C#" %>
<%@ Register TagPrefix="Chapter11" TagName="MyControl"
     Src="MyControl.ascx" %>

<html>
<head><title>MyPage</title></head>
<body>
<Chapter11:MyControl runat="server" />

</body>
</html>
```

Basic Gotchas

The code in Listings 11.1 and 11.2 will yield the simple message displayed in the browser "This is MyControl." Did you get any errors? Here's what might have gone wrong.

Missing End Tag or End-Tag Marker

All ASP.NET server controls require an end tag. User Controls are a form of server control that you custom-create, so the same rules apply. Forgetting to include either an end tag `</Chapter11:MyControl>` or and end-tag marker `/>` will generate an error like this:

```
Parser Error Message: Literal content ('</body> </html>') is not allowed within a
'ASP.MyControl_ascx'
```

Of course, the exact syntax of the error will vary, depending on what literal content is present directly after your User Control reference. In this case, it was the `</body></html>` HTML tags.

Missing *Runat* Attribute

What if your User Control doesn't show up at all? This almost always means that that you forgot to include the `runat="server"` attribute on your User Control. This is a requirement, as it is with all other ASP.NET server controls. A quick way to verify this is to right-click the screen in Internet Explorer and select View Source. You'll most likely see that your User Control tag was mistaken for plain-old HTML tags and was sent directly to the browser. Without the `runat` attribute, the ASP.NET engine does not know that it is supposed to do anything with it, so it completely ignores it.

Unknown Server Tag

Occasionally, you'll get a message that doesn't make any sense at first glance. For instance, you might get this error:

```
Parser Error Message: Unknown server tag 'Chapter11:MyControl'.
```

It doesn't seem to make any sense because that is the `TagPrefix` and `TagName` that you specified. Or is it? Take another look at your `@Register` tag at the top of your ASP.NET page. Odds are, you misspelled either the `TagPrefix` or the `TagName` attribute. If the situation were reversed, it would have been easier to spot the issue because the ASP.NET sourcecode surrounding the error is shown. If the error resides in the `@Register` tag, the solution is not always so obvious.

Adding Properties and Methods

Now that you can debug the basic issues with User Controls, let's add some complexity. One of the nicest things about User Controls is that they can expose properties, making their underlying content more dynamic. They can also expose methods.

Although it's not a requirement, it is good design practice to implement methods in User Controls only when they are needed to influence the appearance of the content of the User Control itself. Use code-behind methods of your ASP.NET page, .NET components, or Web Services if you need more utilitarian functionality.

Add a Property

Listings 11.3 and 11.4 show your MyControl User Control with a Name property implemented.

Listing 11.3   *MyControl* **with Property (C#)**

```
<%@ Control Language="C#" %>

<script language="C#" runat="server">
    private string _name;

    public string Name
    {
        get
        {
            return _name;
        }
        set
        {
            _name = value;
        }
    }
</script>

This control belongs to <%= Name %>.
```

Listing 11.4   *MyControl* **with Property (Visual Basic .NET)**

```
<%@ Control Language="VB" %>

<script language="VB" runat="server">
    Private _name As String

    Public Property Name As String
        Get
            Return _name
        End Get
```

```
        Set

                _name = Value

            End Set

        End Property

    </script>


    This control belongs to <%= Name %>.
```

To access the Name property of your User Control from your ASP.NET page, simply add a Name attribute to your MyControl tag, like this:

```
<Chapter11:MyControl Name="Jon" runat="server" />
```

Property Gotchas

You'll face two primary gotchas when it comes to dealing with User Control properties: the scope modifier and the order in which properties are assigned.

Improper Scope Modifier

When testing your User Control with properties, you might notice that the property is not appearing, even though you are setting it in your server tag definition. The problem could be due to the scope modifier (or lack thereof) attached to your property definition.

For the properties of your User Control to be available to your ASP.NET page, they must have public scope. If you leave off the scope modifier completely in Visual Basic, the default is public, so your property will appear just fine. However, if you leave off the scope modifier in C#, the default is private, so your property will not appear. Worse yet, it won't even throw an error because you are setting the property in your server tag definition and are not programmatically in a script block (discussed next).

If you wanted to assign your User Control properties programmatically, you could add a script block to your ASP.NET page as shown in Listings 11.5 and 11.6.

Listing 11.5   **Assign User Controls Properties Programmatically (C#)**

```
<%@ Page Language="C#" %>
<%@ Register TagPrefix="Chapter11" TagName="MyControl"
    Src="MyControl_cs.ascx" %>


<script language="C#" runat="server">
    protected void Page_Load(object sender, EventArgs e)
    {
        myControl1.Name = "Jon";
    }
```

continues

Listing 11.5 **Continued**

```
</script>

<html>
<head><title>MyPage</title></head>
<body>
<Chapter11:MyControl id="myControl1" runat="server" />
</body>
</html>
```

Listing 11.6 **Assign User Controls Properties Programmatically (Visual Basic .NET)**

```
<%@ Page Language="VB" %>
<%@ Register TagPrefix="Chapter11" TagName="MyControl"
    Src="MyControl_vb.ascx" %>

<script language="VB" runat="server">
    Protected Sub Page_Load(sender As Object, e As EventArgs)
        myControl1.Name = "Jon"
    End Sub
</script>

<html>
<head><title>MyPage</title></head>
<body>
<Chapter11:MyControl id="myControl1" runat="server" />
</body>
</html>
```

Note that the Name attribute of the server tag has been replaced with an id attribute. This enables you to reference it from the code block. The error thrown for an improper scope modifier at this point is a little more intuitive:

Compiler Error Message: CS0122: 'ASP.MyControl_cs_ascx.Name' is inaccessible due to its protection level

or (Visual Basic .NET)

Compiler Error Message: BC30390: 'ASP.MyControl_vb_ascx.Private Property Name() As String' is Private, and is not accessible in this context.

It is always better if you do not rely on default behaviors of the programming language you are using. You should always specify scope modifiers. For the purposes of exposing User Control properties, be sure to use public scope.

Order of Property Assignment

You might experience what appears to be some strange behavior with your User Control properties if you don't know the order in which events occur in your ASP.NET page. For instance, take the following code examples shown in Listings 11.7 and 11.8.

Listing 11.7 **Property Assignment Order (C#)**

```
<%@ Page Language="C#" %>
<%@ Register TagPrefix="Chapter11" TagName="MyControl"
    Src="MyControl_cs.ascx" %>


<script language="C#" runat="server">
    protected void Page_Init(object sender, EventArgs e)
    {
        myControl1.Name = myControl1.Name + "Brian";
    }

    protected void Page_Load(object sender, EventArgs e)
    {
        myControl1.Name = myControl1.Name + "Jon";
    }
</script>


<html>
<head><title>MyPage</title></head>
<body>
<Chapter11:MyControl id="myControl1" Name="Brad" runat="server" />
</body>
</html>
```

Listing 11.8 **Property Assignment Order (Visual Basic .NET)**

```
<%@ Page Language="VB" %>
<%@ Register TagPrefix="Chapter11" TagName="MyControl"
    Src="MyControl_vb.ascx" %>


<script language="VB" runat="server">
    Protected Sub Page_Init(sender As Object, e As EventArgs)
        myControl1.Name = myControl1.Name & "Brian"
```

continues

Listing 11.8 **Continued**

```
    End Sub

    Protected Sub Page_Load(sender As Object, e As EventArgs)
            myControl1.Name = myControl1.Name & "Jon"
    End Sub
</script>

<html>
<head><title>MyPage</title></head>
<body>
<Chapter11:MyControl id="myControl1" Name="Brad" runat="server" />
</body>
</html>
```

As you can see, the Name attribute has been added back to the User Control tag. This example also added the Page_Init event handler. When you run the previous code listings in a browser, it will display the following text:

```
This control belongs to BradBrianJon.
```

This exercise is meant to show the order in which code is executed in an ASP.NET page. Tag attributes are evaluated and applied first, the Page_Init event fires next, and the Page_Load event fires last. You can trap a few other page-level events, but you get the idea.

If you hadn't been concatenating the Name property in each of the event handlers, then only the one in the Page_Load event would survive. The point to remember is that if you don't get the expected results displayed for your User Control, it sometimes helps to check the sequence in which the code is executed. This can give you clues on what happened, as well as how to fix it.

Add a Method

Now that you know some of the issues with User Control properties, let's add a method to your User Control. Listings 11.9 and 11.10 show what your User Control code looks like now:

Listing 11.9 *MyControl* **with Method (C#)**

```
<%@ Control Language="C#" %>

<script language="C#" runat="server">
    private string _name;

    public string Name
    {
```

```
        get
        {
                return _name;
        }
        set
        {
                _name = value;
        }
    }


    public void DisplayNewDateTime()
    {
            panel1.Controls.Add(
                new LiteralControl(DateTime.Now.ToString() + "<br />"));
    }
</script>


This control belongs to <%= Name %>.

<asp:panel id="panel1" runat="server" />
```

Listing 11.10   *MyControl* with Method (Visual Basic .NET)

```
<%@ Control Language="VB" %>

<script language="VB" runat="server">
    Private _name As String

    Public Property Name As String
        Get
            Return _name
        End Get
        Set
            _name = Value
        End Set
    End Property

    Public Sub DisplayNewDateTime()
        panel1.Controls.Add( _
            New LiteralControl(DateTime.Now.ToString() + "<br />"))
    End Sub
</script>
```

continues

Listing 11.10 **Continued**

```
This control belongs to <%= Name %>.

<asp:panel id="panel1" runat="server" />
```

The code required to call this method from your ASP.NET page is fairly simple. It is done in the same manner as any other method call on an object (see Listings 11.11 and 11.12).

Listing 11.11 **Calling a User Control Method (C#)**

```
<%@ Page Language="C#" %>
<%@ Register TagPrefix="Chapter11" TagName="MyControl"
    Src="MyControl_cs.ascx" %>

<script language="C#" runat="server">
    protected void Page_Load(object sender, EventArgs e)
    {
        myControl1.Name = "Jon";
        myControl1.DisplayNewDateTime();
        myControl1.DisplayNewDateTime();
    }
</script>

<html>
<head><title>MyPage</title></head>
<body>
<Chapter11:MyControl id="myControl1" runat="server" />
</body>
</html>
```

Listing 11.12 **Calling a User Control Method (Visual Basic .NET)**

```
<%@ Page Language="VB" %>
<%@ Register TagPrefix="Chapter11" TagName="MyControl"
    Src="MyControl_vb.ascx" %>

<script language="VB" runat="server">
    Protected Sub Page_Load(sender As Object, e As EventArgs)
        myControl1.Name = "Jon"
        myControl1.DisplayNewDateTime()
```

```
                myControl1.DisplayNewDateTime()
       End Sub
</script>

<html>
<head><title>MyPage</title></head>
<body>
<Chapter11:MyControl id="myControl1" runat="server" />
</body>
</html>
```

Method Gotchas

There really aren't any tricky things about calling User Control methods themselves (besides the scope modifier and the code execution order issues discussed in the previous "Property Gotchas" section). The actions performed by your User Control methods can cause problems, however.

Modifying the Controls Collection

One of the most common things that your User Control methods will do is dynamically create new server controls. This is exactly what the `DisplayNewDateTime` method defined previously does. You'll notice that instead of adding your new `LiteralControl` directly to the `Controls` collection of your User Control, you created a `Panel` server control to act as a placeholder. There are two reasons for this. Because you have already used code blocks in your User Control, you cannot dynamically add any more controls to it. Doing so would result in an error that looks like this:

```
Exception Details: System.Web.HttpException: The Controls collection cannot be
modified because the control contains code blocks (i.e. <% ... %>).
```

If you had not used a code block to display the `Name` property of your User Control, then you would have been able to add your new `LiteralControl` objects directly to the `Controls` collection of your User Control. The other reason why you shouldn't do this, though, is because when you add items to the `Controls` collection, by default, it adds the item to the end of the User Control. This might not be the desired outcome. An `AddAt` method of the `Controls` collection enables you to specify an insertion index, but it can be difficult to determine which index position to specify. It is much easier (and less likely to contain bugs) if you use a `Panel` or `Label` server control as a placeholder for the new dynamic controls that you want to add to your User Control.

Accessing Out-of-Scope Controls

A common pitfall in using User Control methods trying to access a control that is contained in the ASP.NET page itself. For instance, if you placed a `Label` server control named `label1` after your `MyControl` tag in your ASP.NET page and then tried to reference it in a method of your User Control, you would get an error that looks like this:

```
Compiler Error Message: CS0246: The type or namespace name 'label1' could not be
found (are you missing a using directive or an assembly reference?)
```

or (Visual Basic .NET)

```
Compiler Error Message: BC30451: The name 'label1' is not declared.
```

The easiest solution is to put any controls that you want your User Control to manipulate inside the User Control definition file itself. That way, the controls will be within the scope of your User Control methods.

Dynamic User Controls

Inevitably, you'll run into a situation in which you want to create an entire User Control dynamically. This often occurs when it is uncertain how many instances of the User Control will be required on your ASP.NET page. Dynamically generated User Controls can be a powerful tool, but you must be aware of a few snags.

Defining a Class Name

To be able to reference the properties and methods of your dynamically loaded User Controls in your ASP.NET page, you must be able to cast them to a strong type. This requires you to define a class name in your User Control definition file. This is a relatively painless process. All it takes is to add a `className` attribute to the `@Control` directive, like this:

```
<%@ Control Language="C#" className="MyControl" %>
```

or (Visual Basic .NET)

```
<%@ Control Language="VB" className="MyControl" %>
```

Failure to specify a `className` attribute will yield an error that looks like this:

```
Compiler Error Message: CS0246: The type or namespace name 'MyControl' could not
be found (are you missing a using directive or an assembly reference?)
```

or (Visual Basic .NET)

```
Compiler Error Message: BC30002: Type is not defined: 'MyControl'
```

Your User Control is now all set up to be dynamically loaded and cast to a strong type.

Referencing User Control Classes

The code in your ASP.NET page that will dynamically load your User Control changes significantly from the code used to display User Controls using server control tags. Listings 11.13 and 11.14 illustrate what the code should look like:

Listing 11.13 **Dynamically Loading User Controls (C#)**

```
<%@ Page Language="C#" %>
<%@ Reference Control="MyControl_cs.ascx" %>

<script language="C#" runat="server">
    protected void Page_Load(object sender, EventArgs e)
    {
        MyControl mc1 = (MyControl)LoadControl("MyControl_cs.ascx");
        mc1.Name = "Jon";
        mc1.DisplayNewDateTime();
        panel1.Controls.Add(mc1);
    }
</script>

<html>
<head><title>MyPage</title></head>
<body>
<asp:panel id="panel1" runat="server" />
</body>
</html>
```

Listing 11.14 **Dynamically Loading User Controls (Visual Basic .NET)**

```
<%@ Page Language="VB" %>
<%@ Reference Control="MyControl_vb.ascx" %>

<script language="VB" runat="server">
    Protected Sub Page_Load(sender As Object, e As EventArgs)
        Dim mc1 As MyControl = _
            CType(LoadControl("MyControl_vb.ascx"),MyControl)
        mc1.Name = "Jon"
        mc1.DisplayNewDateTime()
        panel1.Controls.Add(mc1)
    End Sub
</script>
```

Listing 11.14   **Continued**

```
<html>
<head><title>MyPage</title></head>
<body>
<asp:panel id="panel1" runat="server" />
</body>
</html>
```

Notice the use of the @Reference directive instead of the @Register directive (which is now gone). Because you won't be adding User Controls as server control tags, you don't need the @Register directive. The @Reference directive enables you to cast the generic Control object reference returned by the LoadControl method to the specific strong type of your User Control (in this case, MyControl).

Another interesting thing to point out is that the server control tag you used to declare your User Control on the page is now gone, replaced by a Panel server control that serves as a placeholder for your dynamically loaded User Control object.

When Dynamic User Controls Go Wrong

Some interesting things can go wrong if you don't follow the rules of dynamic User Controls. For instance, if you forget to include the @Register directive, you'll end up with an error that looks like this:

Compiler Error Message: CS0246: The type or namespace name 'MyControl' could not be found (are you missing a using directive or an assembly reference?)

or (Visual Basic .NET)

Compiler Error Message: BC30002: Type is not defined: 'MyControl'

Likewise, if you forget to cast the generic control object returned by the LoadControl method to the strong type of your User Control, then you'll see one of these errors:

Compiler Error Message: CS0029: Cannot implicitly convert type 'System.Web.UI.Control' to 'ASP.MyControl'

or (Visual Basic .NET)

Compiler Error Message: BC30512: Option Strict disallows implicit conversions from System.Web.UI.Control to ASP.MyControl.

Note that the second of these two errors is the Visual Basic flavor and will occur only if you are using the Strict="True" attribute of the @Page directive. Otherwise, Visual Basic will implicitly cast the Control object for you. C# does not offer a setting to turn off option strict, so an explicit cast is always necessary.

If you try to access the properties and methods of a generic Control object returned from the LoadControl method, you'll get an error message like this:

> **Compiler Error Message:** CS0117: 'System.Web.UI.Control' does not contain a
> definition for 'Name'

or (Visual Basic .NET)

> **Compiler Error Message:** BC30456: The name 'Name' is not a member of
> 'System.Web.UI.Control'.

To see the properties and methods specific to your User Control, you must cast it to
the proper strong type specified in your @Reference directive.

One final thing to note is that if you want to add multiple instances of your User
Control, you must call the LoadControl method for each one. Simply changing the
properties of an existing User Control instance and then adding it to the Controls
collection of your Panel server control will not suffice; it merely changes the properties of the original User Control that you added. Even though you add the User
Control instance to the Panel server control, your variable still maintains a reference
to it and can manipulate it.

Summary

In this chapter, you looked at some of the idiosyncrasies of dealing with User Controls
in ASP.NET web applications. We started by discussing some of the basic errors and
problems that you might run into with User Controls. We then added a property to
your User Control and took a look at some of the errors that can occur if proper
scope modifiers and code execution order rules are not followed. We then covered
problems encountered by User Control methods, including how to handle problems
with modifying the Controls collection of the User Control and how to access out-
of-scope controls. We rounded out the chapter by creating a dynamically loaded User
Control. Some of the issues covered here included class name declaration, User
Control references, and explicit strong type casting to custom User Control types.

The next chapter discusses caching issues that you might encounter while
debugging your web applications.

12

Caching Issues and Debugging

ONE OF THE MOST IMPORTANT NEW FEATURES that ASP.NET makes available is a fairly extensive caching engine. This removes the need for "home-grown" caching solutions that often contain memory leaks. ASP.NET's caching capabilities are integrated at the ISAPI level, so they are much better equipped to handle cached resources.

Although caching in ASP.NET is relatively easy to implement, there are a few intricacies and "gotchas" that we'd like to cover. One of the things that might not be so obvious is that, by nature, caching can make debugging your web application particularly troublesome. For instance, if your web application contains a bug that displays the wrong content on a page, that content could end up trapped in cache. At that point, you would be forced to make a change to the underlying ASP.NET page or user control so that it would refresh itself. That's not a very elegant solution at all. There is a better way to handle this issue, using a validation callback, which we'll discuss a bit later.

Let's take a look at a few techniques for how to deal with both output caching and the Caching API.

Output Caching

The easiest way to implement caching in your ASP.NET web applications is through directives at either the page or the user control level. Unfortunately, this method is also the most limiting and frustrating to work with.

@*OutputCache* Directive

The basis for output caching at both the page and the user control level is the `@OutputCache` directive. Although you can use many different possible attributes (a few of which you'll see in a bit), two are mandatory: `Duration` and `VaryByParam`. `VaryByControl` can be substituted for `VaryByParam` in user controls, however.

Duration Attribute

The `Duration` attribute is fairly straightforward, but you must realize that the number it accepts is the number of "seconds" that you want your content to be cached for. Accidentally specifying a value of `10`, for instance, would cache your data only for 10 seconds instead of 10 minutes (which is what you might expect).

If you forget to specify the `Duration` attribute, you'll get an error like this:

➥**Parser Error Message:** The directive is missing a 'duration' attribute.

VaryByParam Attribute

Misuse of the `VaryByParam` attribute can lead to some strange behavior by your ASP.NET page. This is the second mandatory attribute of the `@OutputCache` directive. Failure to include it will yield an error message like this:

Parser Error Message: The directive is missing a 'VaryByParam' attribute, which ➥should be set to "none", "*", or a list of name/value pairs.

If you specify `none` as a value for this attribute, you must be aware that the same cached page will be served up for all requests for that page. For instance, if you intended to cache product information pages on your web application, and set the `VaryByParam` attribute to `none`, then the first product that was requested would be served up for all subsequent requests, regardless of any changes that were made to the query string. The following two page requests would both return the data for the product with an `ID = 10`:

```
http://www.yourdomain.com/product.aspx?ID=10

http://www.yourdomain.com/product.aspx?ID=20
```

You might choose to fix this anomaly by specifying a value of `*` for the `VaryByParam` attribute. Although this might appear to solve the problem, what happens if you are passing information on the query string that is personal to the current user—say, perhaps a user ID? You would then get a cached version for each user that browsed each product. Take the following two page requests:

```
http://www.yourdomain.com/product.aspx?ID=10&user=1234
```

```
http://www.yourdomain.com/product.aspx?ID=10&user=5678
```

You would want both of these requests to be served up from the same item in cache. This is where you would want to specify exactly which QueryString parameters you want the cache to key off. In this case, it would be the ID parameter only.

It is useful to note that, in the scenario just discussed, you would likely want to place your @OutputCache directive in a user control that contains your product-rendering code so that the user QueryString parameter could be used by other sections of the page to personalize the output. Then, only the product information itself would be served up from cache.

If you need to specify more than one QueryString parameter as a caching key, make sure that you use a semicolon as the delimiter instead of a comma. The value ID,user would be interpreted as one QueryString parameter, thereby causing the wrong caching behavior. The tricky part is that no errors are generated when you make this mistake. Instead, use ID;user.

VaryByCustom Attribute

When using the VaryByCustom attribute to customize the key used to store your page or user control in cache, you must remember to override the GetVaryByCustomString method in your web application's global.asax file. No errors will be generated if you forget to do this, but your custom parameter will not take part in the cache key.

VaryByHeader Attribute

The most common error that you will run into with the VaryByHeader attribute occurs if you try to use it in the @OutputCache directive of a user control. This is not allowed and will generate an error like this:

```
Parser Error Message: The 'VaryByHeader' attribute is not supported by the
➥'OutputCache' directive.
```

Use the VaryByHeader attribute only at the page level.

Manipulation of Cached User Controls

If you implement the @OutputCache directive in a user control, you cannot manipulate its properties externally. Dynamically assigning the properties of a user control in one of the page's events (such as Page_Load) works only if a copy does not already exist in the fragment cache. Subsequent attempts to dynamically modify one of the properties of a user control that has output caching enabled will generate an error like this:

```
Exception Details: System.NullReferenceException: Value null was found where an
➥instance of an object was required.
```

As you can see, this error message isn't very intuitive. To be safe, always set the properties of a cached user control in the Page_Load event inside the user control itself. The
exception to this is when you want to use declarative attributes; specifying attributes in
the user control tag itself is permitted. An example might look like this:

```
<chapter12:MyControl UserName="Jon" runat="server" />
```

Validation Callbacks

Remember the issue mentioned at the beginning of the chapter, pertaining to data
being trapped in the output cache? Here is where we'll put that issue to rest. Here
you'll wire up a validation callback so that each time the page is requested from the
cache, you'll get a chance to establish whether the cached item is still good. You'll do
this by checking for the existence of a password QueryString parameter. Take a look at
the code in Listings 12.1 and 12.2, which demonstrate the technique.

Listing 12.1   **Invalidating the Output Cache Through a Validation Callback (C#)**

```
<%@ Page Language="C#" %>
<%@ OutputCache Duration="10000" VaryByParam="none" %>

<script language="C#" runat="server">
    protected void MyHttpCacheValidateHandler(HttpContext context,
        object data, ref HttpValidationStatus validationStatus)
    {
        //initialize the password variable
        string password = "";

        //set the password variable if the user specified the
        //"password" QueryString parameter
        if(context.Request.QueryString["password"]!=null)
        {
            password = (string)context.Request.QueryString["pass
            ➥word"];
        }

        //if a password was specified, then determine if it is
        //correct. If it is, then evict the page from the cache.
        //If the password is incorrect or wasn't
        //specified, then validate the cached page
        switch(password)
        {
            case "mypassword":
                validationStatus =
                ➥HttpValidationStatus.Invalid;
```

```
                        break;
                default:
                        validationStatus = HttpValidationStatus.Valid;
                        break;
                }
        }

        protected void Page_Load(Object sender, EventArgs e)
        {
                //create an instance of the HttpCacheValidateHandler
                //delegate so that we can wire up the validation callback
                HttpCacheValidateHandler myHandler =
                        new HttpCacheValidateHandler
                        ➡(MyHttpCacheValidateHandler);

                //wire up the callback
                Response.Cache.AddValidationCallback(myHandler, null);

                //by displaying the current date and time on the screen,
                //we can see when the cache is being invalidated
                label1.Text = DateTime.Now.ToString();
        }
</script>

<html>
<head>
<title>Validation Callback</title>
</head>

<body>
<asp:label id="label1" runat="server" />
</body>
</html>
```

Listing 12.2   **Invalidating the Output Cache Through a Validation Callback (Visual Basic .NET)**

```
<%@ Page Language="VB" %>
<%@ OutputCache Duration="10000" VaryByParam="none" %>

<script language="VB" runat="server">
        Protected Sub MyHttpCacheValidateHandler( _
```

continues

Listing 12.2 **Continued**

```
        context As HttpContext, data As Object, _
        ByRef validationStatus As HttpValidationStatus)

        'initialize the password variable
        Dim password As String = ""

        'set the password variable if the user specified the
        '"password" QueryString parameter
        If context.Request.QueryString("password") <> Nothing Then
            password = CStr(context.Request.QueryString("password"))
        End If

        'if a password was specified, then determine if it is
        'correct. If it is, then evict the page from the cache.
        'If the password is incorrect or wasn't
        'specified, then validate the cached page
        Select Case password
            Case "mypassword"
                validationStatus = HttpValidationStatus.Invalid
            Case Else
                validationStatus = HttpValidationStatus.Valid
        End Select
    End Sub

    Protected Sub Page_Load(sender As Object, e As EventArgs)
        'create an instance of the HttpCacheValidateHandler
        'delegate so that we can wire up the validation callback
        Dim myHandler As HttpCacheValidateHandler = _
        New HttpCacheValidateHandler( _
        AddressOf MyHttpCacheValidateHandler)

        'wire up the callback
        Response.Cache.AddValidationCallback(myHandler, Nothing)

        'by displaying the current date and time on the screen,
        'we can see when the cache is being invalidated
        label1.Text = DateTime.Now.ToString()
    End Sub
</script>

<html>
```

```
<head>
<title>Validation Callback</title>
</head>

<body>
<asp:label id="label1" runat="server" />
</body>
</html>
```

In Listings 12.1 and 12.2, you can see that we start off by specifying the @OutputCache directive with a duration of 10,000 seconds. This is plenty of time to demonstrate the validation callback. Also notice the fact that the VaryByParam attribute is set to none. Be sure not to specify a * for this attribute—if you do, you will never be able to reset the correct output cache. When the cache is invalidated, it immediately stores a new copy. With the * value for VaryByParam, the password QueryString parameter would become part of the new cache key. This is not the desired outcome. You can set the VaryByParam attribute to specific QueryString parameters. Just don't include the password parameter as one of them.

Below the @OutputCache directive, you define a handler for the validation callback. In it, you check for the presence of the password QueryString parameter. If it exists, then you assign it to the password variable. If the password is correct, you set an Invalid status value to the validationStatus variable. Otherwise, you set a Valid status value.

Notice the use of a switch statement (Case statement, in Visual Basic .NET) instead of an if statement. As originally stated in Chapter 4, "code Structure that Eases Debugging," this enhances the readability of the code and enables you to add more options if needed at a later time.

Next, you define your Page_Load event. You create an instance of the HttpCacheValidateHandler delegate, using the address of the handler function just defined. You can then wire up the callback through the AddValidationCallback method of the Cache property of the Response object.

To visually see when the cache is being invalidated, you assign the current date and time to a label server control on the page. To see the validation callback in action, you can navigate to the page in your browser. The first time you hit the page, it is stored in cache. This is evident when you refresh the page and the same date and time appear on the page. Now add the password=mypassword QueryString parameter to the URL and hit the Enter key. You can see that the cache is refreshed with a new version of the page because the date and time change. If you now remove the password QueryString parameter and hit the Enter key again, you'll see that the newly cached page is fetched and displayed.

By using this technique, you can force a reset of the output cache, eliminating the problem of invalid debugging data (or any other incorrect data, for that matter) being trapped in cache.

The Caching API

The Caching API is much more flexible than the @OutputCache directive, in that you are in direct control of inserting items into cache and specifying exactly when and how they should be removed. For this reason, you will not run into as many issues while using the Caching API. The trade-off is that it is not quite as convenient and it takes a bit more code to get working. This section of the chapter helps you with some of the issues that you might encounter while using the Caching API.

Dependencies

Setting up dependencies for cached items is usually pretty straightforward. A couple situations, however, might be a bit confusing. When you are setting up a file dependency, you might get an error that looks like this:

Exception Details: System.Web.HttpException: Invalid file name for monitoring: {0}

This error means that the Cache object cannot find the file that you want to base the dependency on. The cause of this error is almost always that you attempted to use a virtual path to your dependency file or that you just specified a filename, without a path. Unlike most other references in ASP.NET web applications, file dependencies require you to specify that absolute path to the file. An easy way to get the absolute path is to use the Server.MapPath() method call. The code in Listings 12.3 and 12.4 demonstrates both the incorrect and correct methods of specifying a file dependency.

Listing 12.3 **Wrong and Right Ways to Use a File Dependency (C#)**

```
<%@ Language="C#" %>

<script language="C#" runat="server">
      protected void Page_Load(object sender, EventArgs e)
      {
             //this causes an error
             Cache.Insert("someKey", "someValue",
                    new CacheDependency("keyfile.txt"));

             //this is the correct way
             Cache.Insert("someKey", "someValue",
                    new CacheDependency(Server.MapPath("keyfile.txt")));

      }
</script>
```

Listing 12.4 **Wrong and Right Ways to Use a File Dependency (Visual Basic .NET)**

```
<%@ Language="VB" %>

<script language="VB" runat="server">
    Protected Sub Page_Load(sender As Object, E As EventArgs)
        'this causes an error
        Cache.Insert("someKey", "someValue", _
            new CacheDependency("keyfile.txt"))

        'this is the correct way
        Cache.Insert("someKey", "someValue", _
            new CacheDependency(Server.MapPath("keyfile.txt")))
    End Sub
</script>
```

Some tricky situations can arise when you are attempting to set up a dependency based on another item in cache through its key. To do this, you use the overloaded signature of the `CacheDependency` class that accepts two parameters. Leave the first parameter `null` (unless you want the dependency to be file-based as well). The second parameter is an array of strings correlating to the keys upon which you want this cached item to be dependent. The tricky part comes in when you try to base the dependency on a single key. Ideally, you could just specify the single string value as a parameter. If you do this, however, you will get an error like this:

Compiler Error Message: CS1502: The best overloaded method match for
➥'System.Web.Caching.CacheDependency.CacheDependency(string[], string[])' has
➥some invalid arguments

or (Visual Basic .NET)

Compiler Error Message: BC30311: A value of type 'String' cannot be converted to
➥'1-dimensional Array of String'.

Even though you are specifying only a single cache key as a dependency, it must still be in an array. Listings 12.5 and 12.6 provide examples of both incorrect and correct ways to handle a single-cache key dependency:

Listing 12.5 **Wrong and Right Ways to Use a Single-Cache Key Dependency (C#)**

```
<%@ Language="C#" %>

<script language="C#" runat="server">
    protected void Page_Load(object sender, EventArgs e)
    {
```

continues

Listing 12.5 **Continued**

```
                //this causes an error
                Cache.Insert("someKey", "someValue",
                        new CacheDependency(null, "depKey"));

                //this is the correct way
                string[] dependency = {"depKey"};

                Cache.Insert("someKey", "someValue",
                        new CacheDependency(null, dependency));
        }
</script>
```

Listing 12.6 **Wrong and Right Ways to Use a Single-Cache Key Dependency
(Visual Basic .NET)**

```
<%@ Language="VB" %>

<script language="VB" runat="server">
        Protected Sub Page_Load(sender As Object, E As EventArgs)
                'this causes an error
                Cache.Insert("someKey", "someValue", _
                        new CacheDependency(Nothing, "depKey"))

                'this is the correct way
                Dim dependency As String() = {"depKey"}

                Cache.Insert("someKey", "someValue", _
                        new CacheDependency(Nothing, dependency))
        End Sub
</script>
```

A final point about dependencies that might cause you problems is that the Cache
object enables you to set up a dependency on a cache key that does not exist. This
means that the item that you are trying to insert into the cache is immediately invalidated. One suggestion to avoid that situation is to check for the existence of an item
in the cache before you use it as a dependency for another item. Interestingly, if you
set up a file-based dependency based on a file that doesn't exist, the item IS is inserted
into the cache and can be referenced later.

Date and Time Expirations

Two of the overloaded signatures of the `Insert` method of the `Cache` class, as well as one signature of the `Add` method, enable you to specify an absolute expiration date/time for the cached item or a sliding expiration time. The key word to note in the previous sentence is *or*. If you attempt to specify both at the same time, you will get the following error message:

```
Exception Details: System.ArgumentException: absoluteExpiration must be
➡DateTime.MaxValue or slidingExpiration must be timeSpan.Zero.
```

The error message tells you to use `DateTime.MaxValue` or `TimeSpan.Zero` so that only an absolute expiration *or* a sliding expiration is implemented. As an alternative, the `Cache.NoAbsoluteExpiration` constant can be used, which is equivalent to `DateTime.MaxValue`, and the `Cache.NoSlidingExpiration` constant can be used, which is equivalent to `TimeSpan.Zero`.

Retrieving Cached Items

Because all items returned from the cache are of the `Object` type, you must cast it to the appropriate type before assigning it, like this:

```
string someValue = Cache["someValue"].ToString(); //C#
```

or

```
Dim someValue As String = Cache("someValue").ToString() 'VB
```

If you do not cast it to the proper type and you are not assigning the item from `Cache` to a variable of the `Object` type, you will get an error like this:

```
Compiler Error Message: CS0029: Cannot implicitly convert type 'object' to
➡'string'
```

If you attempt to retrieve an item from the cache using a key that doesn't exist, it does not generate an error. Instead, it returns a `null` reference (`Nothing`, in Visual Basic .NET). If this is the case, then when you attempt to cast it to the proper type (as you just saw), you will get an error like this:

```
Exception Details: System.NullReferenceException: Value null was found where an
➡instance of an object was required.
```

To get around this, always verify that the item that you want to retrieve from the cache exists. The following code demonstrates this:

```
//C#
if(Cache["someValue"] != null)
{
        someValue = Cache["someValue"].ToString();
}
```

or

continues

```
'Visual Basic .NET
If Cache("someValue") <> Nothing Then
        someValue = Cache("someValue").ToString()
End If
```

Removing Cached Items

You can run into trouble if you attempt to remove an item from the cache using an invalid key. This might happen more often than you think because you can never tell when a resource that the cached item is dependent on changes, thereby evicting it from the cache. Normally, the return value of the `Remove` method of the `Cache` class is the item that was removed from the cache. If the key is invalid, however, the return value is `null` (`Nothing`, in Visual Basic .NET). Therefore, if you plan to use the item that you are removing from the cache, you should verify that it exists first, using the same method demonstrated previously.

Summary

In this chapter, we covered some of the more common problems that you will encounter while leveraging caching in your web applications. We started with a look at output caching, using the `@OutputCache` directive at both the page and user control levels. Problems associated with several of its attributes were discussed. We also covered the error generated by manipulating an output cached user control.

Next, you learned how to use validation callbacks to manually evict a page from the output cache. This capability is key to being able to effectively debug web applications without having to worry about incorrect data being trapped in cache. It is also a useful feature that enables you to manually refresh an incorrect page that is in production.

Issues related to the Caching API were discussed next. Specifically, you learned about the intricacies of both file- and key-based dependencies, as well as date and time expirations, and errors associated with retrieving and removing items from the cache.

The next chapter discusses Web Services in the context of debugging your ASP.NET web applications.

IV

Debugging Related Technologies

13   Debugging Web Services

14   Debugging .NET Components and HttpHandlers

15   COM+ Issues

16   Debugging ADO.NET

13

Debugging Web Services

Web Services provide an amazing new stride forward in distributed architecture. These new capabilities enable developers to extend the reach of web applications. They give you the capability to reach any web server. But what about debugging a Web Service?

You probably have had the pleasure of debugging a DLL. Debugging a Web Service might seem similar, but there are some important differences to keep in mind while doing the debugging. This chapter identifies the key areas in building and debugging Web Services. We will show you what tools are available and different techniques to assist you in finding those bugs.

Web Services Stumbling Blocks

Microsoft has done a great deal to ease the process of building Web Services, especially in Visual Studio .NET. But let's focus on using just the .NET framework tools here.

First you'll take a look at a simple Web Service. Then we'll identify areas where you might have problems. Listings 13.1–13.4 serve as examples of the code that you will need to get started.

Listing 13.1 **ASMX Code (C#)**

```
<%@ WebService Language="c#" Codebehind="Service1.asmx.cs"
Class="chap_13_c.TimeService" %>
```

Listing 13.2 **Simple Web Service (C#)**

```
using System;
using System.Web.Services;

namespace chap_13_c
{
        //Create a class and inherit the WebService functionality
public class TimeService : System.Web.Services.WebService
    {
            //Constructor
            public TimeService()
            {
            }
//This is required to make the following method SOAP   enabled
            [WebMethod]
            public string GetTime()
            {
                return DateTime.Now.ToString();
            }
    }
}
```

Listing 13.3 **ASMX Code (Visual Basic .NET)**

```
<%@ WebService Language="vb" Codebehind="Service1.asmx.vb"
Class="chap_13_vb.Service1" %>
```

Listing 13.4 **Simple Web Service (Visual Basic .NET)**

```
Imports System
Imports System.Web.Services

Public Class TimeService
    Inherits System.Web.Services.WebService

    <WebMethod()> Public Function GetTime() As String
```

```
        HelloWorld = Date.Now.ToString()
    End Function


End Class
```

If you look at Listings 13.1–13.4, you will notice that you have to produce very little code to create a simple Web Service. Let's take a look at where you might run into problems and how to resolve them.

Error Messages

You might run into a variety of error messages, but we'll try to focus on some of the more common areas where problems might arise.

Let's start off by looking at a couple common error messages. You might run into this one right off the bat:

```
System.IO.FileInfo cannot be serialized because it does not have a default public
➥constructor.
```

If you manage to get past that error, you might run into the following one:

```
System.Exception: There was an error generating the XML document. — ->
System.Exception: System.IO.FileInfo cannot be serialized because it does not have
➥a default public constructor.
    at System.Xml.Serialization.TypeScope.ImportTypeDesc(Type type, Boolean
    ➥canBePrimitive)
    at System.Xml.Serialization.TypeScope.GetTypeDesc(Type type)
    at System.Xml.Serialization.TypeScope.ImportTypeDesc(Type type, Boolean
    ➥canBePrimitive)
    at System.Xml.Serialization.TypeScope.GetTypeDesc(Type type)
    atSystem.Xml.Serialization.XmlSerializationWriter.CreateUnknownTypeException
    ➥(Type type)
    at System.Xml.Serialization.XmlSerializationWriter.WriteTypedPrimitive(String
    ➥name, String ns, Object o, Boolean xsiType)
    atn2499d7d93ffa468fbd8861780677ee41.XmlSerializationWriter1.Write4_Object
    ➥(String n, String ns, Object o, Boolean isNullable, Boolean needType)
    atn2499d7d93ffa468fbd8861780677ee41.XmlSerializationWriter1.Write9_Object
    ➥(Object o)
    at System.Xml.Serialization.XmlSerializer.Serialize(XmlWriter xmlWriter, Object
    ➥o, XmlSerializerNamespaces namespaces)
    at System.Xml.Serialization.XmlSerializer.Serialize(TextWriter textWriter,
    ➥Object o)
    at System.Web.Services.Protocols.XmlReturnWriter.Write(HttpResponse response,
    ➥Stream outputStream, Object returnValue)
    at System.Web.Services.Protocols.HttpServerProtocol.WriteReturns(Object[]
    ➥returnValues, Stream outputStream)
    at System.Web.Services.Protocols.WebServiceHandler.WriteReturns(Object[]
    ➥returnValues)
    at System.Web.Services.Protocols.WebServiceHandler.Invoke()
    at System.Web.Services.Protocols.WebServiceHandler.CoreProcessRequest()
```

If you get either of those messages, whether while your service is just starting or as you invoke the method that returns the data that caused the error, most likely you are trying to return a complex data set or array that the system cannot serialize. If you take a look at Listings 13.5 and 13.6, you can see that it would be easy to overlook what type of data the system can return.

Listing 13.5 **Complex Return Type (C#)**

```
[WebMethod]
            public DirectoryInfo[] Dir(string dir)
            {
                    DirectoryInfo di = new DirectoryInfo(dir);

                    DirectoryInfo[] diList = di.GetDirectories("*.*");

                    return diList;


            }
```

Listing 13.6 **Complex Return Type (Visual Basic .NET)**

```
    <WebMethod()> Public Function Dir(ByVal dir As String) As
    ➥DirectoryInfo()

        Dim di As New DirectoryInfo(dir)

            Dim diList as di.GetDirectories("*.*")

        Return diList
    End Function
```

The code in Listings 13.5 and 13.6 looks fine, but it won't work. So now what do you do? Well, one way to work around this is to build your own array and then pass it back to the client. If you do this, you must make sure that the array structure is published to public so that the users know what they are working with. This gets accomplished in Listings 13.7 and 13.8.

Listing 13.7 **Custom Return Type (C#)**

```csharp
using System;
using System.Collections;
using System.ComponentModel;
using System.Data;
using System.Diagnostics;
using System.Web;
using System.Web.Services;
using System.Xml.Serialization;
using System.IO;

namespace DirectoryTools
{
    /// <summary>
    /// Summary description for Service1.
    /// </summary>
    public class Service1 : System.Web.Services.WebService
    {
        public Service1()
        {
            //CODEGEN: This call is required by the ASP.NET Web
Services Designer
            InitializeComponent();
        }

        #region Component Designer generated code
        /// <summary>
        /// Required method for Designer support - do not modify
        /// the contents of this method with the code editor.
        /// </summary>
        private void InitializeComponent()
        {
        }
        #endregion

        /// <summary>
        /// Clean up any resources being used.
        /// </summary>
        protected override void Dispose( bool disposing )
        {
        }
```

continues

Listing 13.7 **Continued**

```
                        // WEB SERVICE EXAMPLE
                        // The HelloWorld() example service returns the string
                        ➥Hello World
                        // To build, uncomment the following lines and then save
                        ➥and build the project
        // To test this web service, press F5

                        [WebMethod]
                        public string HelloWorld()
                        {
                                return "Hello World";
                        }

                        [WebMethod()]
                        [XmlInclude(typeof(DirObject))]
                        public DirObject Test( string sPath)
                        {
                                DirectoryInfo di = new DirectoryInfo(sPath);
                                DirectoryInfo[] diList = di.GetDirectories("*.*");
                                DirObject temp = new DirObject();
                                int x = 0;
                                foreach ( DirectoryInfo d in diList)
                                {
                                        temp[x] = d;
                                        x++;
                                }
                                return temp;
                        }
                }

        [XmlInclude(typeof(DirItem))]
        public class DirObject
        {
                [XmlElement("Item")]

                public  ArrayList Data
                {
                        get { return data;}
                        set { data = value;}
                }
```

```
protected ArrayList data = new ArrayList();

public object this [int idx]
{
      get
      {
            if (idx > -1 && idx < data.Count)
            {
                  return (data[idx]);
            }
            else
            {
                  return null;
            }
      }

      set
      {
            if (idx > -1 && idx < data.Count)
            {
                  data[idx] = value;
            }
            else if (idx == data.Count)
            {
                  DirItem  x = new DirItem();
                  DirectoryInfo temp =
                  ➥(DirectoryInfo)value;
                  x.FileName = temp.FullName;
                  data.Add(x);

            }
            else
            {
                  //Possibly throw an exception here.
}
      }
}

} // MyClass

public class DirItem
{
```

continues

Listing 13.7 **Continued**

```
        protected string filename;

        public DirItem()
        {
        }

        [XmlAttribute("FileName")]
        public string FileName
        {
                get { return filename;}
                set { filename = value;}
        }
    }

} //Name space
```

Listing 13.8 **Custom Return Type (Visual Basic .NET)**

```
Imports System.Web.Services
Imports System.IO
Imports System.Xml
Imports System.Xml.Serialization


<WebService(Namespace:="http://microsoft.com/webservices/")> Public Class
➥Service1
    Inherits System.Web.Services.WebService

#Region " Web Services Designer Generated Code "

    Public Sub New()
        MyBase.New()

        'This call is required by the Web Services Designer.
        InitializeComponent()

        'Add your own initialization code after the
        ➥InitializeComponent() call

    End Sub
```

```
'Required by the Web Services Designer
Private components As System.ComponentModel.Container

'Do not modify it using the code editor.
<System.Diagnostics.DebuggerStepThrough()> Private Sub
➥InitializeComponent()

    components = New System.ComponentModel.Container()

End Sub

Protected Overloads Overrides Sub Dispose(ByVal disposing As
➥Boolean)
    'Do not modify it using the code editor.
End Sub

#End Region

    '
    <WebMethod()> Public Function Test(ByVal path As String) As
    ➥DirObject
        Dim di As DirectoryInfo = New DirectoryInfo(path)
        Dim diList() As DirectoryInfo
        Dim d As DirectoryInfo
        Dim temp As DirObject = New DirObject()
        Dim x As Integer = 0

        diList = di.GetDirectories("*.*")

        For Each d In diList
            temp(x) = d
            x = x + 1
        Next
        Return temp
    End Function


    <XmlInclude(GetType(DirItem)), XmlRoot("Root")> Public Class
    ➥DirObject

        Private pdata As ArrayList = New ArrayList()

        <XmlElement("Item")> Public Property Data() As ArrayList
```

continues

Listing 13.8 **Continued**

```vb
Get
        Return pdata
    End Get

    Set(ByVal Value As ArrayList)
        pdata = Value
    End Set
End Property

Default Public Property base(ByVal idx As Integer) As Object
    Get
        If (idx > -1 And idx < Data.Count) Then

            Return pdata(idx)

        Else

            Return Nothing

        End If

    End Get

    Set(ByVal Value As Object)
        If (idx > -1 And idx < pdata.Count) Then
            pdata(idx) = Value

        ElseIf (idx = pdata.Count) Then
            Dim x As DirItem = New DirItem()
            Dim temp As DirectoryInfo

            temp = CType(Value, DirectoryInfo)
            x.FileName = temp.FullName
            x.LastAccessDate = temp.LastAccessTime
            pdata.Add(x)

        Else
            'Possibly throw an exception here.
        End If

    End Set

End Property
```

```
End Class

Public Class DirItem

    Private pfilename As String
    Private pLastAccessDate As Date

    Sub DirItem()

    End Sub

    <XmlElement("FileName")> Public Property FileName() As String
        Get
            Return pfilename
        End Get

        Set(ByVal Value As String)
            pfilename = Value
        End Set

    End Property

    <XmlElement("LastAccessDate")> Public Property LastAccessDate() As
    ➥Date
        Get
            Return pLastAccessDate
        End Get

        Set(ByVal Value As Date)
            pLastAccessDate = Value
        End Set

    End Property

End Class

End Class
```

In Listings 13.7 and 13.8, you will notice a few new elements that you might not have seen before: <XmlAttribute> and <XmlInclude>. These additional features define the output when this class is serialized. This is a great way to rename elements in the XML structure to something more meaningful.

Problems Working with XMLSerializer

You just saw one way to pass back data, but you might say that it involves a bit of work; there must be a simpler way to do it. Why not use the XMLSerializer class to generate the returning data in an XML valid format? Well, if you try this, you might get the following error message:

```
System.Exception: There was an error reflecting 'System.IO.DirectoryInfo'. —->
System.Exception: System.IO.DirectoryInfo cannot be serialized because it does
➡not have a default public constructor.
    at System.Xml.Serialization.TypeScope.ImportTypeDesc(Type type, Boolean
➡canBePrimitive)
    at System.Xml.Serialization.TypeScope.GetTypeDesc(Type type)
    at System.Xml.Serialization.ModelScope.GetTypeModel(Type type)
    at System.Xml.Serialization.XmlReflectionImporter.ImportTypeMapping(Type type,
➡XmlRootAttribute root, String defaultNamespace)
    at System.Xml.Serialization.XmlReflectionImporter.ImportTypeMapping(Type type,
➡XmlRootAttribute root, String defaultNamespace)
    at System.Xml.Serialization.XmlSerializer..ctor(Type type)
    at chapter13_c.Service1.Dir(String dir) in c:\documents and
➡settings\brad\vswebcache\digital-laptop\chapter13_c\service1.asmx.cs:line 110
```

Let's look at the line of code where the error occurred and see why this is happening. Listings 13.9 and 13.10 provide a fix.

Listing 13.9 **Fix for the *XMLSerializer* problem (C#)**

```
[WebMethod]
    public Object[] Dir(string dir)
    {
     XmlSerializer serializer =        new XmlSerializer(typeof(DirectoryInfo));
     Return serializer;
    }
```

Listing 13.10 **Fix for the *XMLSerializer* problem (Visual Basic .NET)**

```
<WebMethod()> Public Function Dir(ByVal dirname As String) As Object()

    Dim serializer =   new XmlSerializer(typeof(DirectoryInfo))
    Return serializer

    End Function
```

The XmlSerializer cannot serialize the structure into XML. That is why you must define the different classes to mimic the DirectoryInfo object.

Working with Errors in SOAP

While working with Web Services, you eventually will need to handle errors in a more constructive way. The question is, how do you want to handle the errors that pop up? The following error message is an example of what you would see if you did not have any mechanism for handling errors:

```
System.IndexOutOfRangeException: Exception of type System.IndexOutOfRangeException
➥was thrown.
at chap_13_c.TimeService.ErrorString() in
c:\inetpub\wwwroot\chap_13_c\service1.asmx.cs:line 38
```

This error message is typical of what you would see if your Web Service ran into an error. To keep this from happening, Listings 13.11 and 13.12 show a simple example to catch the error and return it inside the contents of the SOAP message.

Listing 13.11   **WebMethod Error (C#)**

```
[WebMethod]
    public object ReturnErrorString()
    {
// Catch the error then return it inside a SOAP message.
            string[] sret = new string[3];
            try
            {
                sret[0] = "one";
                sret[1] = "two";
                sret[3] = "three";//Error
            }
            catch(Exception e)
            {
                sret[0] = e.Message;

            }
            return sret;
        }
```

Listing 13.12   **WebMethod Error (Visual Basic .NET)**

```
<WebMethod()> Public Function ErrorStringCatch() As String()

    ' Catch the error then return it inside a SOAP message.Dim sret(3) As
    ➥String

        Try
```

continues

Listing 13.12 **Continued**

```
        sret(0) = "Hello"
        sret(1) = "Bye"
        sret(13) = "Testing" 'This will generate an error


    Catch e As Exception

        sret(0) = e.Message

    End Try

    ErrorStringCatch = sret
End Function
```

If you look closely at the code in Listings 13.11 and 13.12, you will notice that we intentionally added a runtime error while adding the third item to the array.

Now when you run into an error, it will be returned inside the SOAP message. This is one way to approach handling errors and sending them back to the client, but this is not the preferred method for doing so. Instead, one of two things should be done. First, you cannot catch the exception that will send it back to the client to handle. Second, you can identify what the problem is inside the catch and try to resolve the problem or throw another exception that will be sent back to the client. This gives you the capability to identify the error inside your Web Service client and deal with it there. Otherwise, if you just returned the error message inside the array, you would need to check the first item of the array and try to identify whether it is an error message. If you did this, the return message might look something like Listing 13.13.

Listing 13.13 **SOAP Return Values**

```
<?xml version="1.0" encoding="utf-8" ?>

<Object n1:type="ArrayOfString" Listing 13.12
➥xmlns:n1="http://www.w3.org/2001/XMLSchema-instance"
➥xmlns="Debugging_Asp.NET_webservices">
<string>Exception of type System.IndexOutOfRangeException was
thrown.</string>
    <string>Bye</string>
    <string>xmlns:xsd="http://www.w3.org/2001/XMLSchema" n1:nil="true" />
</Object>
```

What if you are working only with numbers? Then how do you go about sending back error messages? If you look at Listings 13.14 and 13.15, you will see that you can use the try-catch method and then rethrow the error.

Listing 13.14 **Throw Exception (C#)**

```csharp
[WebMethod]
        public object ReturnErrorString()
        {
        // Catch the error then return it inside a SOAP message.
                string[] sret = new string[3];
                try
                {
                        sret[0] = "one";
                        sret[1] = "two";
                        sret[3] = "three";//Error
                }
                catch(Exception e)
                {
                        Throw(e);//Return the exception to the client

                }
                return sret;
        }
```

Listing 13.15 *Throw* **Exception (Visual Basic .NET)**

```vb
<WebMethod()> Public Function ErrorStringCatch() As String()

    ' Catch the error then return it inside a SOAP message.Dim sret(3) As
    ➥String

        Try

            sret(0) = "Hello"
            sret(1) = "Bye"
            sret(13) = "Testing" 'This will generate an error


        Catch e As Exception

            Throw(e) 'Return the exception to the client
```

continues

Listing 13.15   **Continued**

```
        End Try

        ErrorStringCatch = sret
    End Function
```

If you look at the Catch statement, the Throw method is being called to pass the error on to the client. By adding this line of code, you change the behavior of the Web Service dramatically. A simple change in one line of code can make a world of difference when it comes to debugging. Don't forget that you need to use the try-catch statement on the client side as well, to be able to handle the exception being passed back by the server. To show how the client should be implemented, take a look at the code in Listings 13.16 and 13.17.

Listing 13.16   **The *try-catch* Statement on the Client Side (C#)**

```
private void Button2_Click(object sender, System.EventArgs e)
        {
                try
                {
                        localhost.Service1 s = new localhost.Service1();
                        s. ErrorStringCatch ();

                }
                catch(Exception ex)
                {
                        TextBox1.Text =  ex.Message;
                }

        }
```

Listing 13.17   **The *try-catch* Statement on the Client Side (Visual Basic .NET)**

```
Private Sub Button1_Click(ByVal sender As System.Object, ByVal e As
➥System.EventArgs) Handles Button1.Click
        Try
            localhost.Service1(s = New localhost.Service1())
            s.ErrorStringCatch()

            catch(Exception ex)
            TextBox1.Text = ex.Message
```

```
        End Try

    End Sub
```

In Listings 13.16 and 13.17, the user clicks the button to invoke the method of the Web Service. If there is an error on the server side, the Web Service passes back the error information, and it can be received in the catch statement. When an error does get caught, it is displayed in the text box that is on the page.

Error Returning Certain Types of Data

One of the errors we ran into was simple because we were not paying attention to the details of the code. The code compiled fine—we're not sure whether it was a compiler issue or, as a software developer would say, it is a problem "as designed," meaning that this is the way it is supposed to be. Take a look at the following error message and see if you can identify why we received this message:

```
System.Exception: There was an error generating the XML document. — ->
➥System.Exception: The type System.Object[] may not be used in this context.
   at System.Xml.Serialization.XmlSerializationWriter.WriteTypedPrimitive(String
   name, String ns, Object o, Boolean xsiType)
   atn2499d7d93ffa468fbd8861780677ee41.XmlSerializationWriter1.Write1_Object
   ➥(String n, String ns, Object o, Boolean isNullable, Boolean needType)
   atn2499d7d93ffa468fbd8861780677ee41.XmlSerializationWriter1.Write3_Object
   ➥(Object o)
   at System.Xml.Serialization.XmlSerializer.Serialize(XmlWriter xmlWriter, Object
   ➥o, XmlSerializerNamespaces namespaces)
   at System.Xml.Serialization.XmlSerializer.Serialize(TextWriter textWriter,
   ➥Object o)
   at System.Web.Services.Protocols.XmlReturnWriter.Write(HttpResponse response,
   ➥Stream outputStream, Object returnValue)
   at System.Web.Services.Protocols.HttpServerProtocol.WriteReturns(Object[]
   ➥returnValues, Stream outputStream)
   at System.Web.Services.Protocols.WebServiceHandler.WriteReturns(Object[]
   ➥returnValues)
   at System.Web.Services.Protocols.WebServiceHandler.Invoke()
   at System.Web.Services.Protocols.WebServiceHandler.CoreProcessRequest()
```

This message contains a lot of repetitive information here, but it also has some very specific bits that narrow down where the problem is coming from. You'll notice that Object and Serialize are used several times. Now you know from the error message at the beginning that the problem originates with the System.Object class. Passing simple types back and forth is very simple to do. Now you are taking the next step to passing arrays in Web Services. When working with any sort of array, you must make sure to define your WebMethod as returning an array, not just a single value or object.

Listings 13.18–13.21 give some examples of problems that you might run into when returning array's of objects.

Listing 13.18 **Code with Error (C#)**

```
[WebMethod]
public object ErrorStringCatch()// Missing [] from object
```

Listing 13.19 **Correct Syntax (C#)**

```
[WebMethod]
public object[] ErrorStringCatch()
```

Listing 13.20 **Code with Error (Visual Basic .NET)**

```
<WebMethod()> Public Function ErrorStringCatch() As Object
```

Listing 13.21 **Correct Syntax (Visual Basic .NET)**

```
<WebMethod()> Public Function ErrorStringCatch() As Object()
```

This might seem like a trivial item, but don't forget that most errors that you will run into probably are simple errors that you overlooked.

Working with Streams

While playing around with Web Services, you might have experimented with different types of data that could be returned by a Web Service. If you tried to do some basic functions such as getting a directory listing or finding out some information on a file, you might have run into some problems.

Listings 13.22 and 13.23 give a simple example of how you might attempt to pass back a `FileStream` object.

Listing 13.22 *GetFile WebMethod (C#)*

```
[WebMethod]
    public FileStream GetFile()
    {
    FileStream fs = new FileStream("c:\\winnt\\greenstone.bmp",
    ➥FileMode.Open);

    byte[] buf;// = new byte[fs.Length];

buf = new Byte[fs.Length];
```

```
fs.Read(buf,0,(int)fs.Length);

    return fs;
    }
```

Listing 13.23   *GetFile WebMethod* (**Visual Basic .NET**)

```
<WebMethod()>public function GetFile() as FileStream

    FileStream fs = new FileStream("c:\\winnt\\greenstone.bmp",
    ➥FileMode.Open);

    Dim buf() as byte();// = new byte[fs.Length];

buf = new Byte(fs.Length);

    fs.Read(buf,0, fs.Length);

    return fs;

    End Function
```

The code in Listings 13.22 and 13.23 looks like it should work. But when you try to use it, you end up getting an error. Take a look at the error shown in Figure 13.1 to see what the end result will be.

Figure 13.1 Serialization problems.

This error seems to be very popular with Web Services, but each case needs to be handled in a different way because Web Services need to pass the data in one of two basic forms: text or binary. As for the text format it, needs to be in an XML format of some sort. The data format can be binary or, in this case, an array of bytes.

There is a simple resolution to this problem. Because you are already dealing with an array of bytes, just pass that array back to the client. Take a look at Listings 13.24 and 13.25 to see how this would be done in the code.

Listing 13.24 **Returning Binary Data (C#)**

```
[WebMethod]
            public Byte[] GetFile()
            {
                    FileStream fs = new FileStream("c:\\winnt\\green
                    ➥stone.bmp", FileMode.Open);


                    byte[] buf;

                    buf = new Byte[fs.Length];

                    br.Read(buf,0,(int)fs.Length);
```

```
            fs.Close();

            return buf;
    }
```

Listing 13.25   **Returning Binary Data (Visual Basic .NET)**

```
<WebMethod()>public Function GetFile() as Byte()

        FileStream fs = new FileStream("c:\\winnt\\greenstone.bmp",
        ➥FileMode.Open)


        Dim buf as byte()

        buf = new Byte(fs.Length)

        br.Read(buf,0,fs.Length)

        fs.Close()

        return buf;
End Function
```

With a simple change to the way the method returns the data, the problem is solved. As you can see, you simply need to change the return type of the method to an array of bytes. Not all your problems will be this simple though.

If you start playing around with the writing of the array of bytes, you might run into the error message shown in Figure 13.2, as we did.

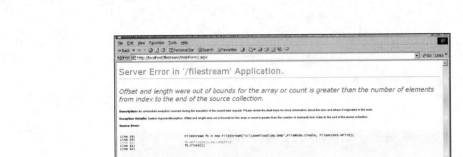

Figure 13.2 Writing to a binary file.

If you take a close look at Listings 13.26 and 13.27, you will notice that we were trying to change the offset of where the file started to write.

Listing 13.26 **Offset Error (C#)**

```
private void Button1_Click(object sender, System.EventArgs e)
     {
     localhost.Service1 svc = new localhost.Service1();
     Byte[] ba = svc.GetPicture();
     FileStream fs = new
     ➥FileStream("c:\\download\\my.bmp",FileMode.Create,
FileAccess.Write);

     fs.Write(ba,1,ba.Length);//error on the offset
     fs.Close();

     }
```

Listing 13.27 **Offset Error (Visual Basic .NET)**

```
private Function Button1_Click(sender as object, e as System.EventArgs )

     dim svc as new localhost.Service1()
     dim ba as byte()
ba = svc.GetPicture()
     Dim fs as new FileStream("c:\\download\\my.bmp",FileMode.Create,
     ➥FileAccess.Write)
```

```
fs.Write(ba,1,ba.Length) 'Error on the offset
fs.Close()

end Function
```

Tools

Microsoft has provided some additional tools to simplify the process of consuming or building client applications for Web Services. If you are using Visual Studio .NET, some of these tools won't be necessary to use because Visual Studio .NET has most of these command-line tools built into the IDE.

What Should I Use—WSDL.exe or SoapSuds.exe?

If you are having problems using the WSDL.exe tool to generate a proxy class for you, try using the Soapsuds.exe program. Because SOAP and remoting are basically the same thing, the Soapsuds tool also can generate the source code to communicate with the Web Service.

Soapsuds.exe

The Soapsuds tool helps you compile client applications that communicate with Web Services using a technique called remoting. Soapsuds.exe performs the following functions:

- It creates XML schemas describing services exposed in a common language runtime assembly.
- It creates runtime assemblies to access services described by XML schemas. A schema definition can be a local file, or it can be dynamically downloaded from the Internet.

WSDL.exe

The Web Services Description Language tool generates code for ASP.NET Web Services and Web Service clients from WSDL contract files, XSD schemas, and .discomap discovery documents.

Web Service Descriptor Language

The WSDL file provides you with all the necessary interface information to consume a Web Service. One problem that you might run into is that there are different versions of WSDL floating around. So far, the latest version is WSDL 1.1, but we'll take a look here at how these differences can affect your client's communication with the Web Service.

Many sites on the web promote Web Services, but if you try to run the WSDL.exe tool to generate a proxy stub for yourself, it might give you one of many errors. This is because there are several versions of WSDL or SDL or even SDC. The WSDL tool is designed to work with wsdl 1.1. If you try to use the WSDL.exe tool on a WSDL file and it gives you an error, that is probably because the files versions are different.

Errors While Using WSDL.exe

One of the most common problems that you might run into involves trying to generate the proxy code for a remote Web Service. Because this is an evolving technology, people are building Web Services and putting them on the web as fast as they can make them. This is great in some cases because this provides developers with many consumable resources. But, on the flip side, the technology and standards for SOAP are evolving just as fast. As soon as you get a new Web Service out there, a newer version of the standard might have been released. So now there is the issue of different formats (SDC, SDL, WSDL-1.0/1.1) floating around on the web.

Universal Discovery Descriptor Interface (UDDI)

You will start to run into the Universal Discovery Descriptor Interface (UDDI) more often. This is yet another new standard being developed for SOAP-enabled users to find and use other SOAP-enabled users—or, more likely, businesses. The best way to look at UDDI is as the Yellow Pages for Web Services.

Basic Web Services Debugging

As with any program, you can use some common methods, no matter what type of environment you are in. The most basic of these involves logging all your debugging information to a file that can be reviewed later. Because the Web Service has very little interaction with the user interface, this is one approach to take. The other approach is to build your own exception class that you can customize. Then, whenever an error occurs ,you can throw your custom exception.

Common SOAP Errors

You might encounter this common error:

```
The underlying connection was closed: Unable to connect to the remote server."
```

This is typically the result of problems on the network, not necessarily in your code. But don't rule out your code—have someone else look at it to see if you have over-looked something. A second pair of eyes is always beneficial.

Another error is the SoapException error, which looks like this:

```
The request reached the server machine, but was not processed successfully.
```

If you run into this one, you might be wondering, what wasn't processed successfully? Why didn't it tell me what wasn't processed? If you are using the standard exception class to handle errors, you could be missing out on some important information provide by the SoapException class. Let's take a closer look at this class in the next section.

Getting the Most Out of *SoapException*

Up to this point, you have looked at various problems that might arise and learned how to work around them. But one of the key elements of debugging Web Services is the SoapException class. Not only does the class handle exceptions that were thrown, but, within the properties of the exception, there are some very useful pieces of data that can help to identify what the problem is.

Take a look at Listings 13.28 and 13.29 to see how you can use the SoapException class to catch errors.

Listing 13.28   **Using *SoapException* (C#)**

```csharp
private void Button2_Click(object sender, System.EventArgs e)
            {
                try
                {
                    localhost.Service1 s = new
                    ➥localhost.Service1();
                    s.HelloWorld(2);//This will throw an exception



                }
                catch(SoapException ex)
                {
                    //Display the main message
                    TextBox2.Text = ex.Message;

                    //Get any additional detailed information
                    System.Xml.XmlNode xn = ex.Detail;

                    //How many Attributes are there
                    TextBox3.Text = xn.Attributes.Count.ToString();

                    //The name of the app or object that caused
                    ➥the problem
    TextBox4.Text = ex.Source;

                    //Display the piece of code that caused the problem
```

continues

Listing 13.28 **Continued**

```
TextBox5.Text = ex.Actor;

                        //Get the type of SOAP fault code
                        System.Xml.XmlQualifiedName qn = ex.Code;

                        //Get the XML qualified name
                        TextBox6.Text = qn.Name;

                        //Get the XML namespace
                        TextBox7.Text = qn.Namespace;

                        //Get the method that throws the exception
                        System.Reflection.MethodBase r = ex.TargetSite;

                        System.Type st = r.DeclaringType;

                        //Get the assembly name where the exception
                        ➥came from
TextBox8.Text = st.AssemblyQualifiedName;



                }



        }
```

Listing 13.29 **Using** *SoapException* **(Visual Basic .NET)**

```
Private Sub Button2_Click(ByVal sender As Object, ByVal e As
System.EventArgs)

    Try

        localhost.Service1(s = New localhost.Service1())
        s.HelloWorld(2) 'This will throw an exception



        catch(SoapException ex)
```

```vb
        'Display the main message
TextBox2.Text = ex.Message

        'Get any additional detailed information
        System.Xml.XmlNode(xn = ex.Detail)

        'How many Attributes are there
        TextBox3.Text = xn.Attributes.Count.ToString()

        The name of the app or object that caused the problem
        ➥TextBox4.Text = ex.Source

        'Display the piece of code that caused the problem
        ➥TextBox5.Text = ex.Actor

        'Get the type of SOAP fault code
        Dim qn As System.Xml.XmlQualifiedName
        qn = ex.Code

        'Get the XML qualified name
        TextBox6.Text = qn.Name

        'Get the XML namespace
        TextBox7.Text = qn.Namespace

        'Get the method that throws the exception
        Dim r As System.Reflection.MethodBase
        r = ex.TargetSite

        Dim st As System.Type
        st = r.DeclaringType

        'Get the assembly name where the exection came from
        ➥TextBox8.Text = st.AssemblyQualifiedName
    End Try

End Sub
```

Listings 13.28 and 13.29 demonstrate how to extract the additional elements that are part of the `SoapException` class. These additional properties could help you identify the problem, either directly or indirectly.

Problems Deploying Your Web Service?

When you are ready to deploy your Web Service, there is not very much that you need to do. But you still might run into some problems. After you have developed you Web Service, copy all the files and subdirectories to the server that the service will be hosted on. One of the first things that you should check is that the .NET framework is installed on the server where you are deploying your Web Service. If it is not on that server, your Web Service will not work.

Summary

Web Services are an exciting new development in the distributed application space. As you can see, creating a Web Service can be very simple, but as soon as you start to push the limits of the technology, you need to roll up your sleeves and do the rest of the work. This becomes more apparent when you start trying to return complex structures of data such as `FileStreams` and `DirectoryInfo` objects. Many components can be serialized into XML, but that's not true for everything yet. You have to admit that Microsoft has done a good job so far, though. If you really look at the amount of work that must have been put into .NET to make all of this work, it is really astonishing.

In Chapter 14 we move on into debugging of the .NET components.

14

Debugging .NET Components
and HttpHandlers

COMPONENTS ARE THE HEART OF THE .NET framework. Sooner or later you will need to create a component to accomplish a unique task. But how do you debug a component? Let's take a look at some techniques that you can use and some common pitfalls that you might run into.

The Component

You'll start by creating a simple component with a method that returns the date. This is the minimal amount of code to create a basic component in the .NET framework. As you look at the listings that follow, take notice of which class was inherited, and keep your eyes open for areas in the code that use the `Container` class; this plays an important role in a component. Also take a closer look at the `ComponentModel` namespace—this will give you a better idea of the core pieces that make up a component, not just a class (See Listings 14.1 and 14.2).

Listing 14.1   **Basic Component (C#)**

```csharp
using System;
using System.ComponentModel;
using System.Collections;
using System.Diagnostics;

namespace WebProject1
{
    /// <summary>
    /// Summary description for DateStuff.
    /// </summary>
    public class DateStuff : System.ComponentModel.Component
    {
        /// <summary>
        /// Required designer variable.
        /// </summary>
        private System.ComponentModel.Container components = null;

        public DateStuff(System.ComponentModel.IContainer container)
        {
        /// <summary>
        /// Required for Windows.Forms Class Composition Designer
        ➥support
        /// </summary>
            container.Add(this);
            InitializeComponent();

        //
        // TODO: Add any constructor code after InitializeComponent
        ➥call
        //
        }

        public DateStuff()
        {
        /// <summary>
        /// Required for Windows.Forms Class Composition Designer
        ➥support
        /// </summary>
        InitializeComponent();

          // TODO: Add any constructor code after InitializeComponent
          ➥call
```

```
        }

        /// <summary>
        /// Required method for Designer support - do not modify
        /// the contents of this method with the code editor.
        /// </summary>
        private void InitializeComponent()
        {
            components = new System.ComponentModel.Container();
        }

        public string GetToday()
        {
            return DateTime.Now.ToString();
        }
    }
}
```

Listing 14.2 **Basic Component (Visual Basic .NET)**

```
Public Class getdate
    Inherits System.ComponentModel.Component


    Public Overloads Sub New(Container As System.ComponentModel.IContainer)
        MyClass.New()

        'Required for Windows.Forms Class Composition Designer support
        Container.Add(me)
    End Sub

    Public Overloads Sub New()
        MyBase.New()

        'This call is required by the Component Designer.
        InitializeComponent()

        'Add any initialization after the InitializeComponent() call

    End Sub
```

continues

Listing 14.2   **Continued**

```
'Required by the Component Designer
Private components As System.ComponentModel.Container

'NOTE: The following procedure is required by the Component Designer
'It can be modified using the Component Designer.
'Do not modify it using the code editor.
<System.Diagnostics.DebuggerStepThrough()> Private Sub
➥InitializeComponent()
    components = New System.ComponentModel.Container()
End Sub


Public Function GetDate() As String
    GetDate = DateTime.Now

End Function
End Class
```

Added in this component is a simple method to return today's date and time in a string. It's not much, but it's a start for now.

You can use several different classes in the System.Diagnostic namespace, including Stacktrace, Tracing, the gui-debugger, Debug, and Debugger. Let's take a look at how you can use these classes to help track down bugs.

If you are working on the server in which the component is running, then you can use the Debugger class. The Debugger class enables you to see whether your process is attached to an existing debugger. If your process is already attached to an instance of a debugger, then there is no need for you to start a new instance; just use the existing one. Otherwise, start a new instance of the debugger and then step through your code using that instance. Next you'll look at how you can use this in your code. Here is a sample of how to check whether the process is already attached to a debugger. If it is not, then you can start the debugger and begin stepping through the process (See Listings 14.3 and 14.4).

Listing 14.3   **Check for Existing Debugger (C#)**

```
//Check to see if this process is attached to a debugger
if (Debugger.IsAttached()== False)
{
    //Check if debugger started successfully
    if (Debugger.Launch() == True)
        {
```

```
                   //The debugger was started successfully
}
      else
          {
          //There was a problem launching the debugger
          }
}
else
      {
      //the process is currently attached to a debugger
      }
```

Listing 14.4   **Check for Existing Debugger (Visual Basic .NET)**

```
Dim db As New Debugger()

'Check if this process is attached to a debugger

      If Not db.IsAttached Then

            'Now start a new debugger instance for this process

            If db.Launch Then

                'The debugger was successfully started

            Else if
                  'There was an error launching the debugger
            End If

            Else
                  'The debugger is already attached to this process
      End If
```

Another very useful class is StackTrace, which enables you to look at the stack frame by frame, or by each step that has been executed. Now two different StackTrace components can be used. System.Diagnostic.StackTrace can be used only if an exception is thrown. If you want to look at the stack before an exception is thrown or just to see what is going on, then you need to use the System.Environment.StackTrace method. This method returns a string that represents the stack. If you need more information, you can use the Stack Trace class in the

System.Diagnostic namespace because it enables you to dig deeper into the stack. The
`Environment` class has some great features that you can use to look at the system's
environment before an exception occurs.

Next we'll cover a few more features that are useful in debugging. Listings 14.5 and
14.6 provide a couple of simple examples of how you can implement this into your
code.

Listing 14.5 **Stack Trace Dump (C#)**

```
Using System;
  string stackdump;
        stackdump = Environment.StackTrace;
        Response.Write(stackdump);
```

Listing 14.6 **Stack Trace Dump (Visual Basic .NET)**

```
Imports System
Dim stackdump As String
        stackdump = Environment.StackTrace()
        Response.Write(stackdump)
```

Now if an exception is thrown, you will probably want to use the
`System.Diagnostics.StackTrace` class. This class works differently than the
Environment Class: you get the `StackTrace` and then navigate through the stack frame
by frame. Take a look at Listings 14.7 and 14.8 to see how to accomplish this.

Listing 14.7 **Get Each Stack Frame (C#)**

```
            try
              {
                    int a=0;
                    int b=1;
                    int c;
                    c = b/a;

                    Response.Write (c);
              }
          catch(Exception ex)
                {
StackFrame sf;
int i;
StackTrace st = new StackTrace();
                for (i = 1; i < st.FrameCount;i++)
```

```
            {
                    sf = st.GetFrame(i);
                    Response.Write (sf);
                    Response.Write ("<BR>");

            }

        }
```

Listing 14.8 **Get Each Stack Frame (Visual Basic .NET)**

```
Try

            Dim a = 0
            Dim b = 1
            Dim c As Integer

            c = b / a
Catch
Dim sf as StackFrame
Dim I as integer
Dim st = new StackTrace()
            for i = 1 to st.FrameCount

                    sf = st.GetFrame(i)
                    Response.Write (sf)
                    Response.Write ("<BR>")

            Next
End Try
```

Several specific pieces of information can be extracted through the
`System.Diagnostic.StackTrace` class by exposing a frame of the stack and information
such as the filename, method, line number, offset, and several other bits of information.

One particular piece of information that you can extract is the method that your
process is currently in. As you jump from function to function, you can keep tabs on
what is being executed. Listings 14.9 and 14.10 both show examples of how this could
be used.

Listing 14.9   **Stack Frame GetMethod (C#)**

```csharp
private void Page_Load(object sender, System.EventArgs e)
{
        // Put user code to initialize the page here
        StackFrame sf = new StackFrame();

        Response.Write(sf.GetMethod());
        Response.Write("<BR>");
        Method2();
}
private void Method2()
{
        StackFrame sf = new StackFrame();
        Response.Write(sf.GetMethod());
}
```

Listing 14.10   **Stack Frame GetMethod (Visual Basic .NET)**

```vbnet
Private sub Page_Load(ByVal sender As System.Object, ByVal e As
➥System.EventArgs)

        ' Put user code to initialize the page here
        Dim sf as new StackFrame()

        Response.Write(sf.GetMethod())
        Response.Write("<BR>")
        Method2()
end sub
private sub Method2()

        Dim sf as new StackFrame()
        Response.Write(sf.GetMethod())
end sub
```

Here's the output you would see from both listings:

```
Void Page_Load(System.Object, System.EventArgs)
Void Method2()
```

As you can see, as the system steps from one function to another, you can keep tabs on what the process is doing. The previous example shows this in the Page_Load method of the aspx page, but it doesn't have to stop there; you can use the functionality in components, services, or Windows applications. Because `StackTrace` and `StackFrame` are part of the System.Diagnostics namespace, these tools can be used pretty much anywhere you need them.

A good example of where to use a stack trace is inside your component. Let's say that you created a component, and whenever you tried to instantiate it, the component throws an exception. Now because the constructor does quite a bit of work, it could be having problems in several places. Let's take a look at Listing 14.11, which shows a scenario in which the stack trace would come in handy.

Listing 14.11   **Pseudocode Example (C#)**

```
public UserActivity(String userX)
        {
                InitializeComponent();
                try
                {
                        //Open a connection to the database
OpenDBConnection();
                        //Open and read our own XML configuration file
                        ReadXMLConfigFile();
//Update the database to show userX has entered a
secure area
UpdateDB();
                }
                catch(Exception ex)
                {
                        Debug.WriteLine(ex.StackTrace);
                }
        }
```

If there was a problem during the creation of this component, this would catch it and write the stack trace to the debug listener. In this particular case, the `ReadXMLConfigFile` function was incapable of opening the file to read it.

You might have noticed that the previous example used the `Debug.Writeline` method. Let's take a closer look at how you can use this method to write to the console or to a file. This can be a tremendous help, especially if you are debugging your components on a remote system (which is most likely what most people will be doing).

A few more useful methods in the `Debug` class are `Writeif`, `Write`, and `Writelineif`. These methods enable you the write to a file or listener, with or without conditions applied. This is great for checking whether a variable falls within the required parameters that you need. If not, you have the option to write to the Listener with the `Writeif` or `Writelineif` method.

The only difference between the Write and Writeline methods is that the Writeline method adds a line terminator, whereas the Write function does not. The use of these methods is illustrated in Listings 14.12 and 14.13.

Listing 14.12 **Debug WriteLineIf example (C#)**

```
public int mydivide( int x , int y)
      {
            int z;
//x= -5
            //y = 100
            //if x < 0 then I want to see the value of x
            //to get an idea of what is happening
            Debug.WriteLineIf(x<0,"x was less than 1 which is BAD: x="+ x );
            z = x/y;
Return z;
      }
```

Listing 14.13 **Debug WriteLineIf example (Visual Basic .NET)**

```
public function mydivide( x as integer , y as integer) as int

            'x= -5
            'y = 100
            'if x < 0 then I want to see the value of x
'to get an idea of what is  happening           Debug.WriteLineIf(x<0,"x
➡was less  than 1 which is BAD: x="+ x )
            z = x/y
            Mydivide = z
End function
```

These methods are very useful if you need to check the condition or state of your variables before writing to the listener. You can also write your debug output to a file as shown in Listings 14.14 and 14.15.

Listing 14.14 **Trace Listener Example (C#)**

```
using System.Diagnostics;
using System.IO;

Debug.Listeners.Add(new
TextWriterTraceListener(File.Create("c:\\debug_output.txt")));
```

```
Debug.Write("Debug output on Page Load");
Debug.Flush();
Debug.Close();
```

Listing 14.15 **Trace Listener Example (Visual Basic .NET)**

```
Imports System.Diagnostics
Imports System.IO

Debug.Listeners.Add(new
TextWriterTraceListener(File.Create("c:\debug_output.txt")))

        Debug.Write("Debug output on Page Load")
        Debug.Flush()
        Debug.Close()
```

If you are writing your debug output to a file, you might come across the following message:

```
The process cannot access the file "c:\debug_output.txt" because it is being used
➥by another process.
```

This message is displayed because the file is still open and is being used by another application or process. This can occur if you don't flush and close your listener. If you fail to do this, you have only accomplished creating a new file and opening it. None of your debug write statements have been sent to the file yet. One way to avoid this is set the AutoFlush property to True when you create your Debug object. Or, as in Listing 14.16, in your Web.Config file you can set the AutoFlush to true by default. This way, you don't have to call the flush method every time you want the contents of the listener to be written to the file. However, you still need to call the close method to close the file as illustrated in Listing 14.16.

Listing 14.16 **Web.config**

```
<configuration>
    <system.diagnostics>
        <debug autoflush="true" />
    </system.diagnostics>
</configuration>
```

Interfaces

Interfaces provide you, the developer, with the most basic of functionality to build upon. All interfaces in the .NET framework are identified with a capital letter *I* at the beginning of the interface class name. If you plan to develop interfaces, you should follow this naming convention. You should consider a few items when developing your own interfaces.

Interfaces can be made from the following types:

- Nested types
- Static members
- Virtual members
- Abstract members
- Properties
- Events

You also should consider a few rules when designing interfaces. The following list of restrictions applies to interfaces:

- Any interface members must have public accessibility.
- Security permissions cannot be attached to the interface or its members.
- Interfaces cannot instance constructors, but they can define class constructors.

The following list includes some of the common interfaces that you might see in some of the components that you use when debugging your web page or building a component. This is just a sample of what is out there. Before you start developing your own components, take a look at a few of these and see what these classes are doing; you might be surprised to find that not a lot is happening in these classes. Still, look at how they provide a strong foundation to build upon.

- IConfigurationSectionHandler
- ICollection
- IHttpAsyncHandler
- IHttpHandler
- IHttpHandlerFactory
- IComponent
- IServiceProvider

In the next section, you will learn how IHttpHandler is used through the HttpHandler component. Also, if you dig deep enough, you will notice that the IComponent and ICollection interfaces are used under the hood.

HttpHandlers

If you have ever programmed in Java and used Struts, then this is very much the same idea. If you haven't used Struts but are more familiar with ISAPI extensions, it's very similar.

HttpHandlers are very cool! You can do some wicked things with custom handlers. So now that we have gotten you all worked up, we had better deliver the goods. First, take a look at how handlers work.

HttpHandlers map incoming URL requests to an HttpHandler class. This is accomplished by modifying the httphandlers section of the Web.config file. This is where you tell the system to map requests to a specific HttpHandler class. Let's break down the important items here.

First, you should identify the parts of the HttpHandler section. Three subtags exist under the HttpHandler section: Add, Remove, and Clear. Table 14.1 provides a description of each subtag.

Table 14.1 **Subtags in the *HttpHandler* Section**

Subtag	Description
<add>	pecifies verb/path mapping to an IHttpHandler or IHttpHandlerFactory class.
<remove>	Removes a verb/path mapping to an IHttpHandler class. The <remove> directive must exactly match the verb/path combination of a previous <add> directive. Wildcards are not supported.
<clear>	Removes all IHttpHandler mappings currently configured or inherited by the specified Web.config file.

With the <add> and <remove> subtags, you can affect specific HttpHandlers. If you just want to remove all handlers, use the <clear> subtag.

Now you can take a closer look at what you need to do to implement your own HttpHandler class. First, you need to add a line to the Web.config file to tell it what to do when it receives a request and which HttpHandler to use. You'll look at using the <add> subtag to accomplish this first step.

The verb identifies if it is a Post or Get, using * for both.

> Verb: verb list ("GET,POST,*")

The path tells the system what specific page or type of page to map the HttpHandler to. This is great because it gives you the capability to map a different HttpHandler for every page, if needed. The potential for this is huge if you step back and look at the big picture. Pay attention to how you configure the path. If you set it up to *.aspx, remember that it will intercept all requests for aspx pages.

> Path: path/wildcard

The next item that needs to be identified is the type. This is where the namespace and class that will be used to handle the request are defined. This is the final item needed to tell the server what component will handle this request.

Type: [Namespace].[Class],[Assembly name]

Listing 14.17 shows what the actual web.config file would look like if you mapped all requests for the MyHandle.aspx page.

Listing 14.17   **<httphandlers> section in Web.Config**

```
<configuration>
    <httphandlers>
<add verb="*" path="MyHandler.aspx" type="MyHttpHandler.MyHandler,
MyHandler" />
    </httphandlers>
</configuration>
```

This is a great feature for creating custom HttpHandlers to intercept specific types of requests and then handle each request with special functionality. This is also an ideal feature for debugging, using filters, and completing a number of other tasks. Let's look at how a request to MyHandler.aspx is intercepted and handled (see Listings 14.18 and 14.19).

Listing 14.18   **Simple HttpHandler class C#**

```
using System;
using System.Web;

namespace MyHttpHandler
{
    public class MyHandler: IHttpHandler
    {

        public void ProcessRequest(HttpContext context)
        {
            context.Response.Write("My HttpHandler");
        }

        public bool IsReusable
        {
            get { return true; }
        }
    }
}
```

Listing 14.19   **Simple HttpHandler class Visual Basic .NET**

```vb
Imports System
Imports System.Web

Namespace MyHttpHandler

    Public Class MyHandler
        Implements IHttpHandler

        ' Override the ProcessRequest method.
        Public Sub ProcessRequest(context As HttpContext) _
        Implements IHttpHandler.ProcessRequest

            context.Response.Write("My HttpHandler")

        End Sub

        ' Override the IsReusable property.
        Public ReadOnly Property IsReusable() As Boolean _
        Implements IHttpHandler.IsReusable

            Get
                Return True
            End Get

        End Property
    End Class
End Namespace
```

Notice that the ProcessRequest method is the point at which you intercept the requests being made to MyHandler.aspx. If you are looking for that page, it doesn't exist. It is a fictitious page; you could create a complete website without one single aspx, html, htm, asp, or any other physical page. You would just have virtual pages, in a manner of speaking.

The other item of importance is the HttpContext that is passed in. This gives you access to all the server components—Request, Response, Session, and Server. With access to these components, you can do anything in an HttpHandler that you could do on an aspx page.

State-Management Issues

State management is an important issue whenever you are designing large-scale websites. Most system designs tend to shy away from maintaining any state on their websites because of the complexities involved when scaling out. Let's take a look at the issues that seem to come up repeatedly.

What Are the Issues?

Scalability is a common issue when designing websites. You can use ASP session state on a web farm in a number of ways. Many companies use routers that use sticky IP, to make sure that each request from a user is routed to the right server and to ensure that session information can be maintained. This seems like a costly method to be able to maintain session state.

The current limitations with ASP session state revolve around three areas:

- Host dependence
- Scalability limitations
- Cookie dependence

To use session state, a user must return to the same host or computer where the information is maintained because this information is maintained in memory and is directly related to the process that it is running.

This brings up the next point: scalability limitations. If the session state is maintained in memory, how can you scale up to handle more traffic? You could always throw more hardware at it, but for how long and at what cost? The preferred method is to use a server farm and some sort of load-balancing appliance, such as Big 5 or Cisco's Load Director. With this type of setup, the load-balancing appliance will distribute the request to the servers with the least amount of load. Just by adding one server, you can cut the load on your website in half. Not only have you decreased the load, but you also now have fault tolerance designed into your architecture.

Now we get to the cookies issue. Without cookies enabled, session states are very difficult to implement. This is not necessarily such a terrible problem, but it's one that should be addressed.

ASP.NET Session State

Let's look at the three issues identified previously in the light of ASP.NET's solution.

Microsoft has solved these problems in ASP.NET by separating the session state into two different modes: in-process and out-of-process. In-process is the old method of state management, and out-of-process is new to .NET.

Why is Microsoft telling you that session variables are okay to use in a scalable architecture? With Microsoft's new .NET Framework, you can use session states in a server farm. How is this possible? Microsoft has added alternative session-management solutions. In addition to the existing session-state management, two more ways exist to manage session data. Now you can store the user's session data in memory on a shared server, and you can store the information in SQL server 7.x or 2000 as well. Take a look at where all this is configured. In the Web.Config file, you will have a section that looks similar to Listing 14.20.

Listing 14.20 **Web.config**

```
<configuration>
    <system.web>

<sessionState
            mode="SqlServer"
            stateConnectionString="tcpip=127.0.0.1:42424"
            sqlConnectionString="data source=127.0.0.1;user
id=sstate;password="
            cookieless="false"
            timeout="20"
        />
    </system.web>
</configuration>
```

If you look at the sessionState section in this listing, you will notice that the web server has been set up to maintain session information in a SQL server database. (One thing to keep in mind when using the SqlServer mode is that you shouldn't use the system administrator account.) Next, you'll take a more detailed look at the parameters that are used in the Session State section.

Session State Section Parameters

Looking at all the parameters used in the session-state section will help you to identify some of the additional features that have been added to the .NET framework. Table 14.2 lists all the available attributes and parameters for the Session State section.

Table 14.2 **Session State Attributes**

Attribute	Option	Description
mode		Specifies where to store the session state.
	Off	Indicates that session state is not enabled.
	Inproc	Indicates that session state is stored locally.
	StateServer	Indicates that session state is stored on a remote server.
	SqlServer	Indicates that session state is stored on a SQL server.
cookieless		Specifies whether sessions without cookies should be used to identify client sessions.
	true	Indicates that sessions without cookies should be used.

continues

Table 14.2 **Continued**

Attribute	Option	Description
	`false`	Indicates that sessions without cookies should not be used. The default is `false`.
`timeout`		Specifies the number of minutes that a session can be idle before it is abandoned. The default is `20`.
`connectionString`		Specifies the server name and port where session state is stored remotely—for example, `127.0.0.1:42424`. This attribute is required when `mode` is set to `StateServer`.
`sqlConnectionString`		Specifies the connection string for a SQL server—for example, `data source=127.0.0.1;user id=sa; password=`. This attribute is required when `mode` is set to `SqlServer`.

Performance and Reliability Considerations with ASP.NET Session-State Modes

When you're building a website, two items should always be at the top of your list: performance and reliability. If your site is slow, no one is going to want to take the time to navigate through it. If your site is down or constantly producing errors, then your customers will find what they need somewhere else. Let's look at session-state modes with these concepts in mind.

In-Process

If you have a small website and don't plan to scale up, this is the fastest, most common method of maintaining a session state. If you use this mode, the client must always return the original web server in which it made its first request. This is because the session information is stored in memory, on the server from which it made the request. This mode is best suited for a single server.

Out-of-Process

If you are looking for a more scalable solution without losing too much performance, then out-of-process mode will be better suited for your architecture. You still get the benefit of maintaining the session-state information in memory, but it is stored on a separate process, which is shared by all your web servers in a web farm. One thing that you might want to consider, though, is what happens if the server that maintains the out-of-process session data goes down?

SQL Server 7.*x* and 2000

If performance is not your top priority and you're more concerned with reliability, this is your best solution. Because all the session data is maintained in a SQL server, your data is stored in a persistent location. What if the server fails? You can set up the SQL server in a clustered solution for redundancy. Granted, this solution involves a lot more overhead, but it is definitely the most reliable.

Required Location for Web.config File

One problem that you might run into is that the session state section in the Web.config file can exist only in the root of the web application. This does not apply to all the settings, but a few must be in the root file.

These new options are great and open up a whole area of functionality that was once considered taboo. Just remember not to go overboard with session data; it still has to be maintained somewhere, whether it is in local memory or remotely. This is data that is either taking up memory or being marshaled back and forth between computers.

.NET Components Versus Registered COM Components

So what is so different about .NET components and COM components? Does DLL Hell ring any bells? This problem is eliminated with .NET components. You no longer have to register your DLL on the server to use it; you just need to copy it to your \bin directory to be executed.

COM components need to be registered in the registry, whereas .NET components only need to be placed in the \bin directory. Another notable point is that assemblies used by several applications on a machine should be stored in the global assembly cache. If an assembly will be stored in the global cache, the assembly must have strong names.

Now let's look at a breakdown of the differences between .NET components and COM components.

Table 14.3 **.NET Comparison to COM**

Characteristics	.NET	COM
Does not require a Registry entry	X	
Is self-describing	X	
Compiles to a binary	X	X
Exposes interfaces	X	X
Uses Xcopy installation	X	
Runs parallel versions	X	
Requires RegSrvr32		X

After this comparison, it looks like .NET has all the benefits of COM, without the hassles. Some of the characteristics might not seem to be a big deal, but others, such as not having to register your managed components, take a huge burden off the developers.

Granted, there are still circumstances in which you have to register your component. We'll be covering this in the next section.

Using Interop to Work with Unmanaged COM Components

.NET does provide a way for managed code to work with unmanaged COM objects. If you are looking to use a COM component in your .NET project, you must use the COM Interop utility (TlbImp.exe) for importing the COM types. This exposes the necessary interfaces to allow them to communicate with each other.

If you want to use your .NET components in an unmanaged project, you can do so with a few extra steps. You need to mimic a typical COM object and how it operates. To do this, use RegAsm.exe. This does two things. First, it exports the managed types into a type library. Second, it puts the information in the registry, as with all other COM objects. This gives your .NET component the capability to imitate a COM object. Otherwise, there is no bridge to communicate from the unmanaged process to the managed process.

COM Component Issues

Surely you have run across one or more of the following issues when trying to debug a new or changed COM object. We'll tackle some issues and solutions here.

Security Issues with Components

You should be asking yourself some common questions when working with any component:

- Where is the component running? Is it local or on a remote system? If it's remote, is the component configured properly to run on the remote computer?

- Is the component accessing other services of the operating system or network? Does the component need to write a file to a directory that has been secured to only a specific group or user? Are you trying to create a network connection to another computer?

- When the component is running as a service, who is the component logged in as? Does the login have all the rights to perform the needed tasks?

One of the annoying tasks of working with COM components is keeping track of references made to the component and making sure that you clean up and release any memory or objects you that have used. This is no longer an issue in the .NET framework because memory management is handled for you.

.NET Components

Microsoft has taken some of the nifty features of Visual Basic and carried them over to the .NET framework. One of these features is memory management. You no longer have to release or dereference your components because the garbage collector will handle it for you.

Garbage Collection

Garbage collection is not new to Visual Basic, but it is new to C#. Although the previous versions of garbage collection might not have been as robust as desired, it looks as if Microsoft has enhanced the process of cleaning up.

The Registry

Now with .NET there is no need to register your component in the registry to use it—with one exception. If you plan to have an existing COM component or a new COM object call in your .NET component, you will need to register your component with the registry. This way, the other COM objects know how to communicate with your component.

Installing a .NET Component Versus a COM Component

One of our favorite things about .NET is how to install and upgrade components. Unlike installing (or, even worse, upgrading) a COM component, this process is simple and straightforward.

So How Do You Install a New .NET Component?

You no longer need to use Regsrv32.exe for .NET components, but you still need to use it for COM components. The only thing that you need to do to install a new or updated version of your .NET component is use Xcopy.exe or your preferred method of copying a file from one location to another. .NET components are self-describing; when a component is running, it makes a copy of itself. Thus, you can copy right over the old version without having to deal with the file being locked by another user because it is in use at the time.

Uninstalling Components

Typical problems with COM components have to do with upgrading them. This involves deregistering the COM object and then deleting it to replace it with the new version. To do this, the COM object typically needs to be deregistered and removed from memory. To do this, you'll end up restarting the web service or computer, depending on what the COM object is being used by.

Another annoying issue is that you must execute this on the computer on which the component is installed. This usually means that you have to be logged onto the system or must be using some sort of remote-control software.

Well, you can kiss all these problems goodbye. Microsoft has finally given you a way to get around these problems. Now the only thing that needs to be done is to copy the new component to your \bin directory, essentially overwriting the old component (assuming that one already exists) and replacing it with the new one. Wow! That wasn't very hard. Because the system will detect that the component is newer, it will release the old copy and load the new version into memory. Presto, change-o—now your system is running with your new component. No need to deregister the old component and register the new one. It couldn't be easier.

One thing to keep in mind is that this technique applies to managed components only. If your component is using the Interop namespace because it needs to simulate a COM object, then you will still have to register your component in the registry as you would any COM component.

Summary

Microsoft has built many cool new features into the .NET framework to help developers. In this chapter, you learned how using components can help in cleaning up your garbage when you are finished with a component. You also learned how the stack trace classes can help you determine where a bug could be coming from, no matter how deep in the code it might be buried. Two more important sections in this chapter addressed the additional features for state management in .NET and showed how managed components are self-describing, which saves developers from having to register them in the registry.

We covered a lot of ground in this chapter, and it is up to you to take it to the next level. Use some of these examples to get a jump-start on debugging your components. Remember, the majority of component issues revolve around containment and cleanup; just keep this in mind when you are developing your component.

15

COM+ Issues

MICROSOFT HAS CONTINUED TO ENHANCE THIS COMPONENT software technology. First there was OLE, then it evolved to COM, and now there's COM+. So much of Microsoft's platform has been built on these technologies that you always have needed to interact with some sort of COM or COM+ component. Now Microsoft is evolving again, and this time the technology is called .NET. Because the .NET framework is new, there needs to be a bridge to COM+ functionality. This bridging brings its own set of issues, and we'll look at those issues in this chapter.

Role-Based Security

Security roles can be supported at the method, class, assembly, and interface levels. As you start to implement different levels of security, you will start to see the power of role-based security. Often in the development process, people look for ways to reuse components. One way to accomplish this is to use the same components but restrict access to portions of the information based on what role the users are in.

As an example, roles would be useful in an application used by stockbrokers. The application might restrict the type of transaction being processed, depending on whether the user is a stockbroker or a manager. Stockbrokers might have authorization to purchase only 1,000 shares of stock, whereas the managers might have an unlimited amount available to them.

Role-based security also can be used when an application requires multiple actions to complete the process. One example is a purchasing system that enables a customer representative to generate a purchase request but that allows only a supervisor to authorize that request, which then becomes a purchase order.

Take a look at Listings 15.1 and 15.2, which use role-based security, to get an idea of what is involved and where you might run into problems.

Listing 15.1   **Simple Role-Based Security (C#)**

```
using System;
using System.Reflection;
using System.Windows.Forms;
using System.EnterpriseServices;


// The ApplicationName attribute specifies the name of the
// COM+ Application that will hold assembly components
[assembly: ApplicationName("RoleBasedApp")]


// The ApplicationActivation.ActivationOption attribute specifies
// where assembly components are loaded on activation
// Library : components run in the creator's process
// Server : components run in a system process, dllhost.exe
[assembly: ApplicationActivation(ActivationOption.Server)]


// AssemblyKeyFile specifies the name of the strong key
// that will be used to sign the assembly.
// The .snk file can be generated with sn.exe from the command prompt

  [assembly: AssemblyKeyFile("RolebasedKey.snk")]



// ApplicationAccessControl is a COM+ security attribute that
// enables and configures application-level COM+ security
// The attribute maps to the Securities tab in a COM+
// application properties page
[assembly: ApplicationAccessControl]


namespace RoleBasedSecurity
{
    // ComponentAccessControl enables security checking
    // at the component level. The attribute maps to the
    // securities tab in a component within a COM+ application
```

```
[ComponentAccessControl]

// SetEveryoneAccess(true) indicates we
// we want the role to be populated with 'Everyone' when created
[SecurityRole("EveryoneRole", SetEveryoneAccess = true)]

public class MySecurityObject : ServicedComponent
{
    public bool IsCallerInRole()
    {
        // Check if the user is in the role
        return ContextUtil.IsCallerInRole("SecurityAppDeveloper");

    }

    public string GetCallerAccountName()
    {
        string ret = "Caller Unknown";

        if (ContextUtil.IsSecurityEnabled)
        {
            SecurityCallContext sec;

            // get a handle to the context of the current caller
            sec = SecurityCallContext.CurrentCall;

            // get the current caller account name
            ret = sec.DirectCaller.AccountName;
        }

        return ret;
    }
}
}
```

Listing 15.2 **Simple Role-Based Security (Visual Basic .NET)**

```
Imports System
Imports System.Reflection
Imports System.Windows.Forms
Imports System.EnterpriseServices
```

continues

Listing 15.2 **Continued**

```
' The ApplicationName attribute specifies the name of the
' COM+ Application that will hold assembly components
<Assembly: ApplicationName("RoleBasedApp")>


' the ApplicationActivation.ActivationOption attribute specifies
' where assembly components are loaded on activation
' Library : components run in the creator's process
' Server : components run in a system process, dllhost.exe

<Assembly: ApplicationActivation(ActivationOption.Server)>


' AssemblyKeyFile specifies the name of the strong key
' that will be used to sign the assembly.
' The .snk file was generated with sn.exe

<Assembly: AssemblyKeyFile("RolebasedKey.snk")>

' ApplicationAccessControl is a COM+ security attribute that
' enables and configures application-level COM+ security
' The attribute maps to the Securities tab in a COM+
' application properties page

<Assembly: ApplicationAccessControl()>


Namespace RoleBasedSecurity

    ' ComponentAccessControl enables security checking
    ' at the component level. The attribute maps to the
    ' securities tab in a component within a COM+ application

<ComponentAccessControl(), SecurityRole("EveryoneRole",
SetEveryoneAccess:=True)> _
    Public Class RBSecurityObject

        ' SecurityRole configures a role named RbSecurityDemoRole
        ' on our component. SetEveryoneAccess(true) indicates
        ' we want the role to be populated with 'Everyone' when created

        Inherits ServicedComponent

        Public Function IsCallerInRole() As Boolean
```

```
      ' Check if the user is in the role

      Return ContextUtil.IsCallerInRole("EveryoneRole")
   End Function


   Public Function GetCallerAccountName() As String
      Dim ret As String = "Caller Unknown"

      If ContextUtil.IsSecurityEnabled Then
         Dim sec As SecurityCallContext

         ' CurrentCall is a static property which
         ' contains information about the current caller
         sec = SecurityCallContext.CurrentCall

         ' retrieve the current caller account name
         ret = sec.DirectCaller.AccountName
      End If


      Return ret
   End Function
   End Class
End Namespace
```

Listings 15.1 and 15.2 should give you a feel for how .NET role-based security can be used, but now take a look at a more real-life scenario.

Let's say that you are building a web-based trading system for a financial firm. One of the issues that you run into first is how you will control security for different people using the system. Here is an example: A stockbroker has an assistant. The assistant needs to be able to add or modify information for clients. But the assistant is not allowed to place trades on the system; only the stockbroker is. This is where roles are really handy. Let's take a look at an example in which the roles are not set up correctly for the situation just described (see Listings 15.3 and 15.4).

Listing 15.3   **Complex Role Configuration (C#)**

```
namespace TradingApp
{
      // ComponentAccessControl enables security checking
      // at the component level. The attribute maps to the
      // securities tab in a component within a COM+ application
```

continues

Listing 15.3 **Continued**

```
[ComponentAccessControl]

// SetEveryoneAccess(true) indicates
// we want the role to be populated with 'Everyone' when created
[SecurityRole("EveryoneRole", SetEveryoneAccess = true)]

public class MyTradingObject : ServicedComponent
{

        public void Buy(string symbol,int shares)
        {
                // Check if the user is in the role
                bool bl;
                bl = ContextUtil.IsCallerInRole("StockBroker");

                if(ContextUtil.IsCallerInRole("StockBroker"))
                {
                        //Allow the trade to go through
                }
                else
                {
                        //Don't allow the trade
                }

        }

        public void Sell(string symbol,int shares, string accountid)
        {
        // Check if the user is in the role and if the account is
        ➥his/hers

                if(ContextUtil.IsSecurityEnabled)
                {
                        string acctname;

                        if (ContextUtil.IsCallerInRole("StockBroker"))
                        {
                                SecurityCallContext sec;
```

```
                          // get a handle to the context of the current
                          ➥caller
                                  sec = SecurityCallContext.CurrentCall;

                                  // get the current caller account name
                                  acctname = sec.DirectCaller.AccountName;

                          //verify if this account belongs to this user
//Do some code to check user name against account
                          //if the account belongs to the user allow
                          ➥the user
                          //to sell the stock
                          }
                  }
                  else
                  {
                          //Don't allow the trade
                  }

              }

      }
}
```

Listing 15.4 **Complex Role Configuration (Visual Basic .NET)**

```
Namespace TradingApp

    ' ComponentAccessControl enables security checking
    ' at the component level. The attribute maps to the
    ' securities tab in a component within a COM+ application
    <ComponentAccessControl()>

    ' SetEveryoneAccess(true) indicates
    ' we want the role to be populated with 'Everyone' when created
    <SecurityRole("EveryoneRole", SetEveryoneAccess = true)>

    Public Class MyTradingObject
        Inherits ServicedComponent
```

continues

Listing 15.4 **Continued**

```
Public Sub Buy(ByVal symbol As String, ByVal shares As Integer)

    ' Check if the user is in the role
    Dim bl As Boolean


    If (ContextUtil.IsCallerInRole("StockBroker")) Then

        'Allow the trade to go through

    Else

        'Don't allow the trade
    End If
End Sub


    Public Sub Sell(ByVal symbol As String, ByVal shares As Integer,
ByVal accountid As String)

    ' Check if the user is in the role and if the account is
    ➥his/hers

    If (ContextUtil.IsSecurityEnabled) Then

        Dim acctname As String

        If (ContextUtil.IsCallerInRole("StockBroker")) Then

            Dim sec As SecurityCallContext

            ' get a handle to the context of the current
            ➥caller
            sec = SecurityCallContext.CurrentCall()

            ' get the current caller account name
            acctname = sec.DirectCaller.AccountName

            'verify if this account belongs to this user
            'Do some code to check user name against account
            'if the account belongs to the user allow the user
            'to sell the stock
```

```
        Else

                'Don't allow the trade
            End If
        End If

        End Sub

    End Class
End Namespace
```

You'll notice that these listings have implemented multiple levels of security based on which role the user is in. This gives you more of a granular approach to applying security to the components, which is great. Now let's take a look at where all these information and configuration settings are maintained and controlled.

Component Services Microsoft Management Console

The Component Services Microsoft Management Console provides you with a way to monitor and manage your components and their properties. Figure 15.1 shows where the different roles can be managed for each component. For the TradingApp, we have defined two roles that the user will fall under.

Figure 15.1 Component services roles for TradingApp.

The roles are basically containers and are not useful unless you add specific users to those roles. In Figure 15.2, you can see that we have added Everyone to the StockBroker role, but no one has been assigned to the Manager role.

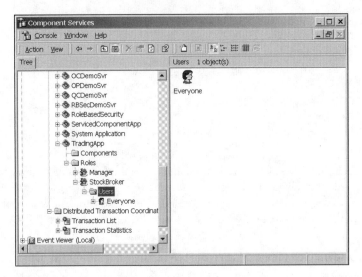

Figure 15.2 StockBroker role.

When setting up roles, make sure that the users within those roles are appropriate. For instance, Bob the stock broker might have an assistant who needs to get in the system and enter data for him. But Bob does not want to give his password and login ID to his assistant because this would allow his assistant to place trades, which the assistant is not licensed to do.

One way to solve this problem is to create another role called Assistants. In this role, you could restrict the type of actions that assistants are allowed to perform.

If you want to exercise more control over your component, you can change the way the component behaves by simply changing the settings in the Security tab of the Properties dialog box (see Figure 15.3).

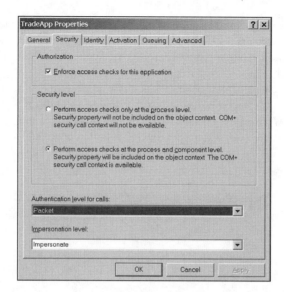

Figure 15.3 Application Properties Security tab.

If you want to force the components to run under a specific login, you can set the user identity in the Application Properties Identity tab, as shown in Figure 15.4.

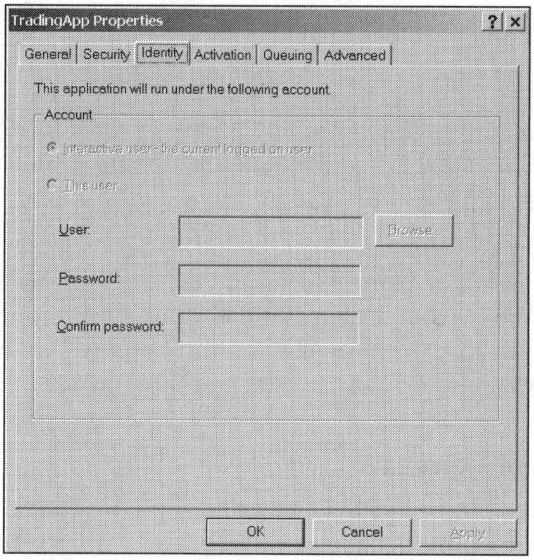

Figure 15.4 Application Properties Identity tab.

If you want the component to run under a specific login, you can enter that information here. If the screen is disabled and grayed out, as it appears here, you will need to make sure that the activation type is set to Server Application; this can be found under the Activation tab.

If you are having problems making changes or deleting the component, check the Advanced tab in the Properties dialog box (see Figure 15.5). If the Disable Deletion box is checked, you will not be able to delete the component until you uncheck it.

If you check the Disable Changes property and then try to add a new user to a role, you will be able to do so. The Disable Changes property applies only to the properties being altered.

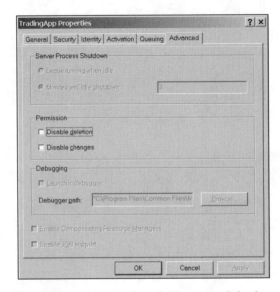

Figure 15.5   Advanced tab in the Properties dialog box.

If the `SetEveryoneAccess` property is set to true, the role Everyone is added as a member. The default is `false`, which means that no users are assigned to a role. Instead, you must configure them manually. This technique is best used for the role of Administrator, which has exclusive control over the system.

Transaction Issues

When you get to the point of utilizing transactions, you must make sure that an action or a series of actions are completed successfully, or you want to make sure that everything gets rolled back if there is a problem during the process. To get started, you'll look at some of the basics of transactions before you look at how to debug them.

Transaction Models

The .NET Framework uses two basic transaction models:

- **Automatic**—Automatically aborts or completes the transaction
- **Manual**—Requires you to call `SetComplete` or `SetAbort`

The amount of control that you want over the processing of your transaction determines which method you use. In most cases, the automatic model should suffice. For a managed object to participate in an automatic transaction, the managed class must be registered with Windows 2000 Component Services. However, not all transactions are automatic.

Automatic transaction processing is a service provided by COM+ that enables you to configure a class at design time to participate in a transaction at runtime. To use this service, the class must derive directly or indirectly from the `System.EnterpriseServices.ServicedComponent` class.

Imagine that you are having problems developing a component to implement transactions. Then take a look at a simple example of a class that implements automatic transaction (see Listings 15.5 and 15.6).

Listing 15.5 **AutoComplete Transaction (C#)**

```
namespace TradeComponent
{
        [Transaction(TransactionOption.Required)]
        public class StockTrade : ServicedComponent
        {
                [AutoComplete]
                public bool Buy(int NumShares, string symbol)
                {
                        try
                        {
                                //Some code that buys x amount of shares
                                //The transaction will automatically SetComplete()
                                ➥if the method call returns normally.
                        }
                        catch(Exception ex)
                        {
                                //If the method call throws an exception, the
                                ➥transaction will be aborted
                        }
                }
        [AutoComplete]
                public bool Sell(int NumShares, string symbol)
                {
```

continues

```
                        try
                        {
                                //Code that Sells x amount of shares
                                //The transaction will automatically
                                ➥SetComplete() if the method call returns
                                ➥normally.
                        }
                        catch(Exception ex)
                        {
                                //If the method call throws an exception, the
                                ➥transaction will be aborted
                        }

        }
}
```

Listing 15.6 **AutoComplete Transaction (Visual Basic .NET)**

```
Imports System.EnterpriseServices

Namespace TradeComponent

    <Transaction(TransactionOption.Required)>
    Public Class StockTrade
        Inherits ServicedComponent


Public Function <AutoComplete()> Buy(ByVal NumShares As Integer, ByVal
➥symbol As String) As Boolean

                        'Some code that buys x amount of shares
                        'The transaction will automatically SetComplete() if
                        ➥the method call returns normally.


                        'If the method call throws an exception, the
                        ➥transaction will be aborted
        End Function


        Public Function <AutoComplete()> Sell(ByVal NumShares As
        ➥Integer, ByVal symbol As String) As Boolean
```

```
'Code that Sells x amount of shares
'The transaction will automatically SetComplete() if
➥the method call returns normally.

'If the method call throws an exception, the
➥transaction will be aborted


        End Function
    End Class
End Namespace
```

In each of the methods in the class, the `AutoComplete` attribute has been assigned. This ensures that the management of the transaction will be handled by the system based on whether the function executes successfully.

Also, if you look closely, you will notice that the `StockTrade` class derives from the `ServicedComponent` class. Deriving the class from `ServicedComponent` ensures that the contexts of `StockTrade` objects are hosted in COM+. Two critical attributes must be applied for this example to work:

- **TransactionAttribute**—Applied to the `StockTrade` class to set the transaction to `Required`, which is equivalent to using the COM+ Explorer to set the transaction support on a COM+ component.

- **AutoCompleteAttribute**—Applied to the `Buy` and `Sell` methods. This attribute instructs the runtime to automatically call the `SetAbort` function on the transaction if an unhandled exception is generated during the execution of the method; otherwise, the runtime calls the `SetComplete` function.

Various assembly-level attributes are also used to supply COM+ registration information. A serviced component must be strong-named and should be placed in the global assembly cache (GAC) for manual registration.

Assemblies
Assemblies cannot be placed in the global assembly cache and should use dynamic registration.

Now that you have looked at the different attributes of a transaction, let's take a look at some known issues with transactions.

Known Issues with Microsoft Transaction Server Components

Microsoft has made some changes in the ASP.NET security model. If you have existing Microsoft Transaction Server components that you plan to use with ASP.NET applications, you might need to change the security access permissions.

One of the common exceptions seen when calling an MTS component without the necessary security permissions is, "Permission denied." If you are running into this, you might want to try the following steps to resolve the problem:

1. In Component Services, bring up the Properties dialog box for the MTS application.

2. Select the Identity tab, and change the account under which the component runs to that of a new local machine account, created solely for this purpose.

3. Run the utility Dcomcnfg.exe.

4. Select the Default Security tab.

5. Under Default Access Permissions, click Edit Default and add the user created in Step 2.

6. Restart IIS to ensure that the changes are recognized.

Going through all these steps should solve your permission problem.

Strong-Named Assemblies

Are you having problems getting your component to work? If so, have you implemented strong-named assemblies? You might have overlooked this requirement. Even though you can build and register your component as a COM object, you might not be able to use it.

To create a strong-named key, use this code:

```
[C#]
sn -k TradeComponent.snk
```

After you have generated a key, you can then reference it in your code to create a strong-named assembly. Without a key, you will not be able to generate the strong-named assembly.

Listings 15.7 and 15.8 illustrate how to properly implement the attributes to make your component a strong-named component.

Listing 15.7   **Strong-Named Component (C#)**

```
// - Registration details -
// Supply the COM+ application name.
[assembly: ApplicationName("TradeComponent")]
// Supply a strong-named assembly.
[assembly: AssemblyKeyFileAttribute("TradeComponent.snk")]

namespace TradeComponent
{
        [Transaction(TransactionOption.Required)]
        public class StockTrade : ServicedComponent
```

```
        {

                public bool Buy(int NumShares, string symbol)
                {
                        try
                        {
                                //Some code that buys x amount of shares
                                //The transaction will automatically
                                ➥SetComplete() if the method call returns
                                ➥normally.
                        }
                        catch(Exception ex)
                        {
                                //If the method call throws an exception
                                //you must call SetAbort so the transaction
                                ➥will be aborted
ContextUtil.SetAbort();
                        }
                        //Everything has completed successfully
                        ContextUtil.SetComplete();

                }
        [AutoComplete]
                public bool Sell(int NumShares, string symbol)
                {
                        try
                        {
                                //Code that Sells x amount of shares
                                //The transaction will automatically
                                ➥SetComplete() if the method call returns
                                ➥normally.
                        }
                        catch(Exception ex)
                        {
                                //If the method call throws an exception, the
                                ➥transaction will be aborted
                        }

                }
        }
}
```

Listing 15.8   **Strong Named Component(Visual Basic .NET)**

```vbnet
Imports System.EnterpriseServices

Namespace TradeComponent

    <Transaction(TransactionOption.Required)> Public Class StockTrade
        Inherits ServicedComponent


        Public Function Buy(ByVal NumShares As Integer, ByVal symbol As
        ➥String) As Boolean

            Try

                'Some code that buys x amount of shares
                'The transaction will automatically SetComplete() if
                ➥the method call returns normally.

            Catch ex As Exception

                'If the method call throws an exception, the
                ➥transaction will be aborted

                    ContextUtil.SetAbort()

            End Try

ContextUtil.SetComplete()


        End Function


        Public Function Sell(ByVal NumShares As Integer, ByVal symbol As
        ➥String) As Boolean

            Try

                'Code that Sells x amount of shares
                'The transaction will automatically SetComplete() if
                ➥the method call returns normally.
```

```
Catch ex As Exception

    'If the method call throws an exception, the
    ➥transaction will be aborted

ContextUtil.SetAbort()
End Try

ContextUtil.SetComplete()


    End Function
  End Class
End Namespace
```

If you look at the method definitions in these listings, you will notice that the `AutoComplete` attribute is missing but that the `Transaction` attribute is still on the `Class` definition.

Now if you are trying to call the `SetComplete` or `SetAbort` methods on the transaction object, the examples above (Listings 15.7 and 15.8) shows how this can be accomplished.

After you have built your component, you probably will want to make sure that it is being executed as you intended it to. To accomplish this, you will need some sort of monitoring program to monitor transactions. The next section looks at how to monitor transactions.

Monitoring Your Transactions

When you start working with transactions, you will probably want to see how many are being processed by the system and see if there are any problems with any of them. Microsoft has provided a very simple, yet informative, tool for you to use to monitor transactions on the system. This can be found under the Distributed Transaction Coordinator. To access this tool, you will need to drill down into the Component Services console. The nice thing about the Distributed Transaction Coordinator is that, if you have permission on a remote server where transactional components are running, you can look at the statistics (see Figure 15.6).

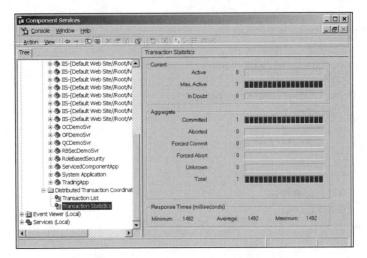

Figure 15.6   Distributed Transaction Coordinator.

Summary

COM+ can be a complicated beast, and with the onset of .NET, some changes are bound to crop up in the future. In this chapter, you learned how permissions play a vital role in the COM+ design. Not only do you have the capability to apply permissions to a whole component, but also you can take it down to the method level, if you need that type of granularity.

Another great feature is role-based security. This gives you the capability to group users by functionality and then administer which users should be in which roles.

Finally, the .NET Framework offers some pretty nifty features that have been added to aid in developing transaction-based components. These new attributes, such as `AutoComplete`, are great for identifying which methods you want to take care of themselves.

To wind up our look at debugging aspects of the of .NET framework, we turn to ADO.NET in Chapter 16, "Debugging ADO.NET."

16

Debugging ADO.NET

So what is so different about ADO.NET that we need to devote a whole chapter of this book to it? Well that's what we were thinking when we started to write this chapter. But as we dug deeper under the hood, we really began to realize the importance of this chapter. It all became very clear to us—and by the end of this chapter, it will be clear to you, too.

Let's first take a look at the differences between the old ADO and the new ADO.NET features. Table 16.1 presents these differences. This should help you identify some of the changes up front.

Table 16.1 **Differences Between ADO and ADO.NET**

Feature	Old ADO	New ADO.NET
Memory-resident data representation	Uses the `RecordSet` object.	Uses the `DataSet` object, which can contain one or more tables represented by `DataTable` objects.
Relationships among multiple tables	Requires the use of a `JOIN` query to return data from tables in a `RecordSet`.	Supports the `DataRelation` object to associate rows in one `DataTable` object with rows in another `DataTable` object.

Data visitation	Scans `RecordSet` rows sequentially.	Uses a navigation paradigm for nonsequential access to rows in a table. Follows relationships to navigate from rows in one table to corresponding rows in another table.
Disconnected access	Available through a `RecordSet`, but supports connected access, represented by the `Connection` object. You communicate to a database by using the OLE DB providers.	Communicates to a database with standardized calls to the DataAdapter object, which communicates to an OLE DB provider, or directly to SQL Server.
Programmability	Uses the `Connection` object to transmit commands to address underlying data structure of a data source.	Uses the strongly typed programming characteristic of XML. Data is self-describing because names for code items correspond to the "real-world" problem solved by the code. Underlying data constructs such as tables and rows do not appear, making code easier to read and write.
Sharing of disconnected data between tiers or components	Uses COM marshalling to transmit a disconnected record set. This supports only those datatypes defined by the COM standard. Requires type conversions, which demand system resources.	Transmits a `DataSet` as XML. The XML format places no restrictions datatypes and requires no type conversions.
Transmission of data through firewalls	Is problematic because firewalls typically are configured to prevent system-level requests such as COM marshalling.	Supported because ADO.NET `DataSet` objects use XML, which can pass through firewalls.
Scalability	Database locks and active database connections for long durations contend for limited database resources.	Disconnected access to database data without retaining database locks or active database connections for lengthy periods limits contention for limited database resources.

Understanding the System.Data Namespace

When accessing data, there are two distinct ways to retrieve information. The two entry points for data access are as follows:

- SqlClient
- OleDb

By using one or both of these classes, you can read and write data to almost any database. Figure 16.1 give you a bird's-eye view of how things in the overall .NET data component are organized.

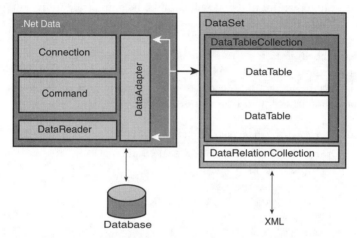

Figure 16.1 Relationships among .NET data components.

The key here is to identify which class will best suit your needs. We will make it very simple for you: If you are using Microsoft SQL Server, you most likely will want to use the SqlClient class for all your work. If you need to connect to any other third-party SQL databases or OLE DB–supported databases such as Oracle, you're stuck using the OleDb class.

Now that we have looked at the big picture, let's start looking at the details by beginning with catching SQL errors.

Catching SQL Errors

Two distinct exception classes exist for catching exceptions, if they are thrown. Depending on which data class you are working with, you will obviously need to use the appropriate exception class. For the examples in this section, we will be using the SqlClient class, so we will use the SqlException class to catch any exception thrown. If you are using the OleDb class, you will need to use the corresponding OleDbException class to catch exceptions.

The `SqlException` class is designed to handle exceptions that are thrown while executing a SQL statement. When an exception is thrown, you can gather enough information in the `SqlException` class to figure out what is happening. We have written a small function (see Listings 16.1 and 16.2) that will display all the properties of the `SqlException` class when an exception is thrown. This gives you a good idea of what is happening when the error occurs.

This function was written to return a string that is formatted with some HTML tags to display on a web page. If you want to use it in a different context, such as writing to a file, you can just change the `nl` (short for "new line") to a carriage return and line feed, if you prefer.

You might find that this function will be more helpful during more complicated SQL errors. Most of the time, you will find the error that you get will be the result of a simple spelling mistake.

This code shown in Listings 16.1 and 16.2 is a simple function that you can include in your program. If you are having problems debugging a SQL problem, this code might shed more light on the situation. The main purpose of this function is to serve as an additional utility to help you debug SQL problems.

Listing 16.1 *GetSqlExceptionDump* **Function (C#)**

```csharp
private string GetSqlExceptionDump(SqlException Ex)
    {    string sDump;
         string nl =   "<br>";
         sDump = "";

         sDump = "Class: " + Ex.Class + nl +
         "Errors: " + Ex.Errors + nl +
         "Help Link: " + Ex.HelpLink + nl +
         "InnerException: " + Ex.InnerException + nl +
         "Line#: " + Ex.LineNumber + nl+
         "Message: " + Ex.Message + nl+
         "Procedure: " + Ex.Procedure + nl+
         "Server: " + Ex.Server + nl+
         "Source: " + Ex.Source + nl+
         "Stack Trace: " + Ex.StackTrace + nl+
         "State: " + Ex.State + nl+
         "Target site: " + Ex.TargetSite + nl;

         return sDump;
    }
```

Listing 16.2 *GetSqlExceptionDump* Function (Visual Basic .NET)

```
private Function GetSqlExceptionDump(Ex as SqlException ) as string
                dim sDump as String
                dim nl =  "<br>"
                sDump = ""

    sDump = "Class: " + Ex.Class + nl & _
            "Errors: " + Ex.Errors + nl & _
            "Help Link: " + Ex.HelpLink + nl & _
            "InnerException: " + Ex.InnerException + nl & _
            "Line#: " + Ex.LineNumber + nl & _
            "Message: " + Ex.Message + nl & _
            "Procedure: " + Ex.Procedure + nl & _
            "Server: " + Ex.Server + nl & _
            "Source: " + Ex.Source + nl & _
            "Stack Trace: " + Ex.StackTrace + nl & _
            "State: " + Ex.State + nl & _
            "Target site: " + Ex.TargetSite + nl

                GetSqlExceptionDump = sDump


        End Function
```

Let's take a look at what happens when an error occurs during the execution of a web page. Listings 16.3 and 16.4 present a small sample of code to connect to the database and select a few rows of data. What could go wrong with that?

Listing 16.3 **Sample Code to Connect to the Database (C#)**

```
try
{
SqlConnection nwindConn = new SqlConnection("Data Source=localhost;
➥Integrated Security=SSPI;Initial Catalog=northwind");

nwindConn.Open();
SqlCommand myCommand = new SqlCommand("SELECT dCategoryID, CategoryName
➥FROM Categories", nwindConn);



SqlDataReader myReader = myCommand.ExecuteReader();//'This command will
➥trigger an error
```

```
while (myReader.Read())
      Response.Write("<br>" + myReader.GetValue(1));

      myReader.Close();

      nwindConn.Close();
}
catch (SqlException Ex)
{
      Response.Write(GetSqlExceptionDump(Ex));
}
```

Listing 16.4 **Sample Code to Connect to the Database (Visual Basic .NET)**

```
Try

Dim nwindConn = new SqlConnection("Data Source=localhost; Integrated
➥Security=SSPI;Initial Catalog=northwind")

nwindConn.Open()
Dim myCommand = new SqlCommand("SELECT dCategoryID, CategoryName FROM
➥Categories", nwindConn)


Dim myReader = myCommand.ExecuteReader()'This command will trigger an
➥error

Do while (myReader.Read())
      Response.Write("<br>" + myReader.GetValue(1))

      myReader.Close()

      nwindConn.Close()
loop

catch Ex as SqlException
      Response.Write(GetSqlExceptionDump(Ex))
End Try
```

Everything seems to look okay. Looking at the code in Listings 16.3 and 16.4, you probably don't see anything wrong. That's because syntactically it is correct—but what about runtime errors? That's what we are really talking about. Those can be the most difficult errors to track down and debug.

Now that you have an example to work with, let's see what happens if this code is executed. Look at the output shown in Listing 16.5.

Listing 16.5 **Sample Output of *GetSqlExceptionDump***

```
Class:16
Errors:System.Data.SqlClient.SqlErrorCollection
Help Link:
InnerException:
Line#:1
Message:Invalid column name 'dCategoryID'.
Procedure:
Server:DIGITAL-LAPTOP
Source:SQL Server Managed Provider
StackTrace: at System.Data.SqlClient.SqlCommand.ExecuteReader(CommandBehavior
➥cmdBehavior, RunBehavior runBehavior, Boolean returnStream) at
System.Data.SqlClient.SqlCommand.ExecuteReader() at
adoerrors.WebForm1.Page_Load(Object sender, EventArgs e) in
c:\inetpub\wwwroot\adoerrors\webform1.aspx.cs:line 53
State:3
Target site:System.Data.SqlClient.SqlDataReader
ExecuteReader(System.Data.CommandBehavior, System.Data.SqlClient.RunBehavior,
➥Boolean)
Line:1Index #0 Error: System.Data.SqlClient.SqlError: Invalid column name
'dCategoryID'.
```

As you can see, we were trying to retrieve data from an invalid column, called dCategoryID. This would not necessarily stand out to another developer debugging your code, so how you organize your code is important. It is not necessarily going the extra mile—it's just taking that extra little step to ensure that your code won't blow up in the client's face. You can still have an error occur, but you can present it in a pleasant way that won't alarm the user but that instead will inform him of the current situation.

New Connection Components

First let's look at the differences in the two connection components. We're not going to cover the basics, but we'll focus instead on just the differences and where you might run into problems. Whether you are using the `SqlConnection` component or the `OleDbConnection` class, keep one thing in mind when developing your application: Are you using integrated security? If so, you might run into some problems when deploying your web page. Don't forget that when your web page is running, the trusted user will be IUSR_COMPUTERNAME because this is the default account for IIS. If you specify a user account, it will be much easier for you to debug because you already know which user account you are using. If you use a separate account to log into the database, you will also have more control over the amount of security that user account has.

SqlClient.SqlConnection

This component was designed to be used specifically with Microsoft SQL Server and nothing else. One of the benefits that you get by using it is speed. `SqlClient` uses its own protocol to communicate with SQL Server. This eliminates the overhead and layers of `OleDbConnection`. Keep that in mind if you want to accomplish any specific task related to SQL Server, such as use a remote server.

One of the features available on `SqlConnection` that you don't have in `OleDbConnection` is the `Packetsize` property. This can be very useful if you need to adjust the size of the network packets being sent. This is not something that you would typically change, but if you were sending large amounts of text or even images, you might want to increase the packet size. On the flip side, let's say that you are developing a wireless site that will use very small chunks of data; you might want to adjust the packet size to a more efficient size because the default value is 8192 bytes. You might not think that this is that important, but when your web site starts to scale up and your traffic increases, attention to details like this will start to add up and make a big difference.

If you are having a problem connecting to SQL Server 6.5, that is because the `SQLClient` namespace does not support it; it supports only SQL Server 7.0 and higher. You will need to use the `OleDb` namespace to connect to earlier versions of SQL Server.

OleDb.OleDbConnection

One of the first problems you might run into is trying to use a data source name (DSN). This option is no longer supported in the .NET Framework, so if you want to transition your code over to .NET, keep in mind that you will have to replace all your connection strings that contain DSN.

If you compare the OleDbConnection string to its counterpart, it is almost identical, except for a few noticeable modifications in the use of keywords and properties. The major difference between the two is that the OleDbConnection component is designed to be backward compatible and to work with all databases that have an OLE DB driver. The following list contains these exceptions:

- You must use the Provider keyword.
- The URL keyword is not supported.
- The Remote Provider keyword is not supported.
- The Remote Server keyword is not supported.

Also if you take a close look at the properties you will notice that the PacketSize property is not available for the OleDbConnection object. If you happen to be using this with SqlConnection object, it will not port over to the OleDbConnection side.

Issues with the *DataReader* Class

The sole purpose of this class is to read a forward-only stream of data from the SQL Server database. The biggest benefit of the data reader is speed.

One of the common problems that we have come across is that developers are trying to open another connection while the data reader is still reading from the database. You might run into this problem if you are trying to make nested database calls: You cannot do this because the connection object is directly connected to the data reader. While the data reader is in use, no other operation can be performed on the connection object except closing it. This might seem like a bug, but Microsoft designed it this way.

In high-volume sites, it might be better to use DataSets or DataTables because they are disconnected and they release the connection back to the pool more quickly. This also gives you the capability to work with nested database calls.

Working with Transactions

When we first started working with transactions, we ran into a few steps that we needed to incorporate into our code to get a transaction to run. There are a few steps that you need to initiate to process an insert, update, or delete in a transaction. Here are the steps to complete a successful transaction:

1. The first thing you will come across is the SqlTransaction class. You can get this only by calling the BeginTransaction method on the Connection object.

2. The connection object passes back a SqlTransaction object with all the necessary information to complete your transaction.

3. Now you can process your database update just as you would normally do.

4. Finally, when you have completed the database operation, you can call commit, or, if there is a problem, you can roll back the transaction. These points are illustrated in Listings 16.6 and 16.7.

Listing 16.6   **Transactions Example (C#)**

```
SqlConnection myConnection = new SqlConnection("Data
➥Source=localhost;initial catalog=Pubs;persist security info=False;user
➥id=sa;workstation id=DIGITAL-LAPTOP;packet size=4096");
      myConnection.Open();

      SqlCommand myCommand = new SqlCommand();

      SqlTransaction myTrans;
      myCommand.Connection = myConnection;

      // Start the transaction
myTrans =
myConnection.BeginTransaction(IsolationLevel.ReadCommitted,"JobTransaction");
      // Assign transaction object for a pending local transaction
      myCommand.Transaction = myTrans;

      try
      {
      myCommand.CommandText = "SET IDENTITY_INSERT Jobs ON ";
      myCommand.ExecuteNonQuery();

      myCommand.CommandText = "Insert into Jobs (Job_id, Job_Desc)
      ➥VALUES (1000, 'MS.NET Programmer')";
      myCommand.ExecuteNonQuery();

      myCommand.CommandText = "Insert into Jobs (Job_id, Job_Desc)
      ➥VALUES (1001, 'QA Tester')";
      myCommand.ExecuteNonQuery();
      myTrans.Commit();

      Response.Write("The Transaction completed successfully.");
      }
      catch(Exception ex)
      {
      myTrans.Rollback("JobTransaction");
      Response.Write("There was an error during the Insert
      ➥process.<br>");
      Response.Write(ex.ToString());
      }
      finally
      {
      myConnection.Close();
      }
```

Listing 16.7 **transactions example (Visual Basic .NET)**

```vb
Dim myConnection = new SqlConnection("Data Source=localhost;initial
➥catalog=Pubs;persist security info=False;user id=sa;workstation
➥id=DIGITAL-LAPTOP;packet size=4096")

myConnection.Open()

Dim myCommand = new SqlCommand()

Dim myTrans as SqlTransaction
myCommand.Connection = myConnection

     ' Start the transaction
myTrans =
myConnection.BeginTransaction(IsolationLevel.ReadCommitted,"JobTransaction")
     ' Assign transaction object for a pending local transaction
myCommand.Transaction = myTrans


     try
          myCommand.CommandText = "SET IDENTITY_INSERT Jobs ON "
          myCommand.ExecuteNonQuery()

          myCommand.CommandText = "Insert into Jobs (Job_id, Job_Desc)
VALUES (1000, 'MS.NET Programmer')"

          myCommand.ExecuteNonQuery()
          myCommand.CommandText = "Insert into Jobs (Job_id, Job_Desc)
VALUES (1001, 'QA Tester')"

          myCommand.ExecuteNonQuery()
          myTrans.Commit()
          Response.Write("The Transaction completed successfully.")

     Catch Ex as Exception

     myTrans.Rollback("JobTransaction")
     Response.Write("There was an error during the Insert process.<br>")
     Response.Write(ex.ToString())

     finally

          myConnection.Close()
     end try
```

You might notice a few things in these examples. First, you might be wondering about the statement `"SET IDENTITY_INSERT Jobs ON"`. We did this because the `job_id` field is an `Identity` field and because we already have a unique identity; we needed to make sure that the unique identity stayed in sync throughout the database. We must use the `"SET IDENTITY_INSERT"` statement to accomplish this; otherwise, it will throw an exception.

Error Codes and How to Debug Them

In the .NET Framework, error handling has been completely revamped. There is such an enormous amount of errors to cover that you could dedicate a whole book to just this subject. Instead, we have tried to focus on the more common areas where you might run into problems and explain the errors that you will probably encounter.

Access Denied

One of the most common errors could be this one:

```
Access Denied: [DBNETLIB][ConnectionOpen (Connect()).]SQL Server does not exist or
access denied.
```

You are trying to connect to a database, and you get this error message. This message seems vague: Is it a security issue or a networking issue? You would think they could have figured this out by now and identify whether it is one or the other. Well, you know that the database exists, and you have all the proper permissions to use it. So what's wrong? Here are the steps you should take to debug this problem:

1. `ping` the server you are trying to connect to. This will help you identify if there is a network problem.

2. Verify that the login ID and password are valid by logging in through a different source.

3. Make sure that the initial catalog or database is spelled correctly.

4. Make sure that the server name and IP address are correct.

Let's take a close look at the connection string. Microsoft has been meddling quite a lot with the ADO portion of .NET, so you need to pay extra attention to details here. Table 16.2 gives you a list of acceptable keywords.

Table 16.2   **Acceptable Keywords**

Keyword	Explanation
Data Source	The hostname, computer name, or network address of the SQL Server
Server	
Address	
Addr	
Network Address	

`User ID` The SQL	Server login account
`Initial Catalog`	The name of the database
`Password`	The SQL Server password
`Pwd`	

Here are a couple of examples of what a basic connection string could look like:

```
SqlConnection ("server=digital-laptop;uid=sa;pwd=;database=northwind)
```

```
SqlConnection("Data Source=localhost; Integrated Security=SSPI;Initial
Catalog=northwind")
```

SELECT Permission Denied

Another common error is exemplified here:

```
SELECT permission denied on object 'Product', database 'Northwind', owner 'dbo'.
```

This error is typically easy to fix. In this case, we were trying to perform a SELECT statement on the product table with the different account. If you take a look at Listings 16.8 and 16.9, you will notice that we're trying to connect to the database with a user named testuser, not system administrator. Because the system administrator account has privileges to do anything that the owner wants, there are really no restrictions. This causes serious problems if you try to change the user connecting to the database.

One of the first things you should do when setting up a new database-driven web site is create a SQL user account for your web site and not use the system administrator account. This way you can control what that user has access to right from the beginning, and you will avoid major headaches if you try to switch the user account that is logging into the database.

Listing 16.8 **Connecting to the Database (C#)**

```
SqlConnection Conn = new SqlConnection();
Conn.ConnectionString = "server=digital-world;initial catalog =
➥northwind;user id= testuser; pwd=password";
Conn.Open();
DataSet ds = new DataSet();
```

Listing 16.9 **Connecting to the Database (Visual Basic .NET)**

```
Dim Conn as SqlConnection = new SqlConnection()
Conn.ConnectionString = "server=digital-world;initial catalog =
➥northwind;user id= testuser; pwd=password"
Conn.Open()
Dim ds as DataSet = new DataSet()
Dim dr as SqlDataAdapter = new SqlDataAdapter("Select * from
➥product",Conn)
```

To see who has permissions on the product table, you will need to do the following steps:

1. Open the SQL Enterprise Manager.

2. Select the Northwind database.

3. Expand the tables.

4. Right-click the Product table.

5. Select Permissions.

If you take a look at Figure 16.2, you will notice that there are no permissions set for any user. What you need to do is check the testuser SELECT column and save the changes. Then everything will work fine.

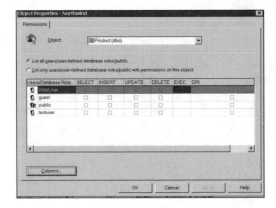

Figure 16.2   SQL Enterprise Manager table permissions.

Now that the problem has been identified, let's look at how to solve it. There are several ways to fix this type of problem, including the following:

- Give the testuser select permissions on the product table.

- Create a new role called WebUsers in SQL server, and then add the testuser to that role. Grant the WebUsers role select permissions on the product table.

- Call a stored procedure and grant execute permission to testuser on that stored procedure.

Column-Level Security

One other point that you might want to consider is column-level security. In SQL Server 7.x and 2000, you can grant access down to the column level. This is very useful if you want to restrict access to sensitive information in a table, such as Social Security numbers. This need would arise only in rare cases, but you should be aware of this feature in SQL server.

IndexOutOfRangeException

Here is an error message that you might run into if you are not careful:

```
An exception of type System.IndexOutOfRangeException was thrown.
[Response.Write("<br>" + myReader.GetValue(2));
```

This is a prime example of stepping outside the boundaries of an array. So how can you prevent this from happening? Let's take a look at your options for this situation. If you will use the GetValue method to retrieve the data from a field, you can use the fieldcount property to identify how many fields were returned. Using that value, you can initiate a loop to iterate through the fields and read them. This is exemplified in Listings 16.10 and 16.11.

Listing 16.10 **Reading Values from the** SqlDataReader **(C#)**

```
SqlConnection nwindConn = new SqlConnection("Data Source=localhost;
Integrated Security=SSPI;Initial Catalog=northwind");


    nwindConn.Open();
    SqlCommand myCommand2 = new SqlCommand("SELECT CategoryID,
    ➥CategoryName FROM Categories", nwindConn);


    SqlDataReader myReader = myCommand2.ExecuteReader();
    int i;
    while (myReader.Read())
        for (i=0;i<myReader.FieldCount;i++)
        {
            Response.Write("<br>" + myReader.GetValue(i));
        }
    myReader.Close();

    nwindConn.Close();
```

Listing 16.11 **Reading Values from the** *SqlDataReader* **(Visual Basic .NET)**

```
Dim nwindConn = New SqlConnection("Data Source=localhost; Integrated
Security=SSPI;Initial Catalog=northwind")


    nwindConn.Open()
    Dim myCommand2 = New SqlCommand("SELECT CategoryID, CategoryName
    ➥FROM Categories", nwindConn)
```

continues

Listing 16.11 **Continued**

```
Dim dsCustomer = New DataSet()

Dim myReader = myCommand2.ExecuteReader()
Dim i As Int32

While myReader.Read()
    For i = 0 To myReader.FieldCount
        Response.Write("<br>" + myReader.GetValue(i))
    Next
End While
myReader.Close()

nwindConn.Close()
```

Using this method, you avoid trying to access an array element outside the valid range.

Another method is to access each field by name. This could require more code than the last example, but it gives you that extra level of manipulation and control.

You still might run into an error if you do not spell the column name correctly or provide an invalid column. If this happens, you should get an error that looks similar to the message shown in Figure 16.3.

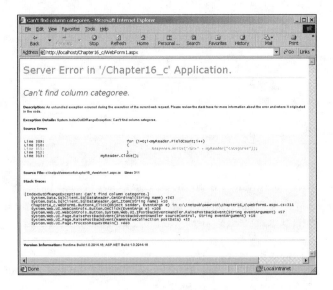

Figure 16.3   Column error.

Make sure that if you use the column names, you have the spelling correct. And if you change the name of a column in the database schema, you will have to make sure that you reflect that change in your code as well.

Listings 16.12 and 16.13 show how you would use the column name instead of the index number.

Listing 16.12 **Accessing Data by Column Name (C#)**

```
    While (myReader.Read())
{

        Response.Write(myReader["CategoryID"].ToString());
        Response.Write(myReader["CategoryName"].ToString());
        Response.Write("<br>");

}
```

Listing 16.13 **Accessing Data by Column Name (Visual Basic .NET)**

```
    Do While myReader.Read()
        Response.Write(myReader("CategoryID").ToString())
        Response.Write(myReader("CategoryName").ToString())
        Response.Write("<br>")
    Loop
```

Invalid Data Source

You can assign a data source to your data control in a couple different ways. This section focuses on just working with the data grid control. While we were working with data grids, we were amazed at how flexible the data source property was. You can pass it a dataset or various types of lists or collections.

When setting up a data grid, you can define the data source property in the aspx code, but you don't have to. You can also set that value in the code behind the aspx page.

If you are working in Visual Studio .NET, you can drag and drop command objects, connection objects, and even datasets. But you need to assign the data source to your data grid. This opens up the possibilities of assigning an incorrect data source if you are not familiar with the process.

If you look at the following code, you will see that it is trying to assign the `sqlcommand1` object as the data source.

```
<asp:DataGrid id="Datagrid2" style="Z-INDEX: 101; LEFT: 25px; POSITION: absolute;
TOP: 59px" runat="server" DataSource="<%# sqlCommand1 %>"></asp:DataGrid>
```

Because the data source is looking for a dataset or a list object, you would need to create a dataset and assign that to the `DataSource` property. Another option is to set the data source in the code behind the page where you do all the database work and initialize your page components. This enables you to add additional debugging code, such as writing to a debug listener or a file to help you with any problems that you might run across. Listings 16.14 and 16.15 illustrate that you make the call to the database during the load process and then bind the results to the data grid.

Listing 16.14   **Setting the data source from behind the aspx page(C#)**

```csharp
private void Page_Load(object sender, System.EventArgs e)
{
        SqlConnection Conn = new SqlConnection();
        Conn.ConnectionString = "server=localhost;initial catalog =
northwind;user id= sa; pwd=";
        Conn.Open();
        DataSet ds2 = new DataSet();
        SqlDataAdapter dA2 = new SqlDataAdapter("Select * from
➥products",Conn);

        //Populate the dataset
        dA2.Fill(ds2,"Products");
        DataGrid1.AllowSorting=true;
        DataGrid1.BackColor = System.Drawing.Color.AliceBlue;

        //Create the association between the data grid and the dataset
        DataGrid1.DataSource = ds2;
        DataGrid1.DataBind();
        //Make sure to close the connection and free unused resources
        Conn.Close();
}
```

Listing 16.15   **Setting the data source from behind the aspx page (Visual Basic .NET)**

```vbnet
Private Sub Page_Load(sender as object, e as System.EventArgs)
        Dim Conn = new SqlConnection()
        Conn.ConnectionString = "server=localhost;initial catalog =
➥northwind;user id= sa; pwd="
        Conn.Open()

        Dim ds2 = new DataSet()

        Dim dA2 = new SqlDataAdapter("Select * from products",Conn)
```

continues

```
        dA2.Fill(ds2)

        DataGrid1.AllowSorting=true
        DataGrid1.BackColor = System.Drawing.Color.AliceBlue

        DataGrid1.DataSource = ds2
        DataGrid1.DataBind()

        Conn.Close()
    End Sub
```

No Data in the Data Grid

What if your data does not show up in your data grid and you don't get any error messages?

If this is the case, you might want to look at your code and make sure that you are using the `DataBind` method after you set your data source. The `DataBind` method initiates a sequence of events that binds the control and all its child controls to the specified data source. This is illustrated in Listings 16.16–16.18.

Listing 16.16 *Databind* method (aspx)

```
<%@ Page language="c#" Codebehind="WebForm1.aspx.cs"
AutoEventWireup="false" Inherits="adoconnection.WebForm1" %>

<HTML>
  <HEAD>
<!DOCTYPE HTML PUBLIC "-//W3C//DTD HTML 4.0 Transitional//EN" >
  </HEAD>
  <body MS_POSITIONING="GridLayout">

    <form id="WebForm1" method="post" runat="server">
<asp:DataGrid id=DataGrid1 style="Z-INDEX: 101; LEFT: 25px; POSITION:
absolute; TOP: 59px" runat="server"></asp:DataGrid>
    </form>
  </body>
</HTML>
```

Listing 16.17   *Databind* method (C#)

```
private void Page_Load(object sender, System.EventArgs e)
      {

      // Put user code to initialize the page here

      SqlConnection Conn = new SqlConnection();
Conn.ConnectionString = "server=localhost;initial catalog =
➥northwind;user id= sa; pwd=";
      Conn.Open();

      DataSet ds = new DataSet();
      SqlDataAdapter dA = new SqlDataAdapter("Select * from
      products",Conn);

      dA.Fill(ds,"Products");

      DataGrid1.AllowSorting=true;
      DataGrid1.BackColor = System.Drawing.Color.AliceBlue;

      DataGrid1.DataSource = ds;
      DataGrid1.DataBind();
      Conn.Close();
            }
```

Listing 16.18   *Databind* method (Visual Basic .NET)

```
private void Page_Load(object sender, System.EventArgs e)


      ' Put user code to initialize the page here

      Dim Conn = new SqlConnection()
      Conn.ConnectionString = "server=localhost;initial catalog =
      ➥northwind;user id= sa; pwd="

      ' Open the connection
      Conn.Open()

      'Create a new dataset to hold the records
      Dim ds = new DataSet()
      Dim dA = new SqlDataAdapter("Select * from products",Conn)
```

```
'Populate the dataset by using the dataAdapters Fill method
dA.Fill(ds,"Products")

DataGrid1.AllowSorting=true
DataGrid1.BackColor = System.Drawing.Color.AliceBlue

DataGrid1.DataSource = ds
DataGrid1.DataBind()
Conn.Close()
```

This applies only to aspx pages, not windows within windows applications.

Problems with Connections

One of the problems that you might run into first involves working with connections. Microsoft has designed the .NET framework to function a little differently than previous versions of ADO. Figure 16.4 provides an example of an error that you might get when trying to work with multiple connections.

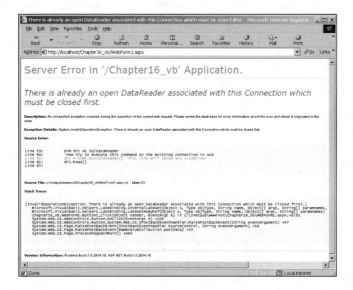

Figure 16.4   Error that can result when working with multiple connections.

This is a good sign that your connection is in use and that you need to either complete the current database operation or close the connection. If you are getting this error, check to see if you have closed the `DataReader` object before executing another operation on the same connection.

This might occur when you are trying to read from one table and then trying to perform an operation on another table. Solutions include closing the `DataReader` before continuing or creating a second connection object and running your process against that.

You will notice in Listings 16.19 and 16.20 that one data reader is open and that we have read the first row of information from it. Then a second command object is created and more data is read from a different table. As soon as the command is executed against the database, however, we get an exception. This is because the connection is right in the middle of reading data from the first `SELECT` statement. At this point, the only thing that can be done is to finish reading the data or close the `DataReader` object.

Listing 16.19   *DataReader* **problem(C#)**

```
SqlConnection Conn = new SqlConnection();
Conn.ConnectionString = "server=localhost;initial catalog =
➥northwind;user id= sa; pwd=";


Conn.Open();
//Create a SqlCommand using the connection that was just created
SqlCommand com1 = new SqlCommand("select * from products",Conn);

//Create a datareader
SqlDataReader dr;
dr = com1.ExecuteReader();

//Now start reading a row at a time
dr.Read();

//Now create a second command that using the same connection
SqlCommand com2 = new SqlCommand("select * from jobs",Conn);

//Create a second datareader
SqlDataReader dr2;
//now try to execute this command on the existing connection in use
dr2 = com2.ExecuteReader(); //This line will throw and exception!
dr2.Read();
```

Listing 16.20   *DataReader* **problem (Visual Basic .NET)**

```
Dim Conn = new SqlConnection()
Conn.ConnectionString = "server=localhost;initial catalog =
northwind;user id= sa; pwd="
```

continues

```
Conn.Open()
//Create a SqlCommand using the connection that was just created
Dim com1 = new SqlCommand("select * from products",Conn)

//Create a datareader
Dim dr as SqlDataReader
dr = com1.ExecuteReader()

//Now start reading a row at a time
dr.Read()

//Now create a second command that using the same connection
Dim com2 = new SqlCommand("select * from Orders",Conn)

//Create a second datareader
Dim dr2 as SqlDataReader
//now try to execute this command on the existing connection in use
dr2 = com2.ExecuteReader() //This line will throw and exception!
dr2.Read()
```

If you need to persist the data to work with it, you will need to pull it into a dataset or some other form. That way you can keep it in memory while you make another connection to the database.

Common Pitfalls

This section looks at some common issues that you might encounter when developing and tells how to work around them.

Working with Multiple Connections and Using Connection Pooling

Connection pooling is built into the .NET Framework. If you create all your connections with the same connection string, the system automatically pools the connections for you. But if the connection strings differ, you will get a new nonpooled connection. Keep this in mind when you are developing. If you create connections all over your code and they all point to the same location, keep a global connection string around so that you don't start creating unmeaningful database connections and wasting resources. A good place to store your connection string would be in the Web.Config file under a custom section called appsettings.

Listings 16.21 and 16.22 illustrate when a new connection will be made and when an existing connection will be used or pooled.

Listing 16.21 **Connection Pooling (C#)**

```
SqlConnection conn = new SqlConnection();
conn.ConnectionString = "Integrated Security=SSPI;Initial Catalog=Store";
conn.Open();        // Pool 1 is created.

SqlConnection conn = new SqlConnection();
conn.ConnectionString = "Integrated Security=SSPI;Initial Catalog=Orders";
conn.Open();        // Pool 2 is created
// The second pool is created due to the differences in connection
➥strings

SqlConnection conn = new SqlConnection();
conn.ConnectionString = "Integrated Security=SSPI;Initial Catalog=Store";
conn.Open();        // pool 1 is used.
```

Listing 16.22 **Connection Pooling (Visual Basic .NET)**

```
Dim conn = new SqlConnection();
conn.ConnectionString = "Integrated Security=SSPI;Initial Catalog=Store";
conn.Open();          ' Pool 1 is created.

Dim conn = new SqlConnection();
conn.ConnectionString = "Integrated Security=SSPI;Initial Catalog=Orders";
conn.Open();          ' Pool 2 is created
// The second pool is created due to the differences in connection strings

Dim conn = new SqlConnection();
conn.ConnectionString = "Integrated Security=SSPI;Initial Catalog=Store";
conn.Open();          ' pool 1 is used.
```

In some cases, you will need to create two separate connections to perform an operation. This might occur when you are in the middle of reading information from a data reader and want to make changes to the database as you iterate the data.

Should I Use a *DataReader* or *DataAdapter*?

You should ask yourself a few basic questions before you start grabbing data from the database. First, what do you need to do with the data? Do you need to change it, add to it, read it, or display it in a data grid? These are important questions to consider because they determine which component you *can* use, as opposed to which one you *want* to use.

If you want to display data in a data grid, your only option is to use the DataAdapter. This is because the DataAdapter is used to populate a dataset, which is the preferred method of populating a data grid.

If you just need to read the data row by row, then, by all means, use a DataReader object. Also note that this is a forward, read-only mechanism; if you want to edit data as you are navigating through the rows, you won't be able to. The DataReader is strictly for reading data—hence, the name DataReader.

How Many Times Do You Really Need to Talk to the Database?

So what is the big deal about calling the database a bazillion times? You don't see any impact while developing it. And some of the stress testing seemed to be fine, so it must be okay to do.

In my experience, the number of trips that you make to the database can have a significant impact on the performance—not to mention the scalability—of your web site. It doesn't matter if it is a very small amount of data that is being retrieved from the database; if it is in a high-traffic page, it can—and usually will—come back to bite you later.

Let's say that you have a web store, and you sell books. On the front page, you want to rotate books from a preselected group of books on sale. Currently all the information that you need is contained in a database. So you figure that you will just query the database every time someone requests the page. But what happens when you start to receive a lot of hits on your web site? I have seen this happen literally overnight! The next day traffic doubles and continues to climb day by day. These are the situations that you thought you saw only in TV commercials. But they are real, trust me!

If you stop to look at this situation, you might be only rotating 30 different books. So, after the 30th time to the database, you start doing redundant work. One solution is to keep on the web server an XML file of the books that are currently on sale. Then your server only needs to look on its own hard drive to retrieve the data that it needs. Now just write some custom code behind the web page to do the rotating and reading the data from the XML file.

If you are worried about new books going on sale and having to update the XML file, don't worry. On MS SQL Server, you can use a trigger or schedule a task to check for new books on sale. If there are new items, the system can export the results to an XML file, and, presto—your web page automatically picks up the new XML file.

This is just one creative way to accomplish this task, but there are many other ways to accomplish the same thing. Just bear in mind the following suggestions:

- Keep it simple.
- Persist common data elements in memory or to a local file.
- Keep the number of trips to the database minimal.
- Keep the number of connection to a minimum.

Keep these points in mind when you are developing your web site, and think through what you are trying to accomplish. As much as you might want to jump in and start coding, it is always beneficial to have a plan can be called in a few different ways without using the parameter components. Here we focus on the issues with the command object and parameter collections, though. We could never understand why people used the parameter object to add parameters to their query when they could simply format a text string to do the same thing and use less code to accomplish the task. So what is the benefit of using parameters? Let's take a look at the type of problems you might run into and how to avoid them.

Using Parameters with *SqlCommand*

When using parameters with `SqlCommand`, the names of the parameters must match the names of the parameter placeholders in the stored procedure. The SQL Server .NET Data Provider treats these as named parameters and searches for the matching parameter placeholders.

The SQLCommand class does not support the question mark (?) placeholder for passing parameters to a SQL statement or a stored procedure call. If you accidentally use the question mark, you will probably get the error shown in Figure 16.5.

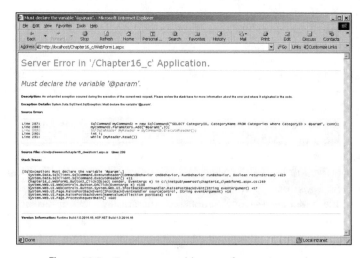

Figure 16.5   Error generated by use of a question mark.

In this case, named parameters must be used. Take a look at Listings 16.22 and 16.23 to see how you would properly implement a parameter using the SqlCommand class.

Listing 16.22   **Implementing a Parameter Using the *SqlCommand* Class (C#)**

```
SqlConnection conn = new SqlConnection("server=(local);database=north-
wind;Trusted_Connection=yes");
conn.Open();
//Build the Command using a named parameter
SqlCommand myCommand2 = new SqlCommand("SELECT CategoryID, CategoryName
FROM
Categories where CategoryID > @param1", conn);

//Add the parameter and value to the command object
myCommand2.Parameters.Add("@param1",3);

SqlDataReader myReader = myCommand2.ExecuteReader();
```

Listing 16.23   **Implementing a Parameter Using the *SqlCommand* Class (Visual Basic .NET)**

```
Dim conn = New
SqlConnection("server=(local);database=northwind;Trusted_Connection=yes")
conn.Open()
'Build the Command using a named parameter
Dim myCommand2 = New SqlCommand("SELECT CategoryID, CategoryName FROM
Categories where CategoryID > @param1", conn)

'Add the parameter and value to the command object
 myCommand2.Parameters.Add("@param1", 3)

Dim myReader = myCommand2.ExecuteReader()
```

In these listings, you will notice that when we created SqlCommand, we included a named parameter called @param1. The next line of code added the parameter value to the command statement by adding it to the parameter collection and specifying the parameter name and value that should replace it. Just remember that the OleDBCommand object does not operate the same way. Let's take a look at the differences in the next section.

Using Parameters with *OleDbCommand*

When using parameters with `OleDbCommand`, the names of the parameters added to `OleDbParameterCollection` must match the names of the parameter in the stored procedure. The OLE DB .NET Data Provider treats these as named parameters and searches for the matching parameter marker.

The OLE DB .NET Data Provider does not support named parameters for passing parameters to a SQL statement or a stored procedure called by a command object. In this case, the question mark (?) placeholder must be used. Take a look at the following example:

```
SELECT * FROM Products WHERE ProductID = ? and price = ?
```

It is important that the order in which parameter objects are added to the `Parameters` `Collection` must directly correspond to the position of the question marks in the SQL statement. Unlike the `SqlCommand` object, in which the parameters have names associated with them, you don't have that option here.

SQL ADO.NET Objects Versus OleDb ADO.NET Objects

So what is the big difference? And why are there two different components to manipulate data?

The biggest difference is not apparent on the outside. It is inside where the differences are tremendous. If you look at how the two components differ, `SQLClient` is native to .NET and MS SQL Server. It communicates to SQL using its own protocol. This enables it to work more quickly and to avoid having to use the ODBC layer or `OleDB` to communicate to legacy database drivers.

When debugging, you need to keep in mind the difference between the two namespaces. Even though most of the features look and act alike, you might run into some problems. For instance, the connection strings differ slightly; if you are working with parameters, you need to make sure that you are formatting the string correctly.

When connecting to a Microsoft SQL Server database, you might want to increase your overall performance by using `SqlDataAdapter` along with its associated `SqlCommand` and `SqlConnection`.

Data Connection Performance Note

If you are concerned about performance, keep in mind the type of connection you will be using. When you are developing a database component, you might think about keeping it flexible enough to work on— say, with Oracle and SQL Server. To get the best performance, you could detect which database you are using and then use the classes that best suit your needs. This would fall under more of a commercial software product feature, but that is one bit of information to think about.

Summary

Let's take a look at what we have covered so far. First we looked at some of the new features Microsoft has added and showed where you might stumble in your transition to .NET. Next we dug into how the system used the `SQLException` class to handle errors that are thrown by the system. This is a very powerful tool for debugging, so get used to using it in your code.

Then the chapter moved into possible problems that you might run into with the `SQLConnection` class and showed how to avoid common mistakes. We also covered some typical error messages and how to fix the errors that they represent. Remember, those data grid controls are a powerful tool, so take advantage of them to do as much work for you as possible.

V

Appendix

A Issues that Arise When Migrating from ASP to ASP.NET

Issues That Arise When Migrating from ASP to ASP.NET

S O NOW THAT YOU HAVE DECIDED TO start writing all your web-based applications in ASP.NET, you must be wondering what issues you will encounter while migrating from ASP to ASP.NET. Unfortunately, this can be a lengthy list, depending on the situation you are in. If you are porting an existing application to the ASP.NET framework, a variety of changes will need to be made to your existing VBScript code. However, of you are starting a project from scratch, you will need to remember only the language and logic changes that are now in the Visual Basic language.

In the next few sections, we discuss the syntactical changes that have been made to Visual Basic. We will also take a look at C# and why you might want to use it for your server-side programming language.

Keep in mind that this is not an exhaustive list of changes between the two versions. This appendix attempts to look at only features that existed in the previous version that have been migrated to the new version. Features in .NET that were not in a previous version will not be discussed here.

Moving from ASP to ASP.NET

Although ASP.NET is based on the ASP technology, a lot of the fundamentals have changed. Here we explore some of the basic changes that you will encounter when migrating from ASP to ASP.NET.

<%%> Versus <script>

In ASP, all server-side code is written between <% and %> tags. This tells the ASP interpreter that everything between the two tags is program code and should be executed on the server.

In ASP.NET, the rules have changed a bit. Now, all variable and function declarations are placed between <script> and </script> tags, while implementation logic is contained in between the <% and %> tags. Listing A.1 shows an example ASP page, and Listing A.2 and Listing A.3 show the same page written in ASP.NET, using Visual Basic .NET and C#, respectively.

Listing A.1   **ASP Page (C#)**

```
<%
    Sub MyFunction(psString)
        If psString <> "" then
            Response.Write psString
        End If
    End Sub


    MyFunction Request.Form("txtText")
%>


<html>
<body>
    <form action="test.asp" method="POST">
        <input type="text" name="txtText">
        <input type="submit">
    </form>
</body>
</html>
```

Listing A.2   **ASP.NET Page (Visual Basic .NET)**

```
<%@ Page Language="vb"%>
<script language="vb" runat="server">
    Sub MyFunction(psString as String)
        If psString <> "" then
            Response.Write(psString)
        End If
    End Sub
</script>
```

```
<%
    MyFunction(Request.Form.Get("txtText"))
%>


<html>
<body>
    <form action="test.aspx" method="POST">
        <input type="text" name="txtText">
        <input type="submit">
    </form>
</body>
</html>
```

Listing A.3 **ASP.NET Page (C#)**

```
<%@ Page Language="c#"%>
<script language="c#" runat="server">
    void MyFunction(String psString)
    {
        if(psString != "")
            Response.Write(psString);
    }
</script>


<%
    MyFunction(Request.Form.Get("txtText"));
%>


<html>
<body>
    <form action="test.aspx" method="POST">
        <input type="text" name="txtText">
        <input type="submit">
    </form>
</body>
</html>
```

You should notice a few things here. First, note the format of the <script> tag, depending on which language you are using as your server-side code. You will want to use the language parameter to specify this. For Visual Basic .NET, you set the language parameter to vb; in C#, you set it to c#.

Second, notice that the function definition is placed between the `<script>` tags, as described previously, but the actual call to it, the implementation logic, is placed between the standard ASP `<%%>` tags. In ASP.NET, you must define all functions within `<script>` tags. However, calls to the function must be placed within the standard `<%%>` tags.

Finally, notice that instead of calling `Request.Form("txtText")` to get the value of the text box upon submission, you use a method of the `Form` object called `Get`. This method exists off the `QueryString` and `Cookie` collections also. Be sure to explicitly specify this in your code when trying to access any of the members of these collections; otherwise, your code will not compile.

Page Directives

The page directives that you are familiar with in ASP are still available in ASP.NET. However, a few new ones are worthy of mention. Table A.1 lists the new directives and what they can do for you.

Table A.1   **ASP.NET Page Directives**

Directive	Description
@ Page	Specifies page-specific attributes
@ Control	Specifies control-specific attributes
@ Import	Imports a namespace into the page
@ Register	Associates aliases with namespaces and class names for concise notation in Custom Server Control Syntax
@ Assembly	Links an assembly with the current page
@ OutputCache	Controls the caching of the page

Response.Redirect Versus *Page.Navigate* Versus *Server.Transfer*

To send the browser to a new page in ASP, the `Redirect` method of the `Response` object is used as shown:

```
Response.Redirect "OtherPage.aspx"
```

In ASP.NET, you have two alternatives to this method. The first is the `Navigate` method of the `Page` object. The function takes the same parameter as `Response.Redirect`: the URL to redirect to. The difference between the two methods is that `Page.Navigate` calls `Response.Redirect`, unloads all controls in the tree, and then calls `Response.End`.

The second method, `Server.Transfer` terminates execution of the current ASP.NET page and then begins execution of the request on the page specified. It takes the following form:

```
Server.Transfer "OtherPage.aspx"
```

At this point in the code, whatever script was being executed stops and then starts at the top of `OtherPage.asp`.

You should use `Page.Navigate` when you want to completely stop execution of one page and immediately move to the other, discarding the results of the current page. The `Server.Transfer` method should be used when you want to start execution on another page without discarding any of the previously computed information.

Cookies

The use of cookies is very different in ASP.NET. Instead of a cookie collection being part of the `Response` and `Request` objects, cookies are now objects that are manipulated individually and tossed into a master collection.

Previously, to add a cookie to the client machine, your code would look similar to Listing A.4.

Listing A.4 **ASP Cookie Code**

```
<%
     Response.Cookies("MyCookie") = "Brian"
%>
<html>
<body>
The cookie is:
<%
     Response.Write(Request.Cookies("MyCookie"))
%>
</body>
</html>
```

The same code in ASP.NET is quite different. What makes it different is that cookies are now treated as objects. You create and instantiate a cookie object, set its value, and then append it onto the cookie collection. Requesting it back out of the collection is very similar to doing so in ASP. Just remember to use the `Get` method, as was shown in the previous section. Listing A.5 illustrates the procedure in Visual Basic .NET, and Listing A.6 illustrates the sequence in C#.

Listing A.5 **Cookies (Visual Basic .NET)**

```
<%@ Page Language="vb"%>
<%
    Dim oCookie As HttpCookie
    oCookie = new HttpCookie("MyCookie")
    oCookie.Values.Add("Name","Brian")
    Response.AppendCookie(oCookie)
%>


<html>
<body>
<%
    Response.Write(Request.Cookies.Get("MyCookie").Value)
%>
</body>
</html>
```

Listing A.6 **Cookies (C#)**

```
<%@ Page Language="c#"%>
<%
    HttpCookie oCookie;
    oCookie = new HttpCookie("MyCookie");
    oCookie.Values.Add("Name","Brian");
    Response.AppendCookie(oCookie);
%>


<html>
<body>
<%
    Response.Write(Request.Cookies.Get("MyCookie").Value);
%>
</body>
</html>
```

Events

Another major change to the way ASP.NET works is that it is based on an event model much like a typical Visual Basic program. Instead of your ASP script being executed from top to bottom, you can respond to events such as button clicks, text box changes, and so on. Of course, all these events will occur on the server side, so you will not be able to hook into every possible event, such as a mouse move or a key-down event.

Moving from VBScript to Visual Basic

You should be aware of quite a few syntactical changes to the Visual Basic programming language before you start any project in this language. This section looks at most of the changes in Visual Basic .NET.

Set

Let's start out with the keyword Set. In short, it is gone. The standard object instantiation in Visual Basic is shown here:

```
Set objMyObj = objSomeOtherObj
```

In Visual Basic .NET, this code has been shortened to more closely match the C# programming language. The same code in Visual Basic .NET looks like this:

```
objMyObj = objSomeOtherObj
```

Properties

Properties have been greatly simplified in the world of the new Visual Basic. Previously, a series of properties looked like the code in Listing A.7.

Listing A.7 **Visual Basic Property Code**

```
Private gsString As String
Private goObject as Object

Public Property Let StringProp(ByVal psData as String)
    gsString = psData
End Property

Public Property Get StringProp() As String
    StringProp = gsString
End Property

Public Property Set ObjectProp(ByVal poObj as Object)
    Set goObject = poObj
End Property
```

In Visual Basic .NET, this is much shorter; an example is given in Listing A.8.

Listing A.8 **Visual Basic .NET Property Code**

```
Private gsString as String
Private goObject as Object

Public Property StringProp as String
    Get
        StringProp = gsString
    End Get

    Set
        gsString = StringProp
    End Set
End Property
```

As you can see, there is no longer a distinction between a `Set` and a `Let` because of the change mentioned in the last section.

Calling Subs

Calls of all types (function, method, and sub) must use parentheses around the parameters, regardless of whether you are doing something with the return value. For example, the code in Listing A.9 would work in Visual Basic or VBScript.

Listing A.9 **Visual Basic Function Calls**

```
dtDate = Date
MyFunction "Value1", 2, plVal
```

However, in Visual Basic .NET, you would need to change these same calls to the code shown in Listing A.10.

Listing A.10 **Visual Basic .NET Function Calls**

```
dtDate = Date()
MyFunction("Value1", 2, plVal)
```

Parameters

A major change to the ways parameters are passed has been introduced into Visual Basic .NET. Previously, all parameters were passed `ByRef` if no method was specified. Now, all intrinsic types are passed `ByVal`. So, the function in Listing A.11 would no longer work in Visual Basic .NET.

Listing A.11 **Visual Basic Function with *ByRef* Parameters**

```
Sub MyFunction(plLng1 As Long, plLng2 As Long, plLng3 As Long)
    plLng3 = plLng1 + plLng2
End Sub
```

In Visual Basic .NET, this subroutine would have to be rewritten as shown in Listing A.12.

Listing A.12 **Visual Basic .NET Function with *ByRef* Parameters**

```
Sub MyFunction(plLng1 As Long, plLng2 As Long, ByRef plLng3 as Long)
    plLng3 = plLng1 + plLng2
End Sub
```

Datatypes

Unlike VBScript, Visual Basic supports a wide range of variable types. The same can be said of Visual Basic .NET. In previous server-side code you have written, all variables were declared as type `Variant`. With your server-side code written in Visual Basic .NET, it is highly recommended that, when you're declaring variables, you define them appropriately so that they will not use excess memory and will be far more efficient. Listing A.13 shows a few examples of how to declare variables of specific types.

Listing A.13 **Visual Basic .NET Variable Declarations**

```
Dim psString As String
Dim plLong as Long
Dim bByte as Byte
```

Also be aware that the Currency datatype has been removed.

Something else to note is that the sizes of certain intrinsic datatypes have changed. Refer to Table A.2 for more information.

Table A.2 **Visual Basic .NET Intrinsic Datatypes**

Datatype	Size
Byte	1 byte (8 bits)
Short	2 bytes (16 bits)
Integer	4 bytes (32 bits)
Long	8 bytes (64 bits)

continues

Table A.2 **Continued**

Datatype	Size
Single	4 bytes (32 bits)
Double	8 bytes (64 bits)
Decimal	12 bytes (96 bits)

Note here that the sizes for Integer and Long datatypes have changed. Long is now 64 bits instead of 32 bits, and Integer is now 32 bits rather than 16 bits.

Variant

The Variant datatype no longer exists in Visual Basic .NET. It has been replaced with the universal Object type. Also removed from Visual Basic .NET is the VarType function. Now, to get the type of a specific variable, you can use the following property that is a member of all the intrinsic datatypes:

```
SomeObj.GetType.GetTypeCode.value
```

Declarations

A new feature of Visual Basic .NET is the capability to initialize variables and arrays at the time of declaration, as shown in Listing A.14.

Listing A.14 **Visual Basic .NET Variable Initializations**

```
Dim psString As String = "Hello!"
Dim piInt as Integer = 123
Const cSTRING = "Goodbye!"
Dim psArray(2) As String = ("Brian", "Jon")
```

Note, however, that the capability to declare strings of a predefined length is missing in Visual Basic .NET. Therefore, the statement Dim psString As String * 5 is no longer valid.

Shorthand Syntax

Visual Basic .NET now supports shorthand assignment much like C, C++, and Java. The code in Listing A.15 illustrates a few examples of the shorthand notation.

Listing A.15 **Shorthand Assignments in Visual Basic .NET**

```
plVal = 100
plVal += 10   ' plVal now equals 110
plVal -= 10   ' plVal now equals 100
```

```
plVal *= 5    ' plVal now equals 500
plVal /= 5    ' plVal now equals 100
```

Error Handling

Although the standard `On Error GoTo XXX` and `On Error Resume Next` exist in Visual Basic .NET, you also might want to take advantage of its built-in structured error handling, which is similar to that of languages such as C++ and Java. The code in Listing A.16 shows an example of structured error handling in Visual Basic .NET.

Listing A.16   **Structured Error Handling in Visual Basic .NET**

```
Try
     ' Some code
Catch
     ' What to run when an error occurs
Finally
     ' Code that always executes after try or catch
End Try
```

Structure Declaration

In Visual Basic, structures were defined using the `Type...End Type`, as shown in Listing A.17.

Listing A.17   **Visual Basic .NET Structure**

```
Type Employee
     EmpName As String
     EmpNumber As Long
     EmpAge As Integer
End Type
```

In the new Visual Basic .NET, this same structure would be declared using the `Structure...End Structure` keywords, as shown in Listing A.18.

Listing A.18   **Visual Basic .NET Structure**

```
Structure Employee
     EmpName As String
     EmpNumber As Long
     EmpAge As Integer
End Structure
```

Variable Scope

The scope of variables in Visual Basic .NET is slightly different from that of Visual Basic. In Visual Basic, the code in Listing A.19 would be valid.

Listing A.19   **Variable Scope in Visual Basic .NET**

```
For plCount = 0 to 10
    Dim plVal as Long
    plVal = plVal + plCount
Next


plVal2 = 2 ^ plVal
```

In Visual Basic .NET, however, because the variable plVal is declared inside the For...Next loop, its scope is inside that block. Therefore, it cannot be seen outside the loop in the previous example.

Object Creation

In Visual Basic, the following statement would declare an object and set it to Nothing until it was used. At that point, it would reference a new instance of MyObject.

```
Dim poObject as New MyObject
```

In Visual Basic .NET, however, this statement is actually shorthand for the following:

```
Dim poObject As MyObject = New MyObject
```

In this statement, the object is created and references a new instance of the object.

IsMissing

Ironically, in Visual Basic .NET, IsMissing is, well, missing. This means that all optional parameters to a function must be declared with a default value, as follows:

```
Sub MySub(Optional psStr = "Default value!")
```

Control-of-Flow Statements

Certain control-of-flow tatements have been removed from Visual Basic .NET, including these:

- GoSub
- On...GoSub
- On...GoTo (On Error...GoTo is still valid)

A change also has been made to the While loop. Previously, While...Wend was valid; however, now the syntax has changed to While...End While.

And the Rest

To wrap this all up, here is a list of everything that has been removed from the Visual Basic .NET programming language:

- As Any keyword phrase
- Atn function
- Calendar property
- Circle statement
- Currency datatype
- Date function and statement
- Debug.Assert method
- Debug.Print method
- Deftype statements
- DoEvents function
- Empty keyword
- Eqv operator
- GoSub statement
- Imp operator
- Initialize event
- Instancing property
- IsEmpty function
- IsMissing function
- IsNull function
- IsObject function
- Let statement
- Line statement
- LSet statement
- MsgBox function
- Null keyword
- On ... GoSub construction
- On ... GoTo construction
- Option Base statement
- Option Private Module statement
- Property Get, Property Let, and Property Set statements
- PSet method

continues

- Rnd function
- Round function
- RSet statement
- Scale method
- Set statement
- Sgn function
- Sqr function
- String function
- Terminate event
- Time function and statement
- Type statement
- Variant datatype
- VarType function
- Wend keyword

Opting for C#

If you are more familiar with the syntax of C, C++ or Java, you might be interested in using C# (pronounced "C sharp") as your server-side programming language. If you are currently a Visual Basic programmer wanting to move to C#, you should be aware of a few syntactic changes. We will look at some of these differences in the next sections; however, be aware that this is not a comprehensive look at the entire C# programming language—it's merely a guide to ease you into the C# language.

Case Sensitivity

One of the main differences between the languages is that C# is case-sensitive, while Visual Basic is not. Therefore, although the code in Listing A.20 is acceptable in Visual Basic, the code in Listing A.21 would be needed in C#.

Listing A.20 **Valid Code (Visual Basic .NET)**

```
psStr = psstr & "Hello"
plVAL1 = plval1 + plval2
```

Listing A.21 **Valid Code (C#)**

```
psStr = psStr & "Hello"
plVal1 = plVal1 + plVal2
```

Semicolons

One of the very first things to be aware of is the use of semicolons to end programming statements. In Visual Basic, statements are terminated by a carriage return; in C#, they are terminated with a ; character. Listing A.22 shows a few lines of code in Visual Basic, and Listing A.23 shows the equivalent code in C#.

Listing A.22   **Some Statements (Visual Basic .NET)**

```
n += 10
MyFunction("Brian", "Jon")
MyLongerFunction("Brian", _
    "Jon")
```

Listing A.23   **The Same Statements (C#)**

```
n += 10;
MyFunction("Brian", "Jon")
MyLongerFunction("Brian",
    "Jon");
```

Brackets

Another syntactical change is the type of brackets that are used for collection and array indexers. In Visual Basic, parentheses—(and)—are used around these values; in C#, square brackets—[and]—are used. Listing A.24 shows the use of brackets in Visual Basic.

Listing A.24   **Use of Brackets (Visual Basic .NET)**

```
MyArray(0) = "Brian"
MyArray(1) = "Jon"

MyCollection("Brian") = "Cool"
MyCollection("Jon") = "Not So Cool"
```

In C#, these same statements would be written as shown in Listing A.25.

Listing A.25   **Use of Brackets (C#)**

```
MyArray[0] = "Brian";
MyArray[1] = "Jon";

MyCollection["Brian"] = "Cool";
MyCollection["Jon"] = "Not So Cool";
```

Functions

Functions are declared very differently in C# than in Visual Basic. Listing A.26 illustrates a typical function implementation in Visual Basic.

Listing A.26   **Function (Visual Basic .NET)**

```
Public Function MyFunction(psStr As String) As String
    MyFunction = psStr
End Function
```

Now let's look at that same function in C#. Listing A.34 is a listing of the same function in C#.

Listing A.27   **Function (C#)**

```
public String MyFunction(String psStr)
{
    return psStr;
}
```

Let's talk about the differences. First, note the case difference in each of the languages. It is extremely important that you remember that C# is a case-sensitive language. Second, you will notice that, in Visual Basic, the type of the function is noted at the end of the function line with the words As String. In C#, however, the type of the function is declared before the name of the function as String. Third, you will see that the Visual Basic function is closed with the End Function statement. In C#, all statements of a function are enclosed around curly braces—{ and }. Fourth, you'll see that the parameters passed in the Visual Basic version are typed after the variable name, just like the function. In C#, the variables are typed before the variable name, again like the type of the function. Finally, the Visual Basic version of the function returns the value of psStr by assigning it to the name of the function, MyFunction. In C#, however, to return a value, you use the return statement, which does the same thing.

Control-of-Flow Statements

All the standard flow-control statements that you are familiar with in Visual Basic exist in C# and have the same functionality; however, their syntax is different. In this section, we look at all the flow-control statements and their syntax in C#.

If Statement

In Visual Basic, the standard If statement takes the form of the code in Listing A.28.

Listing A.28   *If* **Statement (Visual Basic .NET)**

```
If plVal < 10 Then
    ...
Else
    ...
End If
```

In C#, this format is somewhat modified. Listing A.29 shows the same statement in C#.

Listing A.29   *if* **Statement in (C#)**

```
if (plVal < 10)
{
    ...
}
else
{
    ...
}
```

Although it isn't drastically different, you should pay attention to the parentheses around the test statement and the use of curly braces to enclose the code statements. Also you will see that the End If clause is missing. Finally, note the case of the words if and else.

For **Statement**

The For loop is written very differently in C# than it is in Visual Basic. Listing A.30 shows a Visual Basic for loop, and Listing A.31 shows the same loop written in the C# programming language.

Listing A.30   *For* **Statement (Visual Basic .NET)**

```
For plCount = 0 to 100
    plVal = plVal + 1
Next
```

Listing A.31   *For* **Statement (C#)**

```
for(plCount = 0; plCount < 100; plCount++)
{
    plVal = plVal + 1;
}
```

Both of these loops perform the exact same function; however, they each have a very different syntax. Generically, the C# version of the for loop is written as shown in Listing A.32.

Listing A.32 **Generic C#** *for* **Loop**

```
for(initialization; test; increment)
{
    ...
    statements;
    ...
}
```

While **Loop**

The while loop is very similar in both programming languages. Listing A.33 shows a typical while loop in Visual Basic.

Listing A.33 *While* **Loop (Visual Basic .NET)**

```
While plVal1 < plVal2
    plVal1 = plVal1 + 1
Loop
```

In the C# programming language, this same loop would be written as shown in Listing A.41.

Listing A.34 *While* **Loop (C#)**

```
while(plVal1 < plVal2)
{
    plVal1 = plVal1 + 1
}
```

This syntax is very similar to that of the for loop discussed previously. The two things to remember are the parentheses around the test statement and the curly braces in place of the Loop statement to enclose the statements to be executed while the conditional is true.

Switch **Versus** *Select*

In the world of Visual Basic, one of the most useful flow-control statements is the Select...Case..End Select statement. It looks like the code in Listing A.35.

Listing A.35   *Select...Case...End Select* **Statement (Visual Basic .NET)**

```
Select Case plVal
    Case 1
        psStr = "Brian"
    Case 2
        psStr = "Jon"
    Case Else
        psStr = "Else!"
End Select
```

In C#, this same statement is called a `switch` and is written like the code in Listing A.36.

Listing A.36   *switch* **Statement (C#)**

```
switch(plVal)
{
    case 1:
        psStr = "Brian";
        break;
    case 2:
        psStr = "Jon";
        break;
    default:
        psStr = "Default!";
        break;
}
```

Summary

This appendix looked at the ways in which the Visual Basic programming language has changed from the language that you know and love, for better or worse. It also discussed some of the very basic syntactical changes that exist between the Visual Basic and C# programming languages. With this information, you will be prepared to convert any existing Visual Basic code to Visual Basic .NET—or even potentially into the C# programming language. You will also be ready to start writing Visual Basic .NET or C# code from scratch without having to battle with the new syntax changes inherent in both languages. This will certainly help you when you're trying to figure out why your new programs aren't compiling properly.

Index

Symbols

() (parentheses) characters, 319

? (question mark) character, 298

; (semicolon) character, 319

[] (square brackets) characters, 319

<asp:></asp> style tags, 141

#error directive, 77-78

  Listing 5.8, 78

#if...#endif directives (C#), 76

#If...Then...#End If directives (Visual Basic .NET), 76

@OutputCache directive, 190

  Duration attribute, 190

  VaryByCustom attribute, 191

  VaryByHeader attribute, 191

  VaryByParam attribute, 190-191

@Page directive, 80

#undef directive, 77

  Listing 5.7, 77

__VIEWSTATE form variable, 151

#warning directive, 77-78

  Listing 5.8, 78

A

Access Denied error, 284

  acceptable keywords, 284

  connection strings, 285

  debugging, 284

AddAt method, 35

ADO recordsets

  retrieving, 11

  SQL objects versus OleDb objects, 300

ADO.NET, 26, 273

  connecting to data source

    Listing 3.1, 26

    Listing 3.4, 27

  new features, 273-274

  versus ADO, 273-274

Application_Error event handler, 60-63

  Listing 4.26, 60

  Listing 4.27, 60

<asp:></asp> style tags, 141

ASP

  cookies, 309

    Listing A.4, 309

  creating a debug object, 16-21

    Listing 2.4, 16

    Listing 2.5, 20

  debugging strategies, 14

    creating an ASP debug object, 16-21

    Response object, 14

    Server object, 14-16

  drawbacks, 13

  function libraries, 11-12

  includes, 13

  migrating from to ASP.NET, 305

    <%%> versus <script>, 306-308

    cookies, 309

    events, 310

page directives, 308
  Response.Redirect, 308-309
pages, 10
  Listing 2.1, 10
  structure, 10-12
retrieving an ADO recordset,
  Listing 2.2, 11
use of events, 13
versus ASP.NET, 306-310
  Listing A.1, 306
  Listing A.2, 306

ASP.NET versus ASP, 306-310
  Listing A.1, 306
  Listing A.2, 306

ASPError object, 14
  debugging with, Listing 2.3, 15

aspx
  implementing classes in a web
    page, 167
      Listing 10.12, 167
      Listing 10.13, 168
  ItemTemplate tag, 162-163

assemblies, 267
  strong-named, 268-271
    Listing 15.7, 268
    Listing 15.8, 270

attributes
  @OutputCache directive
    Duration, 190
    VaryByCustom, 191
    VaryByHeader, 191
    VaryByParam, 190-191
  function, 70-72
  runat, 175
  Trace, 80
  transactions, 267

authorization, role-based security,
  253-261

AuthorLogic class, 45
  code-behind classes
    Listing 4.14, 50
    Listing 4.15, 52
  using
    Listing 4.12, 48
    Listing 4.13, 49

B

binary files, 224
breakpoints, VS.NET, 99-100
  setting, 106-107
business objects, 45-53
  Listing 4.10, 46
    compiling, 48
  Listing 4.11, 47
    compiling, 48
  tiers, 26-28

C

C#
  #if...#endif directives, 76
  as server-side programming
    language, 318
  For statements, 321-322
    Listing A.32, 322
  If statements, 320
    Listing A.29, 321
  listings
    #error directive, 78
    #undef directive, 77
    #warning directive, 78
    accessing data by column name, 289
    Application_Error event handler, 60
    *assigning User Control properties
      programmatically, 177*
    *author search page using AuthorLogic
      object, 48*
    automatic transaction processing, 265
    basic component, 232

business object code, 46

calling a User Control method, 182

Case/Switch block, 54

checking for existing debuggers, 234

code with a single exit point, 57

code with multiple exit points, 55

code-behind class for author search page using AuthorLogic object, 50

code-behind class referencing user controls, 44

code-behind file for Visual Studio .NET inline debugging example, 105

complex return type (Web Services), 206

complex role-based security, 257

conditional compiling with function attributes, 70

conditional compiling with preprocessor directives, 73

connecting to the database, 285

connection pooling , 296

custom return type (Web Services), 207

Data Reader connections errors, 294

DataBind method, 292

Debug WriteLineIf method, 240

debugging arrays, 287

dynamically loading User Controls, 185

dynamically setting the IsEnabled property, 86

Emailer component, 113

event handler for paging through a data grid, 161

fix for XMLSerializer error in Web Services, 214

GetSqlExceptionDump function, 276

grid paging event handler, 159

If statement, 321

implementing a parameter using the SqlCommand class, 299

implementing TraceContext.Write (string), 87

implementing TraceContext.Write(string, string), 88

implementing TraceContext.Write(string, string, Exception), 90

invalidating output caches through validation callbacks, 192-193

large If statement block, 53

modified code for btn Submit_ServerClick, 115

MyControl with a property, 176

MyControl with method, 180

namespace errors, 165-166

navigating the stack frame by frame, 236

offset error, 224

passing a FileStream object, 220

property assignment order (User Controls), 179

returning binary data, 222

sample code to connect to the database, 277

server controls, code-behind files, 148

server-side events, 5

setting the data source from behind the aspx page, 290

setting up file dependencies, 196

simple data grid control, 158

simple HttpHandler class, 244

simple role-based security, 254

simple Web Services code, 204

single-cache key dependencies, 197

SoapException, 227

Stack Trace dump, 236

stack trace inside component, 239

StackTrace GetMethod, 238

strong-named assemblies, 268

tab controls in creating server controls, 142

testing controls, 147
throwing a handled exception, 62
throwing exceptions, 217
trace listener, 240
tracing within components, 93
tracing within components, 94
transactions, 282
trapping a specific exception type, 59
try-catch method on the client
side, 218
use of square brackets, 319
user controls and code-behind classes,
42-43
using XML as data source, 169
validating input, 30
validating output, 31
validation controls, adding, 33
validation controls, dynamically
creating, 33
validation controls, placement and
behavior, 35
Web Services code, 204
Web Services data type error, 220
Web Services data type error,
corrected, 220
WebMethod error, 215
operators, testing whether an item
has been defined, 76
preprocessor directives, 76
#error, 77-78
#undef, 77
#warning, 77-78
server-side events, Listing 1.2, 5
Switch statements, 322
use of semicolons, 319
use of square brackets, 319
Listing A.25, 319
using as server-side programming
language, 305
versus Visual Basic
brackets, 319
case sensitivity, 318

control-of-flow statements, 320-322
functions, 320
semicolons, 319
While statements, 322

caching, 189
Caching API, 196
date and time expirations, 199
dependencies, setting up, 196-197
dependencies, single-key, 197-198
removing cached items, 200
retrieving cached items, 199-200
output, 190
@OutputCache directive, 190
Use Controls, 191-192
validation callbacks, 192-196

Caching API, 196
date and time expirations, 199
dependencies
setting up, 196-197
single-key, 197-198
removing cached items, 200
retrieving cached items, 199-200

call stack, Visual Studio .NET,
98, 111
tracing functions, 111

case sensitivity, Visual Basic versus
C#, 318

Case/Switch constructs
control-of-flow guidelines, 53-55
Listing 4.18, 54
Listing 4.19, 55
replacing If statements, 54

classes
class names
defining for dynamic User Controls,
184-186
code-behind, 40-41
DataReader, 281
Debugger, 234
Environment, 236

Exception
  use in structured exception
    handling, 58
HttpApplication, 60
OleDb, 275
  catching errors, 275
OleDbException, 275
SoapException, 227
SqlClient, 275
  catching errors, 275
SqlException, 275
  displaying properties, 276-277
  functionality, 277-279
  runtime errors, 279
StackTrace, 235
TraceContext, 79
  methods, 87
  properties, 86-87
User Control, referencing, 185

**client-side events compared to
server-side, 4**

**CLR (Common Language
Runtime), 103**

clsDebug, 16

code
  code partitioning, 39
    user controls, Listing 4.4, 42
  structuring, 39
    code partitioning, 39
    control-of-flow guidelines, 53
    global exception handling, 59
    structured exception handling, 58

code partitioning, 39
  business objects, 45-53
  code-behind classes, 40-41
    Listing 4.1, 40-41
    Listing 4.2, 40
    Listing 4.8, 44
    Listing 4.9, 45
    using AuthorLogic object
  user controls, 41-45
    Listing 4.4, 42

code-behind classes, 40-41
  Listing 4.1, 40-41
  Listing 4.2, 40
  Listing 4.8, 44
  Listing 4.9, 45
  using AuthorLogic object
    Listing 4.14, 50
    Listing 4.15, 52

COM components
  Interop utility, 250
  security issues, 250
  versus .NET, 249-251

COM+
  automatic transaction processing,
    265-267
  bridging to .NET functionality, 253

**command window, Visual Studio
.NET, 98-99, 109**
  functions, executing, 109
  variables
  viewing, 109
  variables, changing values, 109

**Common Language Runtime
(CLR), 103**

compiling conditional, 69
  displaying messages during
    compiles, 77
  function attributes, 70-72
    Listing 5.1, 70
    Listing 5.2, 71
  preprocessor directives, 73-76
    Listing 5.3, 73
    Listing 5.4, 74

**Component Services Microsoft
Management Console, 261-264**

ComponentModel namespace, 231

components, 231
  COM, security issues, 250
  connection, 280

creating, 231-234
Listing 14.1, 232
Listing 14.2, 233
garbage collection, 251
HttpHandlers, 243-245
implementing, 243
Listing 14.18, 244
Listing 14.19, 245
subtags, 243
installing, 251
Interop utility, 250
memory management, 251
.NET versus COM, 249-250
installing, 251
OleDb.OleDbConnection, 280-281
registry, 251
relationships among .NET data
components, 275
SqlClient.SqlConnection, 280
stack traces, 239
Listing 14.11, 239
tracing within, 93-95
Listing 6.11, 93
Listing 6.12, 94
Listing 6.13, 94
Listing 6.14, 94
uninstalling, 251-252

conditional compiling, 69
displaying messages during
compiles, 77
function attributes, 70-72
Listing 5.1, 70
Listing 5.2, 71
preprocessor directives, 73-76
Listing 5.3, 73
Listing 5.4, 74

**config.web files, setting up custom
error pages, 63**
Listing 4.30, 64
modifying existing, 64

connection pooling, 295-296
Listing 16.21, 296
Listing 16.22, 296

connections, multiple
common pitfalls, 295-296
errors, 293

**Control Tree section (TraceContext
class), 83**

control-of-flow statements
guidelines, 53
Case/Switch contructs, 53-55
function and loop exit points, 55-58
If statements, 53-55
VBScript versus Visual Basic, 316
Visual Basic versus C#, 320
For statements, 321-322
If statements, 320-321
*Select...Case...End Select
statements, 322*
While statements, 322

controls
data grid, 157-159
paging, 159-162
data-bound, 157
server, 141
creating, 142-144, 147-151
tab, creating server controls, 142-144

cookies, 83, 309
ASP versus ASP.NET, 309

**Cookies Collection section
(TraceContext class), 83-84**

custom error pages, 63
building, 64
Listing 4.31, 64

D

data grid controls, 157-159
Listing 10.1, 158
Listing 10.2, 158
paging, 159-162
Listing 10.3, 159
Listing 10.4, 160

Listing 10.5, 161
Listing 10.6, 162

data grids
assigning data sources, 289
Listing 16.14, 290
Listing 16.15, 290
No Data in Data Grid error, 291

data link files, 26

data tiers, 24–26

data types
cached items, 199
Variant, 314
VBScript versus Visual Basic, 313
Visual Basic .NET intrinsic, 313
Web Services errors, 219–220

data-bound controls, 157

DataAdapter object versus DataReader, 297

databases, overusing, 297
common pitfalls, 298

DataBind method, 291
Listing 16.16, 291
Listing 16.17, 292
Listing 16.18, 292

DataBinder, 163
used in place of a recordset,
Listing 10.7, 163

DataReader class, 281

DataReader object
connections errors, 294
Listing 16.19, 294
Listing 16.20, 294
versus DataAdapter, 297

date and time expirations (Caching API), 199

Debug.Writeline method, 239

Debug.WriteLineIf method
Listing 14.12, 240
Listing 14.13, 240

Debugger class, 234

debuggers
checking for existing, 234
Listing 14.3, 234
Listing 14.4, 235
starting a new instance, 234

debugging
clsDebug, 16
creating an ASP debug object, 16–21
strategies, 14
Response object, 14
Server object, 14-16

declarations, VBScript versus Visual Basic, 314

dependencies
setting up with Caching API,
196–197
Listing 12.3, 196
Listing 12.4, 197
single-key, 197–198
Listing 12.5, 197
Listing 12.6, 198

Distributed Transaction Coordinator, 271–272

Duration attribute (@OutputCache directive), 190

dynamic User Controls, 184
class names, defining, 184–186
errors, 186–187
User Control classes,
referencing, 185

E

Emailer component, 112
Listing 7.4, 113
Listing 7.5, 114

end tags (User Controls), 175

Environment class, 236

#error directive, 77-78
  Listing 5.8, 78
error handling, 284
  Access Denied, 284
    acceptable keywords, 284
    connection strings, 285
    debugging, 284
  connections problems, 293
  IndexOutOfRangeException,
    287-288
    column names, 288
    debugging, 287
  invalid data source, 289-290
  no data in data grid, 291
  SELECT Permission Denied, 285
    column-level security, 286
    debugging, 285-286
    Listing 16.8, 285
    product table permissions, 286
  VBScript versus Visual Basic, 315
    Listing A.16, 315
errors, Web Services, 205-213
  XMLSerializer class, 214
event handlers
  Application_Error, 60-63
  grid paging, 159
Event Log. *See* **Windows 2000**
  Event Log
EventLog class, viewing event
  logs, 129
EventLog object, 120-121
  creating custom event logs with,
    121-124
events, 310
  ASP versus ASP.NET, 310
  client-side compared to
    server-side, 4
  handling, 124
    expected events, 124, 127
    Listing 8.5, 124-126

Listing 8.7, 127-128
    unexpected events, 127-129
  logging, accessing event log data via
    the web, 129, 135-136
  server-side, 3-4
    compared to client-side events, 4
    life cycle of pages, 5-7
    types, 4-5
  System.Diagnostics event log
    interface, 120-121
  use of in ASP, 13
  Windows 2000 Event Log, 119-120
Exception class, use in structured
  exception handling, 58
exception handling
  global, 59
    Application_Error event handler,
      60-63
    custom error pages, 63-64
  structured, 58
    catching specific exceptions, 58
    use of Exception class, 58
    when to use, 58
  throwing a handled exception
    Listing 4.28, 62
    Listing 4.29, 63
exit points (loop and function)
  control-of-flow guidelines, 55-58
    Listing 4.20, 55
    Listing 4.21, 56
    Listing 4.22, 57
    Listing 4.23, 57
  status flags, 57
expected events, handling, 124-127

F

files
  binary, 224
  data link, 26
  dependencies
    setting up with Caching API,
    196-197
    single-key, 197-198
  global.asax, 6
  available events, 6
  web.config, 80, 241
  defaultLanguage parameters, 103
  Web.Config, Listing 14.16, 241

FileStream object, 220

For statements, Visual Basic versus C#, 321-322

Form Collection section (TraceContext class), 84

forms, displaying, Listing 3.7, 32

functions
  attributes, 70-72
  calling
    Listing A.10, 312
    Listing A.9, 312
  displaying currently called, 98
  executing in Visual Studio .NET
    command
    windows, 109
  exit points, control-of-flow
    guidelines, 55-58
  testing output, 31
    Listing 3.5, 31
    Listing 3.6, 31
  tracing in Visual Studio .NET call
    stacks, 111
  Visual Basic versus C#, 320

G

garbage collection (.NET components), 251

GetAuthorByName method, 45

GetAuthorByState method, 45

GetBaseException() method, 61

GetEventLogs method, 135

GetLastError() method, 61

GetMethod (StackTrace), 237

GetValue method
  debugging arrays, 287
    Listing 16.10, 287
    Listing 16.11, 287

global exception handling, 59
  Application_Error event handler,
    60-63
  custom error pages, 63-64

global.asax file, 6
  available events, 6

H

Headers Collection section (TraceContext class), 84

HttpApplication class, 60

HttpHandlers, 92, 243, 245
  entries, Listing 6.10, 92
  implementing, 243
  Listing 14.18, 244
  Listing 14.19, 245
  subtags, 243

I

#if...#endif directives (C#), 76

#If...Then...#End If directives (Visual Basic .NET), 76

If statements
control-of-flow guidelines, 53–55
Listing 4.16, 53
Listing 4.17, 54
replacing with Case/Switch
constructs, 54
Visual Basic versus C#, 320–321

includes, 13

**IndexOutOfRangeException error,
287–288**
column names, 288
Listing 16.12, 289
Listing 16.13, 289
debugging, 287

inline debugging
Visual Studio .NET, 103–106,
111–112
adding components, 112-115
debugging components, 116

installing .NET components, 251
uninstalling, 251–252

interface encapsulation, 41

interfaces, 242
common, 242
designing, 242
rules and restrictions, 242

Interop utility, 250

Invalid Data Source error, 289–290

IsEnabled property, 86
Listing 6.2, 86
Listing 6.3, 86

IsMissing, 316

ItemTemplate tag (aspx), 162–163

J-K-L

languages
scripted versus compiled, 13
supported, 7

life cycle of pages, 5–7

listings
#error directive (C#), 78
#undef directive (C#), 77
#warning directive (C#), 78
accessing data by column name
C#, 289
Visual Basic .NET, 289
accessing event log data via the web,
129, 132
Application_Error event handler
C#, 60
Visual Basic .NET, 60
ASP cookie code, 309
ASP page, 306
ASP.NET page (Visual Basic
.NET), 306
assigning User Control properties
programmatically
C#, 177
Visual Basic .NET, 178
author search page using
AuthorLogic object
C#, 48
Visual Basic .NET, 49
automatic transaction processing
C#, 265
Visual Basic .NET, 266
basic component
C#, 232
Visual Basic .NET, 233
business object code
C#, 46
Visual Basic .NET, 47
calling a User Control method
C#, 182
Visual Basic .NET, 182

Case/Switch block
  C#, 54
  Visual Basic .NET, 55
checking for existing debuggers
  C#, 234
  Visual Basic .NET, 235
code with a single exit point
  C#, 57
  Visual Basic .NET, 57
code with multiple exit points
  C#, 55
  Visual Basic .NET, 56
code-behind class for author search
  page using AuthorLogic object
  C#, 50
  Visual Basic .NET, 52
code-behind class referencing user
  controls
  C#, 44
  Visual Basic .NET, 45
code-behind classes to handle user
  input, 40
code-behind file for Visual Studio
  .NET inline debugging example
  C#, 105
  Visual Basic .NET, 106
complex return type (Web Services)
  C#, 206
  Visual Basic .NET, 206
complex role-based security
  C#, 257
  Visual Basic .NET, 259
conditional compiling with
  function attributes
  C#, 70
  Visual Basic .NET, 71
conditional compiling with
  preprocessor directives
  C#, 73
  Visual Basic .NET, 74
connecting ADO.NET to data
  source, 26-27

connecting to the database
  (C#), 285
connection pooling
  C#, 296
  Visual Basic .NET, 296
corrected XML file, 171
creating a custom event log, 122
creating an ASP debug object, 16
custom return type (Web Services)
  C#, 207
  Visual Basic .NET, 210
Data Reader connections errors
  C#, 294
  Visual Basic .NET, 294
DataBind method
  aspx, 291
  C#, 292
  Visual Basic .NET, 292
DataBinder used in place of a
  recordset, 163
Debug WriteLineIf method
  C#, 240
  Visual Basic .NET, 240
debugging arrays
  C#, 287
  Visual Basic .NET, 287
debugging with ASPError, 15
displaying forms, 32
dynamically loading User Controls
  C#, 185
  Visual Basic .NET, 185
dynamically setting the IsEnabled
  property
  C#, 86
  Visual Basic .NET, 86
Emailer component
  C#, 113
  Visual Basic .NET, 114
enabling application-level tracing, 81
event handler for paging through a
  data grid
  C#, 161
  Visual Basic .NET, 162

fix for XMLSerializer error in
Web Services
C#, 214
Visual Basic .NET, 214
generic C# For loop, 322
GetSqlExceptionDump function
C#, 276
Visual Basic .NET, 277
grid paging event handler
C#, 159
Visual Basic .NET, 160
httphandlers section in
Web.Config, 244
HttpHandlers section of
machine.config file, 92
If statement (C#), 321
implementing a parameter using the
SqlCommand class
C#, 299
Visual Basic .NET, 299
implementing classes in a web page
(aspx), 167–168
implementing
TraceContext.Write(string)
C#, 87
Visual Basic .NET, 87
implementing
TraceContext.Write(string, string)
C#, 88
Visual Basic .NET, 89
implementing
TraceContext.Write(string,
string, Exception)
C#, 90
Visual Basic .NET, 90
invalidating output caches through
validation callbacks
C#, 192–193
Visual Basic .NET, 193-195
large If statement block
C#, 53
Visual Basic .NET, 54

logging expected events, 124–126
logging unexpected events, 127–128
modified code for
btnSubmit_ServerClick
C#, 115
Visual Basic .NET, 115
MyControl basics, 174
MyControl with a property
C#, 176
Visual Basic .NET, 176
MyControl with method
C#, 180
Visual Basic .NET, 181
MyPage basics, 174
namespace errors
C#, 165-166
Visual Basic .NET, 165-166
navigating the stack frame by frame
C#, 236
Visual Basic .NET, 237
offset error
C#, 224
Visual Basic .NET, 224
ouput showing
__VIEWSTATE, 151
page for Visual Studio .NET inline
debugging example, 104
passing a FileStream object
C#, 220
Visual Basic .NET, 221
portfolio.xml file, 170
property assignment order (User
Controls)
C#, 179
Visual Basic .NET, 179
retrieving an ADO recordset, 11
returning binary data
C#, 222
Visual Basic .NET, 223
sample ASP page using clsDebug, 20

sample code to connect to the
database
C#, 277
Visual Basic .NET, 278
sample output of
GetSqlExceptionDump, 279
search user-interface code
implementing user controls, 42
server controls, code-behind files
C#, 148
Visual Basic .NET, 149
server-side events
C#, 5
Visual Basic .NET, 5
setting the data source from behind
the aspx page
C#, 290
Visual Basic .NET, 290
setting up custom error pages, 64
setting up file dependencies
C#, 196
Visual Basic .NET, 197
shorthand assignments in Visual
Basic , 314
simple ASP page with form, 4
simple custom error page, 64
simple data grid control
C#, 158
Visual Basic .NET, 158
simple HttpHandler class
C#, 244
Visual Basic .NET, 245
simple role-based security
C#, 254
Visual Basic .NET, 255
simple Web Services code
C#, 204
Visual Basic .NET, 204
single-cache key dependencies
C#, 197
Visual Basic .NET, 198
SOAP return values, 216

SoapException
C#, 227
Visual Basic .NET, 228
Stack Trace dump
C#, 236
Visual Basic .NET, 236
stack trace inside component
(C#), 239
StackTrace GetMethod
C#, 238
Visual Basic .NET, 238
strong-named assemblies
C#, 268
Visual Basic .NET, 270
structure declaration (Visual Basic
.NET), 315
structured error handling (Visual
Basic .NET) , 315
tab controls in creating
server controls
C#, 142
Visual Basic .NET, 144
testing controls
C#, 147
Visual Basic .NET, 147
throwing a handled exception
C#, 62
Visual Basic .NET, 63
throwing exceptions
C#, 217
Visual Basic .NET, 217
trace listener
C#, 240
Visual Basic .NET, 241
tracing within components
C#, 93-94
Visual Basic .NET, 94
transactions
C#, 282
Visual Basic .NET, 283
trapping a specific exception type
C#, 59
Visual Basic .NET, 59

try-catch method on the client side
   C#, 218
   Visual Basic .NET, 218
typical ASP page, 10
use of parentheses (Visual Basic
   .NET), 319
use of square brackets (C#), 319
user controls and code-behind
  classes
   C#, 42-43
   Visual Basic .NET, 43
user-interface code for an author
  search, 40-41
using XML as data source
   C#, 169
   Visual Basic .NET, 169
validating input
   C#, 30
   Visual Basic .NET, 30
validating output
   C#, 31
   Visual Basic .NET, 31
validation controls, adding, 33
validation controls, dynamically
  creating
   C#, 33
   Visual Basic .NET, 34
validation controls, placement and
  behavior
   C#, 35
   Visual Basic .NET, 35
Visual Basic function calls, 312
Visual Basic function with ByRef
  parameters, 313
Visual Basic property, 312
Visual Basic structure
  declaration, 315
Visual Basic variable
  declarations, 313
Visual Basic variable
  initializations, 314
Visual Basic properties, 311

Web Services code
   C#, 204
   Visual Basic .NET, 204
Web Services data type error
   C#, 220
   Visual Basic .NET, 220
Web Services data type
  error, corrected
   C#, 220
   Visual Basic .NET, 220
Web.Config (session state), 247
Web.Config file, 241
WebMethod error
   C#, 215
   Visual Basic .NET, 215
writing messages to the Windows
  2000 Event Log, 120

logging
  accessing event log data via the Web,
  129, 135-136
   Listing 8.9, 129, 132
  traces, viewing logs, 91-92

**loops, exit points, control-of-flow
guidelines, 55-58**

M

**messages, setting (TraceContext
class), 85**
methods
  AddAt, 35
  DataBind, 291
   Listing 16.16, 291
   Listing 16.17, 292
   Listing 16.18, 292
  Debug.Writeline, 239
  Debug.WriteLineIf
   Listing 14.12, 240
   Listing 14.13, 240
  GetAuthorByName, 45
  GetAuthorByState, 45

GetBaseException(), 61
GetEventLogs, 135
GetLastError(), 61
GetValue, debugging arrays, 287
Page.Navigate, 308
RaisePostBackEvent, 150
Render, overriding, 150
Response.Redirect, 308–309
Server.ClearError(), 62
Server.Execute(), 62
Server.Transfer, 309
TraceContext class, 87
   Warn, 87
   Write, 87-91
try–catch, 217–218
User Controls, 175, 180–182
   calling, 182
   creating new server methods, 183
   errors, 183
   out-of-scope controls, 184
Validate(), 34
WriteEntry, 123
WriteEntry(), 61

Microsoft Transaction Server, components, 267–268

migrating from ASP to ASP.NET, 305
<%%> versus <script>, 306–308
cookies, 309
events, 310
page directives, 308
Response.Redirect, 308–309

mission statements, 29

monitoring transactions, 271–272

MyControl.ascx user control, 174
basics, Listing 11.1, 174
building, 174
   errors, 175
methods
   adding, 180-182
   calling, 182
   errors, 183

properties, errors, 177
properties, adding, 176
   Listing 11.3, 176
   Listing 11.4, 176

MYDEBUG constant, 75

MyPage.aspx, 174
basics, Listing 11.2, 174

N

namespaces, 164
ComponentModel, 231
errors, 164
   Listing 10.8, 165
   Listing 10.9, 165
   Listing 10.10, 166
   Listing 10.11, 166
System.Data, 275
System.Diagnostics, 234
   event log interface, 120-121
System.Web.UI.Web-
   Controls.Control, 149

No Data in the Data Grid error, 291

O

objects
business, 45–53
creating, 316
FileStream, 220
Response, 28
   debugging with, 14
Server
   debugging with, 14-16

objects:ASPError, 14

OleDb class, 275
catching errors, 275
OleDbConnection component,
   280–281

OleDb objects versus SQL objects, 300

OleDbCommand, using parameters, 300

OleDbConnection component, 280-281

OleDbException class, 275

@OutputCache directive, 190
Duration attribute, 190
VaryByCustom attribute, 191
VaryByHeader attribute, 191
VaryByParam attribute, 190-191

ouput caching, 190
@OutputCache directive, 190
User Controls, 191-192
validation callbacks, 192-196

output tracing, 81
Control Tree, 83
Cookies Collection, 83-84
Form Collection, 84
Headers Collection, 84
QueryString Collection, 84-85
Request Details, 81-82
Server Variables, 85
Trace Information, 82-83

P

@Page directive, 80

page directives, 308
ASP versus ASP.NET, 308

Page.Navigate methods versus Response.Redirect, 308

pages
ASP, 10
life cycle, 5-7
MyPage.aspx, 174
simple ASP page with form, Listing 1.1, 4
structure, 9
in ASP, 10-12

paging data grid control, 159-162

parameters
? (question mark) placeholder, 298
ByRef, 312
Listing A.11, 313
Listing A.12, 313
OleDbCommand, 300
SqlCommand, 298
VBScript versus Visual Basic, 312

parentheses (())characters, 319

partitioning, 39
business objects, 45-53
code-behind classes, 40-41
user controls, 41-45

performance
data connections, 300
overusing the database, 297-298

preprocessor directives, 73-76
#error, 77-78
#if...#endif, 76
#undef, 77
#warning, 77-78
MYDEBUG constant, 75

programs
executing statements separately from running programs, 98
execution control, Visual Studio .NET, 110-111
stopping execution, 99

properties
IsEnabled, 86
tab controls, 150
TraceContext class, 86-87
User Controls, 175-176
errors, 177
VBScript versus Visual Basic, 311
Listing A.7, 311
Listing A.8, 312

Q-R

QueryString Collection section (TraceContext class), 84-85

question mark (?) character, 298

RaisePostBackEvent method, 150

Register directive, server controls, 150
  registering, 153

registering components, 251

remote debugging
  Visual Studio .NET, 116
    configuring, 116
    installation, 116
    using, 117

remoting, 225

Render method, overriding, 150

Request Details section (TraceContext class), 81-82

Response object, 28
  debugging with, 14

Response.Redirect method, 308
  versus Page.Navigate, 308
  versus Server.Transfer, 309

Response.Write, 79

role-based security, 253
  complex, 257-261
    Listing 15.3, 257
    Listing 15.4, 259
  Component Services Microsoft Management Console, 261-264
    roles, setting up, 262
    settings, changing, 262
  simple, 254-257
    Listing 15.1, 254
    Listing 15.2, 255

roles
  role-based security, 253-261
    Component Services Microsoft Management Console, 261-264
    setting up roles, 262
    settings, changing, 262

runat attributes, 175

runat=server attribute, 153-154

S

scope modifiers (User Controls), 177-178

SELECT Permission Denied error, 285
  column-level security, 286
  connecting to the database, Listing 16.8, 285
  debugging, 285-286
  product table permissions, 286

Select...Case...End Select statements, Visual Basic versus C#, 322

semicolon () characters, 319

server controls, 141, 151
  code-behind files, 152-153
    Listing 9.5, 148
    Listing 9.6, 149
  creating, 142-144, 149-151
  debugging in Visual Studio .NET, 154-155
  end tags, 175
  Register directive, 150
  registering, 153
  runat=server attribute, 153-154
  System.Web.UI.WebControls.Control namespace, 149
  test pages
    Listing 9.3, 147
    Listing 9.4, 147
  ViewState dictionary, 151-152

Server object (ASP), debugging with, 14–16

server variables, 85

Server Variables section (TraceContext class), 85

server-side events, 3–4
C#, Listing 1.2, 5
compared to client-side events, 4
life cycle of pages, 5–7
types, 4–5
Visual Basic, Listing 1.3, 5

Server.ClearError() method, 62

Server.Execute() method, 62

Server.Transfer method versus Response.Redirect, 309

session state, 246
attributes, 247
implementing, 246
in-process versus out-of-process, 246
performance and reliability, 248
limitations, 246
performance and reliability, 248
SQL Server, 249
section parameters, 247

Set keyword, 311

shorthand assignments, 314
Listing A.15, 314

single-key dependencies, 197–198

SOAP
common errors, 226
return values, Listing 13.3, 216
throwing exceptions
Listing 13.14, 217
Listing 13.15, 217
Web Services errors, 215–216

SoapException class, 227
Listing 13.28, 227
Listing 13.29, 228

Soapsuds utility, 225

spaghetti code, 10

SQL objects versus OleDb objects, 300

SQL Server, 249

SqlClient class, 275
catching errors, 275
SqlConnection component, 280

SqlCommand class
implementing parameters, 298
Listing 16.22, 299
Listing 16.23, 299
use of ? (question mark)
placeholder, 298

SqlConnection component, 280

SqlException class, 275
displaying properties, 276
Listing 16.1, 276
Listing 16.2, 277
functionality, 277–279
Listing 16.3, 277
Listing 16.4, 278
runtime errors, 279
Listing 16.5, 279

square brackets ([]) characters, 319

stack traces, 235
inside components, 239
Listing 14.11, 239
navigating frame by frame, 236
Listing 14.7, 236
Listing 14.8, 237
trace listeners, 240
Listing 14.14, 240
Listing 14.15, 241
writing output to a file, 241

StackTrace class, 235
dumps
Listing 14.5, 236
Listing 14.6, 236
GetMethod, 237
Listing 14.10, 238
Listing 14.9, 238

state management, 246
i-process versus out-of-process, 246
session state limitations, 246

status flags, 57

**Step Into (Visual Studio
.NET), 110**

**Step Out (Visual Studio
.NET), 110**

**Step Over (Visual Studio
.NET), 110**

strategies, 23
building complexity from simplicity,
32-34, 36
"divide and conquer", 29
inputs and outputs, 29-32
Listing 3.3, 30
Listing 3.4, 30
mission statements, 29
plan carefully, 36
tier sandboxes, 24
business object tiers, 26-28
data tiers, 24-26
user interface tiers, 28-29
use caution, 37

streams, Web Services, 220-224

strong-named assemblies, 268-271

**structure declaration, VBScript
versus Visual Basic, 315**
Listing A.17, 315

structure of pages, 9
in ASP, 10-12

structured exception handling, 58
catching specific exceptions, 58
Listing 4.24, 59
Listing 4.25, 59
use of Exception class, 58
when to use, 58

structuring code, 39
code partitioning, 39
control-of-flow guidelines, 53

global exception handling, 59
structured exception handling, 58

Switch statement, 322

System.Data namespace, 275

System.Diagnostics namespace
event log interface, 120-121
EventLog class, 129
EventLog object, 120

**System.Web.UI.Web-
Controls.Control namespace,
server controls, 149**

T

tab controls
creating server controls, 142
Listing 9.1, 142
Listing 9.2, 144
declaring, 152-153
properties, 150

templates, 162

tier sandboxes, 24
business object tiers, 26-28
data tiers, 24-26
user interface tiers, 28-29

tiers
business object tiers, 26-28
data tiers, 24-26
tier sandboxes, 24
user interface tiers, 28-29

Trace attribute, 80

**Trace Information section
(TraceContext class), 82-83**

Trace Viewer, 91
accessing, 92
interface, 92-93

TraceContext class, 79
methods, 87
Warn, 87
Write, 87-91
properties, 86-87

setting messages, 85
trace output, 81
   Control Tree, 83
   Cookies Collection, 83-84
   Form Collection, 84
   Headers Collection, 84
   QueryString Collection, 84-85
   Request Details, 81-82
   Server Variables, 85
   Trace Information, 82-83
VIEWSTATE, 84

tracing, 79
enabling, 80
   application-level, 80-81
   page-level, 80
options, 80-81
output, 81
   Control Tree, 83
   Cookies Collection, 83-84
   Form Collection, 84
   Headers Collection, 84
   QueryString Collection, 84-85
   Request Details, 81-82
   Server Variables, 85
   Trace Information, 82-83
setting messages, 85
strategies, 95
trace logs, viewing, 91-92
Trace Viewer, 91
   accessing, 92
   interface, 92-93
TraceContext class, 79
Visual Studio .NET, 101, 110
web.config files, 80
within components, 93-95

transactions, 264, 281
attributes, 267
automatic transaction processing,
  265-267
   Listing 15.5, 265
   Listing 15.6, 266

Distributed Transaction Coordinator,
  271-272
Microsoft Transaction Server
  components, 267-268
monitoring, 271-272
.NET transaction models, 265
strong-named assemblies, 268-271
successful, 281
   Listing 16.6, 282
   Listing 16.7, 283

try-catch method, 217-218
client-side
   Listing 13.16, 218
   Listing 13.17, 218

U

**UDDI (Universal Discovery
Descriptor Interface), 226**

#undef directive, 77
Listing 5.7, 77

**unexpected events, handling,
127-129**

**Universal Discovery Descriptor
Interface (UDDI), 226**

User Controls, 41-45, 173
building, 174
   errors, 175
dynamic User Controls, 184
   class names, defining, 184-186
   errors, 186-187
   Listing 11.13, 185
   Listing 11.14, 185
   User Control classes, referencing, 185
end tags, 175
Listing 4.5, 42
Listing 4.6, 43
   compiling, 44
Listing 4.7, 43
   compiling, 44

methods, 175
  adding, 180-182
  calling, 182
  creating new server methods, 183
  errors, 183
  Listing 11.10, 181
  Listing 11.11, 182
  Listing 11.12, 182
  Listing 11.9, 180
  out-of-scope controls, 184
modifying cached, 191–192
MyControl.ascx, 174
properties, 175
  adding, 176
  assigning programmatically, 177
  assignment order, 179-180
  errors, 177
  Listing 11.5, 177
  Listing 11.6, 178
  Listing 11.7, 179
  Listing 11.8, 179
  scope modifiers, 177-178
runat attributes, 175
unknown server tags, 175
user interface tiers, 28–29
utilities
Interop, 250
Soapsuds, 225
UDDI (Universal Discovery Descriptor Interface), 226
Web Services, 225
WSDL (Web Services Description Language), 225–226

V

Validate() method, 34
validation callbacks, 192–195
invalidating output caches, 195–196
  Listing 12.1, 192-193
  Listing 12.2, 193, 195

validation controls
adding, Listing 3.8, 33
dynamically creating
  Listing 3.10, 34
  Listing 3.9, 33
placement and behavior, 35
  Listing 3.11, 35
variable declarations VBScript versus Visual Basic, 313
variables
changing values in Visual Studio .NET command windows, 109
changing values in Visual Studio .NET watch windows, 108
monitoring in Visual Studio .NET watch windows, 108
scope, 316
server, 85
viewing in Visual Studio .NET command windows, 109
watching contents, 100
Variant data type, 314
VaryByCustom attribute (@OutputCache directive), 191
VaryByHeader attribute (@OutputCache directive), 191
VaryByParam attribute (@OutputCache directive), 190–191
VB.NET. See Visual Basic .NET
VBScript
in ASP pages, 10
versus Visual Basic, 311, 317–318
  control-of-flow statements, 316
  data types, 313
  declarations, 314

error handling, 315
IsMissing, 316
object creation, 316
parameters, 312
properties, 311
scope of variables, 316
Set keyword, 311
shorthand syntax, 314
structure declaration, 315
subroutines, calling, 312
Variant data type, 314

__VIEWSTATE form variable, 151

VIEWSTATE, 84

ViewState dictionary, 151–152
output showing __VIEWSTATE,
Listing 9.7, 151

Visual Basic .NET
#If...Then...#End If directives, 76
benefits compare to VBScript, 7
bridging to COM+ functionality,
253versus C#
brackets, 319
case sensitivity, 318
control-of-flow statements, 320-322
functions, 320
semicolons, 319
error handling, 315
For statements, 321–322
function calls
Listing A.9, 312
If statements, 320
initializing variables, 314
Listing A.14, 314
intrinsic datatypes, 313
listings
accessing data by column name, 289
Application_Error event handler, 60
ASP.NET page, 306
assigning User Control properties
programmatically, 178
author search page using AuthorLogic
object, 49

automatic transaction processing, 266
basic component , 233
business object code, 47
calling a User Control method, 182
Case/Switch block, 55
checking for existing debuggers, 235
code with a single exit point , 57
code with multiple exit points, 56
code-behind class for author search
page using AuthorLogic object, 52
code-behind class referencing user
controls, 45
code-behind file for Visual Studio
.NET inline debugging
example, 106
complex return type (Web
Services), 206
complex role-based security, 259
conditional compiling with function
attributes, 71
conditional compiling with preprocessor directives, 74
connection pooling, 296
custom return type (Web
Services), 210
Data Reader connections errors, 294
DataBind method, 292
DataBinder used in place of a
recordset, 163
Debug WriteLineIf method, 240
debugging arrays, 287
dynamically loading User Controls,
185
dynamically setting the IsEnabled
property, 86
Emailer component, 114
event handler for paging through a
data grid, 162
fix for XMLSerializer error in Web
Services, 214
function calls, 312
function with ByRef parameters, 313

GetSqlExceptionDump function, 277

grid paging event handler, 160

implementing a parameter using the SqlCommand class, 299

implementing TraceContext.Write(string), 87

implementing TraceContext.Write(string, string), 89

implementing TraceContext.Write(string, string, Exception), 90

invalidating output caches through validation callbacks, 195

invalidating output caches through validation callbacks, 193

large If statement block, 54

modified code for btn Submit_ServerClick, 115

MyControl with a property, 176

MyControl with Method, 181

namespace errors, 165-166

navigating the stack frame by frame, 237

offset error, 224

passing a FileStream object, 221

properties, 311-312

property assignment order (User Controls), 179

returning binary data, 223

sample code to connect to the database, 278

server controls, code-behind files, 149

server-side events, 5

setting the data source from behind the aspx page, 290

setting up file dependencies, 197

shorthand assignments, 314

simple data grid control, 158

simple HttpHandler class, 245

simple role-based security, 255

simple Web Services code, 204

single-cache key dependencies, 198

SoapException, 228

Stack Trace dump, 236

StackTrace GetMethod, 238

strong-named assemblies, 270

structure declaration, 315

structured error handling , 315

tab controls in creating server controls, 144

testing controls, 147

throwing a handled exception, 63

throwing exceptions, 217

trace listener, 241

tracing within components, 94

transactions, 283

trapping a specific exception type, 59

try-catch method on the client side, 218

use of parentheses, 319

user controls and code-behind classes, 43

using XML as data source, 169

validating input, 30

validating output 31

validation controls, dynamically creating, 34

validation controls, placement and behavior, 35

variable declarations, 313

variable initializations, 314

Web Services code, 204

Web Services data type error, 220

Web Services data type error, corrected, 220

WebMethod error, 215

object creation, 316

Select...Case...End Select statements, 322

server-side events, Listing 1.3, 5

shorthand assignments, Listing A.15, 314

structure declaration, 315
  Listing A.18, 315
transactions, 264
  models, 265
use of parentheses, 319
  Listing A.24, 319
use of semicolons, 319
variable declarations, 313
  Listing A.13, 313
variable scope, 316
  Listing A.19, 316
versus VBScript, 311, 317–318
  control-of-flow statements, 316
  data types, 313
  declarations, 314
  error handling, 315
  IsMissing, 316
  object creation, 316
  parameters, 312
  properties, 311
  scope of variables, 316
  Set keyword, 311
  shorthand syntax, 314
  structure declaration, 315
  subroutines, calling, 312
  Variant data type, 314
While statements, 322

Visual Studio .NET, 97
attaching to processes, 101–103
breakpoints, 99–100
  setting, 106-107
call stack, 98, 111
  tracing functions, 111
command window, 98–99, 109
  functions, executing, 109
  variables, changing values, 109
  variables, viewing, 109
configuring, 103
debugging server controls, 154–155
execution control, 110–111
features, 97
inline debugging, 103-106, 111-112

  adding components, 112-115
  debugging components, 116
  Listing 7.1, 104
  Listing 7.2, 105-106
  Listing 7.6, 115
  Listing 7.7, 115
remote debugging, 116
  configuring, 116
  installation, 116
  using, 117
Step Into, 110
Step Out, 110
Step Over, 110
tracing, 101, 110
watch windows, 100, 107–108
  variables, changing values, 108
  watching variables, 108

W

Warn method (TraceContext class), 87

#warning directive, 77-78
  Listing 5.8, 78

watch windows (Visual Studio .NET), 100, 107-108
  variables, changing values, 108
  watching variables, 108

Web Services, 203
  basic debugging, 226
  building, 203
  complex return types, 206
    Listing 13.5, 206
    Listing 13.6, 206
  custom return types, 206
    Listing 13.7, 207
    Listing 13.8, 210
  deployment problems, 230
  error messages, 205-213

errors
  data types, 219-220
  Listing 13.18, 220
examples, 203
  Listing 13.1, 204
  Listing 13.2, 204
  Listing 13.3, 204
  Listing 13.4, 204
serialization problems, 222
  Listing 13.24, 222
  Listing 13.25, 223
SOAP, common errors, 215-217, 226
  Listing 13.11, 215
  Listing 13.12, 215
SoapException class, 227
streams, 220-224
  Listing 13.22, 220
  Listing 13.23, 221
  Listing 13.26, 224
  Listing 13.27, 224
utilities, 225
  Soapsuds, 225
  UDDI (Universal Discovery
    Descriptor Interface), 226
  WSDL (Web Services Description
    Language), 225-226
XMLSerializer class, 214
  Listing 13.10, 214
  Listing 13.9, 214

**Web Services Description
Language (WSDL) utility, 225**
  common problems, 226

Web.Config file, 241
  httphandlers section, 243
    Listing 14.17, 244
  implementing HttpHandlers, 243
  Listing 14.16, 241

required location, 249
session state, Listing 14.20, 247

web.config files
  defaultLanguage parameters, 103
  tracing, 80
    Listing 6.1, 81

**While statements, Visual Basic
versus C#, 322**

Windows 2000 Event Log, 119-120
  accessing event log data via the Web,
    129, 135-136
  creating custom event logs, 121-124
    Listing 8.3, 122
  handing events, 124
    expected events, 124, 127
    unexpected events, 127-129
  writing messages to, Listing 8.1, 120

**Write method (TraceContext
class), 87-91**
  Listing 6.4, 87
  Listing 6.5, 87
  Listing 6.6, 88
  Listing 6.7, 89
  Listing 6.8, 90
  Listing 6.9, 90

WriteEntry method, 123
  parameters, 123

WriteEntry() method, 61

**WSDL (Web Services Description
Language) utility, 225**
  common problems, 226

X-Y-Z

XML, 168, 171
errors, 169–170
Listing 10.17, 171
portfolio.xml file, Listing 10.16, 170
using as data sources
Listing 10.14, 169
Listing 10.15, 169

XMLSerializer class, 214

HOW TO CONTACT US

VISIT OUR WEB SITE

WWW.NEWRIDERS.COM

On our web site, you'll find information about our other books, authors, tables of contents, and book errata. You will also find information about book registration and how to purchase our books, both domestically and internationally.

EMAIL US

Contact us at: **nrfeedback@newriders.com**

- If you have comments or questions about this book
- To report errors that you have found in this book
- If you have a book proposal to submit or are interested in writing for New Riders
- If you are an expert in a computer topic or technology and are interested in being a technical editor who reviews manuscripts for technical accuracy

Contact us at: **nreducation@newriders.com**

- If you are an instructor from an educational institution who wants to preview New Riders books for classroom use. Email should include your name, title, school, department, address, phone number, office days/hours, text in use, and enrollment, along with your request for desk/examination copies and/or additional information.

Contact us at: **nrmedia@newriders.com**

- If you are a member of the media who is interested in reviewing copies of New Riders books. Send your name, mailing address, and email address, along with the name of the publication or web site you work for.

BULK PURCHASES/CORPORATE SALES

If you are interested in buying 10 or more copies of a title or want to set up an account for your company to purchase directly from the publisher at a substantial discount, contact us at 800-382-3419 or email your contact information to corpsales@pearsontechgroup.com. A sales representative will contact you with more information.

WRITE TO US

New Riders Publishing
201 W. 103rd St.
Indianapolis, IN 46290-1097

CALL/FAX US

Toll-free (800) 571-5840
If outside U.S. (317) 581-3500
Ask for New Riders
FAX: (317) 581-4663

WWW.NEWRIDERS.COM

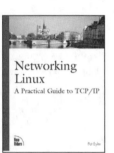

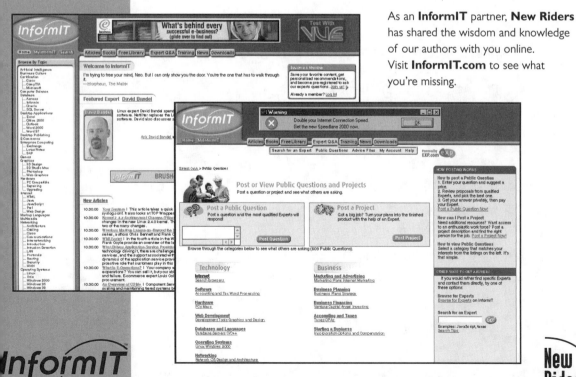

Colophon

Pictured on the cover is a photograph of The Ancient Forum in Rome, Italy. The Forum was the center of Roman life for over 500 years. It was used for political debates, Senate meetings, honoring ancient gods, and as a marketplace. The primary buildings that make up the Ancient Forum are the Temple of Castors, Arch of Titus, Arch of Septimius Severus, and the Temple of Antoninus and Faustina. The Ancient Forum was also home to the first Latin population.

This book was written and edited in Microsoft Word, and laid out in QuarkXPress. The font used for the body text is Bembo and MCPdigital. It was printed on 50# Husky Offset Smooth paper at R.R. Donnelley & Sons in Crawfordsville, Indiana. Prepress consisted of PostScript computer-to-plate technology (filmless process). The cover was printed at Moore Langen Printing in Terre Haute, Indiana, on Carolina, coated on one side.

Please note: All information in blue will need to be verified by the Project Editor just prior to the book's ship date.